recurrent education

selma j. mushkin, editor

NATIONAL INSTITUTE OF EDUCATION
U.S. DEPARTMENT OF HEALTH, EDUCATION AND WELFARE
WASHINGTON, D.C. 20208

For sale by the Superintendent of Documents, U.S. Government Printing Office, Washington, D.C. 20402
Price $3.60 Stock No. 1780-01277

CONTRIBUTORS

Russell Allen
Assistant Director
Labor Studies Center
Washington, D.C.

Homer D. Babbidge, Jr.
Professor
Yale University

Jarl Bengtsson
Centre for Educational Research
and Innovation
Organisation for Economic
Co-operation and Development

Kenneth R. Biederman
Professor of Economics
Georgetown University

Bradley B. Billings
Professor of Economics
Georgetown University

Francis M. Boddy
Professor of Economics
University of Minnesota

Andrew Daly
Director of Management Development
Curriculum
IBM

Jacques Delors
Secretary General
Interministerial Committee on
Vocational Training and Social
Development
France

Stephen P. Dresch
Director
Yale Higher Education Project
Yale University

Friedrich Edding
Director
Max Planck Institute for
Educational Research
Federal Republic of Germany

Kjell Eide
Director
Department of Planning of
Education and Research
Royal Ministry of Church and
Education
Norway

J. R. Gass
Director
Centre for Educational Research
and Innovation
Organisation for Economic Co-
operation and Development

Thomas K. Glennon, Jr.
Director
National Institute of Education
DHEW

A. H. Halsey
Professor
Nuffield College
Oxford

Charles C. Holt
Director
Inflation, Unemployment, and
Manpower Policy Research
The Urban Institute

Caryl M. Kline
Director
Continuing Education for Women
University of Pittsburgh

Herbert Levine
Director
Labor Institute
Rutgers University

S. M. Miller
Chairperson
Department of Sociology
Boston University

Selma J. Mushkin
Director
Public Services Laboratory
Georgetown University

Frank Newman
Director
Department of University Relations
Stanford University

Helen Peston
Senior Research Fellow
Queen Mary College
University of London

Maurice Peston
Professor of Economics
University of London

Gosta Rehn
Director
Swedish Institute for Social Research
University of Stockholm

Thomas I. Ribich
Research Economist
National Institute of Education
DHEW

Gisela Schade
Centre for Educational Research
and Innovation
Organisation for Economic
Co-operation and Development

Berislav Sefer
Professor of Economics
University of Belgrade

Virginia Smith
Director
Fund for the Improvement of Post-
secondary Education
DHEW

foreword from NIE

THOMAS K. GLENNON, JR., ***Director***

In the past decade, the education community has seriously rethought the traditional patterns and concepts in education. This re-examination has given new emphasis to the needs and wants of those whom educators must serve.

The process has stimulated unprecedented demands for a restructuring of educational systems and for examining new approaches to education --approaches which meet those demands more efficiently and with greater equity and access for all segments of the population. Recurrent education is one of the most important alternative educational approaches to have emerged in recent times.

This volume--and the Conference held by the Public Services Laboratory of Georgetown University in Spring 1973 from which the papers printed here are drawn--represents one product of the continuing search for new educational alternatives. The Conference, initiated at the suggestion of the Centre for Educational Reform and Innovation (CERI) and supported by the United States Department of Health, Education, and Welfare (HEW), was the first major meeting on recurrent education to be held in the United States.

The Georgetown meeting was unique in that it brought together for the first time scholars working on a strategy for lifelong learning within CERI and those doing independent research on flexible working-life styles; those involved with recurrent education efforts in the Council of Europe and Organisation for Economic Co-operation and Development (OECD) and those engaged in the preparation of a proposed International Labour Office resolution calling for paid leave to pursue one's education. In short, conference participants represented the broadest possible range of scholars and practitioners in the field of recurrent education.

The Conference was structured around a multifaceted examination of recurrent education as a system starting at the completion of one's formal compulsory schooling and continuing throughout the remainder of a person's active life.

For some time, the OECD community has been developing the definition of recurrent education terminology, but in the United States it was virtually unknown before the Georgetown Conference. A recent OECD publication, for example, defines the essence of such a system as "the distribution of education over the lifespan of the individual in a recurring way." Recurrent education makes it possible to alternate between leisure, work, and education in a way that avoids the rigid sequence that characterizes the structure of educational systems in most nations.

This volume represents the work and findings of the Conference. Findings, I should add, which do not uniformly point to recurrent education as a substitute for existing educational patterns, but which underscore the many problems and issues that argue both for much greater flexibility in the timing of education and for educational systems that give meaning to the broadening of these choices.

The papers of the many European contributors are indicative of the spirited and widespread debate and discussion surrounding recurrent education that has been going on in Europe over the past few years. In part, the intent of the meeting last Spring was to give American policymakers and scholars a sense of what their European colleagues were thinking about recurrent education, and to hope that such exposure would pique their interest at home.

In America there is already a growing consensus among members of national commissions, task forces, and study groups concerning the education/work problem. These groups include the Work in America Task Force, HEW, the Carnegie Commission on Non-Traditional Study, the Kellogg Foundation Commission on the Future of Continuing Education, and the American Assembly. All seem to agree on the need for continuing lifelong education which recognizes the relevance of work to the educational experience starting early in life and the need to involve more retired people in satisfying educational, work, and leisure experiences.

The economists at the Conference undertook new analyses of the economic ramifications of recurrent education. I believe these new analyses in themselves constitute an important contribution to our understanding of recurrent education. The Georgetown Conference was significant in heightening the awareness of the potential offered by recurrent education. In this respect, then, I feel that we have taken yet another step toward the structuring of an educational system for all people that is responsive and excellent. This, in itself, is a worthwhile achievement.

foreword from CERI

J. R. GASS, *Director*

It is a great pleasure to join with Thomas Glennon in the foreword to a report on a conference in the United States on a European educational idea--recurrent education. Since the end of World War II the Europeans and the Japanese have become accustomed to placing U.S. educational experience in the center of their own debate, and it comes as somewhat of a surprise to the outside observer to see how intensively inward-looking the Americans are in educational matters. The OECD Centre for Educational Research and Innovation, therefore, welcomed the opportunity for an exchange of views about the concept of recurrent education, which has been largely pioneered by the Centre.

Recurrent education is a response to trends in Europe flowing from a realization that the vast growth of education of the last 30 years is failing in part to meet its objectives. As an alternative to longer continuous education for youth, leading eventually to access from high school to college for all, it proposes for those who prefer it, an alternation of periods of work and education. Based on something like a civilian GI Bill of Rights, it would give young people the option of leaving the educational system without sacrificing forever the right to higher education. More equity, more relevance, more realistic and open patterns of development for many young people and more opportunities for adults to return to education are the advantages its proponents see.

That the 1973 Conference of the European Ministers of Education in Switzerland decided to adopt recurrent education as the main issue for their 1975 meeting in Sweden testifies to the growing interest in recurrent education in the European countries. This is not to say that recurrent education can be considered as an alternative to the present system but rather that it provides an overall strategy for educational change in relation to which many specific policies and approaches can be articulated. Essentially it means new learning environments for youth at the upper end of secondary school, an alternative to immediate university entry via the right to return to higher education, and more flexible postsecondary arrangements which enable flexible and continuous adjustment of careers to ambitions, labor market opportunities and changing social conditions. It is one of the major claims of the advocates of recurrent education that such new relationships between individuals, educational opportunities and working careers would lead to more equity between social classes, ethnic and age groups, and between women and men than is possible with youth education alone.

There is no doubt of the relevance of recurrent education to current U.S. policy problems. But the issue is whether the undoubted variety and vitality of U.S. educational institutions, based on the realities of state, regional and local development, can collectively respond to some new general concept that would change the pattern of U.S. educational growth, and at the same time relate to social and economic development. It is encouraging to note from the exchange of views in Washington that many features of recurrent education already exist in the U.S.--ranging from junior colleges with a wide range of options for young people, widespread participation of adults in postsecondary education, and growing interest of trades unions and employers in granting educational opportunities for working people. Can these be harnessed to a new overall pattern of U.S. education and thereby be considered as a response to the present malaise? That is the central question that remains posed after the Washington Conference.

The stage is now set for deepening discussions between the U.S. and other OECD countries on that central policy issue, and this itself is a result of cooperation between CERI and the U.S. leading to the papers presented here. I would like to express my appreciation to those who sponsored and prepared the conference on the U.S. side, namely, the Department of Health, Education, and Welfare and the Public Services Laboratory at Georgetown University, and to those European and Japanese experts who crossed the Atlantic and the Pacific to engage in sharp but friendly debate with their American colleagues. Special thanks are, of course, due to those whose hard work made the event possible: Selma Mushkin, Violet Gunther and Ann Guillot in Washington and Jarl Bengtsson and Denis Kallen in Paris.

CONTENTS

Education and the World of Work

Financing and Politics of Recurrent Education

Summary

policy directions

the social considerations of recurrent education

FRANK NEWMAN

The United States is moving steadily, if unconsciously, toward recurrent education at the postsecondary level. This movement is less apparent than in Europe, but nonetheless real. In part this is due to the organization of postsecondary education in the U.S., for there is no single government agency charged with indicating clearly our new direction. Not only are there 50 states with responsibilities for education, but within each state higher education responsibilities are often fragmented among several multi-campus systems and coordinating agencies, each of which has some planning responsibilities. In addition to this fragmentation, other policies are initiated from private higher education and the proprietary sector.

Despite the fact there is no single voice for the directions of higher education, a broad trend is discernible. We are returning to a pattern of recurrent education, for there was a time when recurrent education, while not widespread, was in many ways more in vogue than it is today. Particularly in urban areas there were institutions devoted to part-time evening study serving mainly already employed and somewhat older students. These were important vehicles for social mobility, but during the 1950's and 1960's, as higher education grew, many of these institutions lost influence.

The Foundations Already Available

Today there is a new interest in recurrent education, and a foundation on which to build.

Some old, established programs on the periphery of higher education have been quietly flourishing despite concentrations on conventional campus development. Continuing education programs of universities, adult education programs in high schools, and courses run directly in the employers plant by growing numbers of community colleges comprise this foundation. Some are completely new: television colleges, examining universities, and the new Open Universities are a few examples.

Some are expansions of older programs. Programs by large employers (most specifically by the Armed Forces), the expansion of proprietary schools and a host of nonprofit institutes from Esalen to the Institute of Transactional Analysis fall into this category.

But the most important change has been the enormous postwar growth in access to higher education. Open admissions and the steadily broader age rules for admission to many public universities has and will continue to make a major change in the student's perception of how realistic it is to return to college or enter at an older age.

Thus, both educational and social circumstances have changed, but the question of how these changes of the past two and a half decades require new concepts and institutions if recurrent education is to be realistic and useful remains unsolved.

Social and educational changes have of course occurred worldwide. Some, however, are particularly American. The issue in the U.S. is not so much one of equity for the older population relative to the younger and better educated, as it often is in Europe. The widespread availability of 12 or 13 years of schooling, the higher rates of college access, the degree of open admission allowing some recurrent patterns of attendance all mitigate against this becoming a subject of intense political concern in this country.

Close coupling between recurrent education and job training is less applicable here because high rates of college attendance make shortages of highly trained manpower where recurrent programs can be focused hard to find. Finally, many American students already have a long educational experience--recurrent education is needed not to help them into higher education, but to help them out for the sake of effectiveness in their socialization and education.

The Educational Demands In An Egalitarian Era

Since World War II there has been an enormous growth in American college enrollments in response to a broadly held perception of a public policy of educational opportunity.

We have moved through several eras of higher education, each characterized by a dominant social purpose. For a very long period following the founding of the first colleges, education in this country could be described as aristocratic.

What made the American system more democratic than the European was steady expansion in the percent of the college age group that gained access and the ease with which new colleges could be founded. Any well-organized group of individuals could, if it felt excluded from the establishment of the day, establish its own college with its own specific mission. Institutions like City College of New York in the urban areas or the land-grant college movement in the newly-settled areas, made higher education more accessible, and gave it relatively democratic social values. Moreover, there was always access for the student of high ability and motivation who was prepared to work his way. Still, it is important to keep in mind that in 1900 only about four percent of the college age group actually entered college.

Steadily, the aristocratic concept weakened, and by the 1930's we were well into a meritocratic period. Colleges increasingly sought academically able students, whatever their background, and thus began to educate a new elite not of birth, but of talent. But it was in the post-World War II period that the spread of meritocratic values accelerated, and the concept of merit became more and more limited to ability as measured by academic grades and tests. Colleges and universities sorted themselves by "quality" standards. These standards were based on relative selectivity in admissions policies.

Meritocratic values as measured by grades and test scores still dominate, but beginning in the postwar period and accelerating around 1960 we moved into a third period. The assumption has grown that nearly everyone should have some kind of chance at a college education. Increasingly, college is seen not so much as selecting the meritorious as giving each individual a chance to fulfill his or her individual potential. Perhaps the most striking development of this egalitarian policy has been the establishment of the community college. Most of these systems accept any high school graduate and, under certain conditions, non-high school graduates as well.

In the late 1960's the move to open admissions was supplemented by a more direct concern for the less advantaged in society, particularly minorities. Major campaigns were begun to recruit such students into almost all types of institutions from the most selective to those practicing open admissions. A small but significant number of new colleges were established or adapted for these students following the models of black colleges. Recently, open universities brought a new dimension to that minority of students who find attendance on a campus either unattractive or unfeasible.

The shift toward egalitarianism is also evident in public policy on student aid. Whereas earlier in the meritocratic era the establishment of scholarships most often focused on students of high academic ability such as with the National Merit Scholars program founded in 1955, the 1960's saw a growing number of programs based solely on income, such as the Educational Opportunity Grant for work-study programs established in 1965. Perhaps the two most striking examples are a program established by New York State, the New York Scholar Incentive Program, and the new Basic Opportunity Grant Program established by the federal government in the Higher Education Amendments of 1972. The BOG's, as the program is commonly called, entitles every student enrolled in a postsecondary institution to up to one-half the cost of attendance or the difference between his family's contribution and the actual cost of attendance, whichever is less, up to $1,400.

But, of course, the ultimate test of accessibility is the degree to which people actually utilize the opportunity. College entrance has been rising steadily; now over 50 percent of those age 18 to 22 receive some form of higher education. In some states it is over 70 percent.

Yet American higher education is still far from providing equality of opportunity. Not only do access rates still differ significantly by socioeconomic status, there also remain the vexing questions "access to what and to what purpose?"

Equality of opportunity turns out to be simpler to express that to apply. Every student is given a chance to compete, but within the framework of goals and rules established on meritocratic principles by dominant social groups. To achieve true equality, some argue, the rules need changing. In admissions this has come to mean everything from special efforts to recruit low-income and minority groups to quotas and forms of reverse discrimination. But, as has become painfully clear, equality of access has not led to equality of education, or for many to much education at all.

Recent arguments claim that equality of opportunity requires more than access and more compensatory programs--rather, it requires a social responsibility for equality of results. According to this view, the primary purpose of college should be to equalize ability and achievement. At a minimum, this would mean that a substantial proportion of college resources and energies would be devoted to the least advantaged.

But equality of results is an inappropriate and misleading goal. There cannot be equality of results for all, because all students do not want or need the same results. In elementary education, there is a broad social purpose served by students achieving some common skills--mastery of the language, knowledge of civics, familiarity with mathematics--as well as sharing some common social experiences.

But postsecondary education does not attempt such unity. Not only do its students have different abilities and motivations, they also have different goals. There cannot be equality of results between an 18-year-old student studying nursing to prepare for a career and a 40-year-old fully engaged in life studying psychology in order to develop a new and broader outlook toward life.

Public policy cannot and should not strive for equality of results. Yet it should encourage much more than simply access to some kind of "college." Perhaps the best goal is equality of educational opportunity. Under this goal the government would oppose discrimination on grounds we deem socially inappropriate and aid the least financially advantaged students. Beyond that, the goal is more difficult, in part because our understanding and ability to measure effectiveness and usefulness in postsecondary education is limited.

However, part of the new effort should be to encourage differing patterns of attendance so that a student who wishes to go to college when he is ready to learn, not when he is the traditional age, will find this socially acceptable as well as feasible. Another part of the effort should be to encourage differing institutions with multiple standards for selectivity (not just the single standard of academic ability). This requires some concept of the differing dimensions of human excellence. In short, public policy should create an opportunity more realistic than now exists for most students to gain from access to postsecondary education. At the same time this makes the student responsible not only for the type of education he chooses for his career and role as a citizen, but for the match between the educational institution and his own goals and abilities.

The Domain Of Postsecondary Education

In the early postwar era, it was clearer what a college was. There were colleges, universities, and vocational schools, yet higher education was largely recognized as consisting of only the first two. With the advent of the community college, encompassing both liberal arts from the traditional college and vocational studies from the traditional vocational school, that distinction began to blur. Gradually more types of educational programs and institutions developed. Today the spectrum includes research universities, proprietary vocational schools, and off-campus education. Yet this range of institutions represents only a portion of the universe of institutions in America offering noncompulsory formal instruction to individuals who have completed high school. Career and professional training is also offered by industrial and labor organizations, and by governmental agencies such as the Armed Services. Education for personal fulfillment and cultural enrichment is offered by still other institutions from language schools to zoological gardens.

The universe of postsecondary education is broad in an era of egalitarianism. Since all students are of equal concern, then their institutions deserve not only equal concern, but equal eligibility for public funds as well.

Standards For Evaluating Performance

If the purpose of college is essentially meritocratic, then college admissions and the evaluation of student performance are appropriately based on competitive performance according to standards set principally by the faculty. Yet if the purpose of college is egalitarian in nature, the issue is not, "How does the student compare with his peers?" Rather, the issues are, "What is the student's potential? How far has he developed in terms of this potential? What does he want to do, and how can we assist him? What does it take to be a citizen?"

532-819 O - 74 - 2

In judging egalitarian objectives, one would not look merely to the quality of an institution's graduates, for high quality might indicate merely that only potentially successful students were recruited. Rather, one should look for change the college itself brought about in the student from wherever the student initially began. What was the educational value added? A community college which produced significant changes in students of low initial skills would, therefore, be judged more effective than a prestigious university which did little more than admit able students and graduate them undamaged four years later.

This concept has profound implications for testing in higher education and credentialing in American society. Presently, most testing is designed to measure how well the student can do in academic courses, not what he can do as a citizen and worker. Indeed, the wrong factors are being tested, for academic grades often correlate poorly with performance in many careers.

Particularly in career-oriented training, admission criteria ought to be more meaningful to later performance. The use of traditional academic measures is meaningless in some cases; for example, it is uncommon to use grades or a national test to select entrants to music conservatories or theater workshops. For medical training as well--although high grades are essential for admission--there is little attempt to determine what is relevant to success in medical practice. What evidence is available seems to indicate that beyond a point grades are not closely coupled to performance. Yet it is grades which determine which students gain public subsidies.

When we consider expanding public subsidies for other career-oriented and recurrent education, it becomes apparent that factors other than academic performance as measured by grades should be the basis for determining financial assistance. There is a new awkwardness about present standards. Much was taken for granted before that will not necessarily follow under current conditions. Moreover, the growth of recurrent education will make increasingly apparent the limitations of today's emphasis on academic standards in measuring learning of any sort.

Public Expectations Of Higher Education

Particularly since World War II, the gateway to the upper spectrum of American society was thought to be college. Ironically, colleges are losing this social "placement" function as increasing numbers of individuals gain college degrees. The result is that college is an often necessary but no longer sufficient condition of social mobility. Not having the degree may block opportunities. Having it will not insure them.

It is difficult, however, to determine which way the causal relationship works. Is social mobility a function of education, or do people likely to be socially mobile also perceive that education is useful? Are educational credentials required for more middle and upper class jobs because more college credentialled applicants are available?

The rise in college attendance rates leads, of course, to a growing dilemma. Mobility is in general perceived in relationship to someone else. If some move up, others must move down. Somehow it must be made clear that, no matter how socially desirable, everyone cannot join the upper-middle class.

Higher education continues to provide meaningful social mobility in view of this dilemma. Yet social mobility was the basis for so much public support in recent decades.

Education And Jobs

The general public, including students and educators alike, have long believed the maxim, "go to college, get a good job." As a primary goal, that corrupts the concept of higher education. In a society well on its way to an egalitarian mode of postsecondary education, such maxims may no longer even be realistic.

Within the last few years, a number of occupations requiring highly-trained college graduates have been receiving applicants above the normal vacancies. Increasingly, the question is, "Will the requirements of the job market call for all these well-trained people?" It was not always this way. In fact, just a few years ago it was more common to hear the question being put in an entirely different form, "How can the educational system of the country provide the necessary trained manpower to prepare for the post-industrial knowledge-based economy?"

The actual manpower requirements of the economy are extraordinarily difficult to measure. The advancing sophistication of our society does require new levels of education and training that are less difficult to measure. But a second phenomenon complicates the picture. Jobs are often redefined to require higher levels of education simply because more college-trained people are available. For example, it is now more common for policemen to have college training.

Some jobs have precise training and membership levels, and some, nursing and teaching for instance, grow with the population. In another set of jobs, one can tell who has been trained for the role, but not how many are required. Lawyers and architects fall into this category. In most jobs, it is impossible to tell either how many people are trained for the job or how many are required. Stockbrokers, clerical employees, and many government workers fall into this indefinite category.

There have been a number of recent attempts to study carefully the changing make-up of the work force and its relationship to educational training. Such studies indicate there will be more than enough "supply" in almost every field compared to "demand." The few exceptions will be those where restrictions from licensing or the need for very specialized training will limit the number of graduates. Medical training is the obvious example. As a result, most occupations historically considered college-level type jobs will have more trained people than openings.

The actual requirements of the labor force for educated manpower are unclear. Obviously they are flexible. To some degree, the availability of people with certain types of training may in turn affect the shape of the economy. There are, however, two ways to measure whether there is a general shortage of well-trained people.

First, at the current level of college attendance, jobs which individuals take immediately after they finish college must absorb approximately twice the proportion of college graduates as presently exist in the make-up of the total labor force. In addition, these entry-level jobs must absorb an even larger share of non-graduate college attendees.

Second, compared to other developed nations, the American economy currently absorbs at least twice the share of college graduates and somewhat more than that of college attendees.

Balancing supply and demand under current circumstances is more difficult due to changing perceptions of the roles of women. Twenty years ago most women college graduates expected to become full-time wives and mothers. Those that entered the labor force were required to settle for a job that might normally have demanded less than a college education. Now women increasingly want full equality. Since they represent approximately 42 percent of the bachelor's degrees granted in this country, the trend toward entering the work force with new and higher expectations could potentially double the number of those looking for "college level" jobs.

Education And Income

The assumption is widespread in American society that going to college leads to a high-paying job. Obviously this is true in certain cases of restricted entry such as the case of the physician.

The evidence, however, on the relationship between income and education is more complex. There is an earnings gap between college attendees and nonattendees, but several factors must be taken into account. First, the gap is narrowing. A recent census publication indicates a 60 percent overlap between incomes of those with a college education and those without. As the percentage of the work force attending some college continues to rise, one would expect the gap to narrow. Not only are college attendees forced to enter a broader range of jobs, including some that are lower paying, but also the rate of pay of many jobs that have traditionally not required a college education have been moving upward at a rate exceeding the general increase in wage rates, particularly where strong unions are involved.

There is also a small number of studies where the attempt has been made to measure income levels of control groups of young people of roughly comparable ability, one of which attends college and the other does not, where the nonattendees have been drawn so as to include those who would normally have been expected to attend but for some reason could not. Though the evidence is sparse, it seems to indicate that some of those who did not attend college under such circumstances achieve higher incomes than their counterparts.

There is, of course, a conceptual difficulty in any measurements of the relationship between income and education. Those who are aggressive, intelligent and generally capable enough to achieve high incomes perceive the public reverence for college education and act upon it. Presumably they value education for its own sake as well. Consequently, those most likely to gain high incomes are also most likely to go to college. It is extraordinarily difficult to tell whether college itself has much influence on their incomes.

In the question of education and jobs, there is an important public policy concern which must not be overlooked. In several countries, the government has gradually assumed the responsibility for detailed manpower planning. Occasionally, within this country the argument has been put forward that public policy as represented by either the federal or state government has a responsibility to match the numbers of students encouraged to enter into different types of academic training with the numbers required by the work force in those occupations. For example, some years ago, when the first oversupply of physicists became apparent, the cry was raised that the federal government, having encouraged students into long graduate programs in physics, had a responsibility to insure that employment levels in that field were kept high in order to employ those who had undertaken the training in good faith. It was argued that at a minimum the government had the responsibility to provide funding and other support for new training to re-adapt the physicists to fields in which there would be career opportunities.

However, no amount of manpower planning can guarantee the individual that acceptance by an institution, assistance through training and obtaining a credential, will mean that a place will be waiting for him. The responsibility must be for the individual to select his own path. Manpower planning can influence people into careers in short supply, but presently it is not possible for people to be guaranteed a place in life as a result of following those influences.

Since the educational system can no longer insure jobs, it should return to its rational function of instilling a desire to learn rather than offering a ritualistic entry into the job market.

The Need For Diversity

The desire to learn is only part of what is needed to make a more effective system of postsecondary education. The system itself must become much more diverse to accommodate the new range of incoming students. The response on the part of many educators to such a proposition is, "But we are diverse! We have two-year colleges, four-year colleges and graduate schools. We have public and private institutions. We have liberal arts, vocational, and career education. We have institutions, large and small, and student bodies of all different mixes."

This is true, even though in some of these dimensions, diversity is decreasing. Small institutions and private institutions are educating a declining share of the total college population, and the number of single-sex and other specialized institutions is declining. The correlation between the academic selectivity of institutions and the socioeconomic status of their student bodies remains significant though somewhat mitigated.

But the real issue concerns what kind of diversity there is from the perspective of students. To increase the effectiveness of teaching and learning, we need in particular to extend the diversity of educational missions and methods.

As for missions, nearly all colleges impart knowledge organized into disciplines. Yet it can no longer be assumed that the mission of education is to process students through common patterns of academic achievement.

As for methods, a number of colleges are now exploring alternatives to the classroom lecture format. But across the landscape of American higher education, learning is still largely a spectator sport. New methods utilizing outside resources, active learning techniques, and concrete tasks and problems could create the excitement of learning.

The social systems within which teaching and learning occur define the patterns of interaction and roles taken by teachers and learners. The fact that American higher education has institutionalized a single system involving academic years and semesters--in which knowledge is fragmented into courses, attended at fixed times by teachers and students who both play prescribed roles--helps explain the lack of diversity. In this sense, American higher education has become a single, though decentralized, service bureaucracy which like all other bureaucracies is based on habit.

There are two strategies important in encouraging needed diversity. First, it is desirable to develop new institutions. Yet today, educational entrepreneurs find it harder and harder to find funding, overcome accrediting barriers, meet state requirements, and so forth. This is the experience of those new institutions primarily devoted to recurrent patterns of education; the universities without walls and the open universities are good examples of this. Similarly, resources and incentives are needed to encourage the evolution of established institutions within the conventional nonprofit segment of higher education.

Second, society should recognize and legitimize the serious educational activities of peripheral institutions, including those of the armed services, proprietary institutions, and industry. This unsung segment of higher education clearly meets certain adult needs more effectively than the conventional sector. The nation will be served best by a diverse system that includes public and private, nonprofit and proprietary education. All should compete under conditions which encourage a healthy attention to each institution's effectiveness.

By movements in these directions, educational standards can--and should--be raised, not lowered. Standards need not--and should not--be confused with higher and higher levels of abstraction in the content of learning or the degree of similarity to the teaching style of a graduate seminar. The appropriate educational standards for our era should maximize effectively the potential of each student to learn and think. Such skills can be enhanced if the teaching process really engages the student. A mere pass-fail system--rigorous and finely discriminative on purely academic standards--is insufficient.

In summary, higher education is being reshaped by enormous social forces. Today's era of egalitarian opportunity poses serious questions we were able to ignore previously. Public expectations of high paying jobs for every college attendee, regardless of energy, motivation and other skills, must be dispelled lest there be massive social dissatisfaction.

To respond to these new circumstances, higher education must relax the acceptable patterns of college attendance. Since learning depends on motivation, the student should be in college when he is ready to learn and out of college when he is not. If he is unready and unmotivated to learn at an early age, he should not be considered "odd" when he attends college at a later age with better motivation.

Recurrent education must be made available for a full range of educational opportunity. If it is to have a serious impact, a student should not be required to complete all academic work and credentials early in life to place himself in a relatively permanent career trajectory.

Credentialism must not be allowed to block the paths to upward mobility through job opportunity. For example, it must be possible to go from an associate arts degree in nursing to a bachelor's degree in nursing without paying an extraordinary penalty (often today it is necessary for students, after two years of education and several years of experience, to begin as freshmen in order to get a bachelor's degree in nursing). It must also be possible for a nurse to find entrance to medical schools leading to an M.D. degree. Unless this is true, many will feel compelled early to strive to the highest level for fear that they will permanently confine themselves to lower levels. While such a pattern of educational development is appropriate for a certain percentage of students, most students would probably prefer to start with limited goals and expand their horizons as they mature.

Since many consider a conventional campus a place where young people go but where more mature people do not, we should realize that all educational institutions cannot be conventional campuses. There should be a spectrum of choices among institutions, just as there is a spectrum of student interests and needs.

The foundations are already available, and upon them we must build a widespread and flexible system of recurrent education to supplement our conventional system. Today it is neither sensible nor feasible to fit the millions of different student needs and interests into a single plan of organization.

recurrent education—the issues

J.R. GASS

Has education--in terms of quantity, quality and equality--gone so far wrong that major changes are needed? If so, can recurrent education provide the guiding principle for restructuring education in the future?

One of the problems with traditional education is that its expansion to more and more young people limited its social utility. This questions whether the United States model of educational growth is the right one to follow, even if the Japanese and the Europeans are already well down that same road.

Another issue is whether the gap between schooling and the real needs of individuals and society has not reached a point where school and other forms of learning have to be more inter-connected.

Many feel that education has not promoted social equality to the desired extent. Whether a redistribution of educational opportunities, relating them more to adult social and career motivations, would bring about more equality or inequality is a question that requires examination.

A clear diagnosis of the present crisis is needed if we are to come to grips with such complex issues. A crucial point is that we will enhance our educational reform possibilities if we know more about the social functions and reactions of education.

For instance, the socio-education links of today are conceived of in straight line education-career vectors. It hardly ever works that way for any individual. Since the world beyond the school is a strange and somewhat fearful place for many young people, they tend to seek bridges. More bridges could be constructed to meet this sociological phenomenon. In addition, exposure to work or other experience leads many to a crystallization of ambition, hope, and will. Why distribute all the educational opportunities before this takes place?

We also need to know better how education affects--or can affect--certain groups. Women, for instance, are in a particularly difficult box. They are educated more and more to do less and less. Then there is a rapidly growing number of middle-aged professionals who are casualties because their knowledge falls behind the demands of organizational efficiency. Retired persons also constitute another group for which some form of educational preparation is clearly needed.

We all know there must be some sort of a fit between educational output and the needs of the economy. Despite the rapid development of the economics of education, that fit has never been worse. The fundamental reason is that in open, democratic societies, the social demand for education is only partly responsive to the labor market for qualifications. It translates the hopes and aspirations of individuals and families for the vaguely perceived future. It is a cat which will always jump out of the bag of economic forecasting. That is why manpower analysis is at best a partial tool for educational policy.

Is the answer then to improve the fit by better information and guidance about careers and their relationship to educational qualifications? Obviously, this is one sensible thing to do.

But the real issue surely is that choices must be changed. If the fundamental option remains as today--i.e., opt for higher education and the income and status that goes with it, or opt for work and proceed to the other side of the track--then, of course, the social demand for education will pile up beyond the capacity of the economy to absorb it. Relative prices of educated and uneducated manpower may adjust, but are not the social costs of this adjustment too high to justify the Clapham Junction approach to social selection via the educational system?

Moreover, changing social and industrial conditions call for some form of education and training as a necessary service to enable the continuing development and adjustment of the individual. If "participation," "democratic management," "adaptability and mobility," and "creativity" in work--all slogans of the contemporary industrial society--are to be meaningful, is not access to education and training one of the indispensable conditions of work in a modern society?

Possibly the best hope of interconnecting the individual's career, the educational system and the economic system is recurrent education. Access to such education should be an indispensable individual right in a modern democratic society.

The equity issue logically follows the economic issue because--strangely enough--the two are related. The idea of a meritocracy may be seen as a response to disillusionment in the contribution of political ideologies to transforming income and social structure.

"If someone has to win may the best man (or woman?) win--thanks to equal access to education." Equally, "if we (the parents) are unequal, at least our children will be more equal--through education. . . ." To write off by doubtful statistics these fundamental responses to the failure of political ideologies to meet fundamental human aspirations in the 20th Century is perhaps going too far. Can we believe that parents will take seriously the proposition that the persistence of educational inequality is consistent with more equal life chances for children?

The response to the persistence of inequalities does not lie in giving up education as a tool of redistribution, but in relating it more effectively to the other relevant policies, and thereby strengthening its effective role in equality. The struggle for equity has to be across-the-board and penetrate more deeply into the life cycle. To do this we should break the monopoly of the 16-19 age group on access to higher education; encourage firms, trade unions and public administration to accept responsibility for developing individuals through education and training; and allow more flexible certification procedures for professional qualifications. These are some of the steps that might be needed if education is to continue to promote social equity.

If social mobility in the 19th Century came from the self-made man; and in the first half of the 20th Century from the educated child; why cannot it now come from adults who return to education over a good part of their working lives?

Let us not forget that, when all is said and done, learning is an objective of the educational system. But the institutionalization of learning in schools has produced a strange dilemma. If there is one pedagogical truth, it is that animals learn by practice and humans by theory and practice. Not theory _or_ practice, but theory _and_ practice; the acquisition of principles and their incorporation into behavior are part of the _same_ process. Yet most of our educational efforts today are based on theory in the formal educational system _or_ practice elsewhere, later, or perhaps never.

To increase actual learning, many more bridges must be created between the school and real life and between the formal educational system and training activities and experience in industry. This can only be achieved if pedagogical functions are recognized as existing in all social institutions. The monopoly that schools and universities have on education can be dispersed by the general acceptance of a less rigid and more rational view.

What are some of the main options to solve these problems, and is recurrent education one of them?

There are three possible options: reverting to a traditional, elitist form of education; an acceleration of deschooling; and some form of recurrent education which, while incorporating elements of the deschooling movement, maintains and probably reinforces the educational system as a major social institution.

There are already signs that many countries are reverting to elitist education. This occurs mainly in the form of a defense of "quality." Oddly enough, this position often goes hand-in-hand with deschooling, on the understanding that the "less able" children are deschooled. Taken together, these two options are at least a rational response to the diagnosis, in that they represent a maintenance of a successful historical experience with the educational meritocracy. Such options recognize the difficulties and failures of extending this system to all children, and they provide organized exits from schooling into work situations for less able children. But who could pretend this is not a failure of equity?

Why not be equally "realistic" and recognize the dramatic growth of training and education as part of active life? This growth is taking place already in most countries. Why not link this growth with new and more feasible patterns of working life and social participation? This is the option of recurrent education.

Of course, recurrent education could only be a gradual development. It would have to coexist with further extensions of the traditional educational system. Total substitution of traditional by recurrent education may be improbable or far in the future. The essential point is that there should be an option to link the two and make them responsive to a common set of objectives.

The key issue in all strategies is the goal. Is recurrent education to be developed to insure a better integration of education into the labor market, or is it to be designed to allow individuals to renew life chances? Both objectives are clearly present in the development of policies at present. Which should take precedence?

There are two factors which may determine which goal takes precedence. Traditional education has failed to contribute to equity. And industries and public services are beginning to accept that training opportunities in adult life should respond to broader needs than simple up-dating of knowledge or techniques, or retraining in the event of redundancy. These factors suggest that recurrent education should be broadly based rather than narrowly vocational.

If recurrent education becomes one potential response to the problems of equity and quality of life in the increasingly urbanized, organized, technologized industrial societies of today, what would be its essential components?

To begin, recurrent education must be seen as more than continued, lifelong or adult education, since it implies a new pattern of educational opportunities. This pattern will not be realized unless both the formal educational system and training opportunities in adult life are seen as part of an overall commitment to providing renewed life chances. This implies much more intensive interaction between educational institutions and the community, and the acceptance that a much wider range of social institutions offer valid learning experiences. Furthermore, the structural changes themselves will fail unless reinforced by new pedagogies which effectively combine theory and practice, as part of a learning process more meaningful for people with practical as well as academic motivations.

There is a consequent need for a much closer interaction of all social policies affecting life chances: educational, labor market, social, and income distribution.

In the future, resources should be allocated not only to adult education in the _traditional_ system, but also to developing a wider and more flexible range of options for young people. Subsidized work experience or organized social service could become some of the options. But unless policies for upper secondary education are geared to the notion of a _right_ to voluntarily deferred opportunities for higher education, social selection through education is likely to be reinforced. To achieve equality of opportunity, such a right is needed. It would have to be supported by social, labor market and financing policies which provide _incentives_ to participate in recurrent education.

recurrent education general policy options and objectives

KJELL EIDE

It is hardly a consolation that nearly everybody today seems to be in favor of recurrent education. Together with its close terminological relatives, "permanent education" and "lifelong education,"[1] "recurrent education" has come close to being a normative term;[2] we tend per definition to regard it as a good thing. But as is the case with other such terms, it is only inherently good as long as we do not clarify what we mean by it. The moment we attach a more specific meaning to the term, we may find ourselves in full disagreement about its desirability.

Recurrent education is claimed to be a remedy for most current ills of our educational systems. This paper is meant to contribute to an understanding of the concept by discussing certain claims for recurrent education, especially the following:

--Recurrent education will make education more relevant.

--Recurrent education will increase the impact of education on economic performance.

--Recurrent education will serve to counteract inequality in education.

---

1. These terms are favored by the Council of Europe and UNESCO, respectively.

2. Other such terms much in use among educational planners are "rational," "effective," and even "sound."

--Recurrent education will influence the educational system's ability to transfer values.

--Recurrent education will contribute to personal development through education.

If valid, such claims would mean that recurrent education may profoundly influence policy goals for education as stated by the responsible politicians. Such general statements on goals are not, however, very operational, and their mutual interdependencies and relative priorities leave a host of open questions. Perhaps the best we can do is to shed some light on the ends-means relationships in this context. What objectives recurrent education actually will serve may depend decisively on how we develop a system of recurrent education.

What Is New In Recurrent Education?

An essential feature of recurrent education is educational programs primarily prepared for adults who have spent some time at work. Presumably, the existence of major programs of this kind will have repercussions for prework education, that is programs offered to young people who have not left the school system.

These two features are the main characteristics of a system of recurrent education. The term "recurrent" indicates a property of an educational system, not any particular form of education. The features described here are not necessarily new to our educational systems.

In recent years, there has been increasing recognition of the extent to which learning in a modern society occurs outside educational institutions. Attempts to measure resources spent on informal learning of this kind indicate that such inputs may exceed the resources spent on formal education, even if student's foregone income is included.[3]

Large scale learning outside school, and after school-leaving age, is thus no new feature in a modern society. A considerable part of this learning comes through the mass media, and on-the-job training. Thus, even "organized" education is far from a monopoly for what we usually call "the regular school system."

The system of organized adult education also tends to expand. In the Scandinavian countries, voluntary associations for adult

---

3. For such estimates, see Stanley Moses, The Learning Force: An Approach to the Politics of Education (Syracuse, N.Y.: Educational Policy Research Institute, 1970), and Kjell Eide, "The Organization and Financing of Post-Work Education," in Permanent Education (Strasbourg: Council of Europe, 1970).

education have between 20 and 30 percent of the adult population attending their courses every year.

The repercussions of external learning opportunities for education in school may not be so easy to recognize. Yet current tendencies towards a change in the authority position of the school and of individual teachers towards pupils and students may well reflect developments outside school. Educational institutions cannot maintain their near-monopoly in knowledge dissemination. Today, even small children know that the school does not necessarily possess the right answer to all questions. Different answers provided by other sources may be as valid as those offered by the school or the teacher.

Subtly, the school system adapts to the emergence of a vast learning sector outside the school. Educational institutions tend to concentrate on those tasks which they perform best. In the long run, an essential question for the school is whether those tasks are also the ones found least interesting by the rest of society. Yet recurrent education has been referred to in several countries as an essential means of revitalizing the educational systems of today. Thus this concept must include some new features. The following are possible interpretations of this "new" quality.

--A substantial further increase in the amount of time and other resources spent on postwork education.

--A substantially greater share of postwork education taking the form of organized programs.

--A substantially greater role to be played in this field by educational institutions.

Such changes could be brought about in different ways. As few countries seem prepared to make large scale postwork education schemes compulsory, the first alternative would primarily mean the substitution of education for work-time. This could be achieved by paid educational leave or possibly by utilizing other forms of social security measures, such as unemployment or rehabilitation grants.

The second alternative would require, in addition, large scale subsidizing of organized educational programs outside educational institutions, e.g., by firms, professional, and voluntary associations.

The third alternative would require expansion of the existing facilities of educational institutions and a shift in the general orientation of their programs.

These three main alternatives may illustrate why different interest groups, though generally welcoming the principle of recurrent education, are likely to disagree on the practical implementation of such a reform, and even on what the reform really means. Its implications are, in fact, quite open as long as we have not defined how we want to put the reform into practice. Or, in other words, unless we define what purposes we should want a recurrent education system to serve, there is no basis for agreement on strategy.

532-819 O - 74 - 3

The Question Of Relevance

One of the claims of the proponents of recurrent education is that it will make educational programs more relevant. It might be wise to view such claims with a certain amount of scepticism. The educational programs we have today would hardly be offered unless some groups regard them as relevant. A challenge for more relevance, therefore, usually reflects the wish of other groups to become authorized as the ones to define educational relevance.

The quest for relevance may thus be seen as a competition for legitimized power positions in relation to the educational system. Currently industry, and especially manufacturing branches, is strongly represented in this competition. Others are professional groups wishing to control their own recruitment basis in order to fortify their power positions. In some countries, keen spokesmen for local interests are active competitors. The dark horse in this game may be the clients of the educational system themselves, the students and pupils.

In most countries, pupils have rather limited political power. They have the advantage, however, that learning is rather closely related to the feeling of relevance among those who should learn. If relevance is defined by others, a rather strong system of rewards and sanctions will be needed for students to go through an educational process. Even then it is debatable whether the process has led to internalized learning or only to imitation of the behavior rituals needed for certification.

Thus, the question whether recurrent education will lead to more relevant education is mainly a question of whom we would like education to be relevant for. It may be industry, though it would seem somewhat paradoxical if our current concern for social goals other than the purely economic ones should run parallel to an increased industrial control over education. It would be equally paradoxical if, in spite of the increasing scepticism about the established power positions of professional experts and the forms of professionalization that build up such power positions, recurrent education should be developed so as to increase the power of such groups to define what is relevant education. To others, such developments as indicated above may seem to reduce educational relevance, for instance those whose main concern is relevance as felt by pupils and students.

Impact On Work Life

Claims have been made that a system of recurrent education will affect relationships between education and work in the following ways:

--updating skills needed for work performance;

--adapting the existing work force to changes in skill requirements;

--using retraining opportunities as a buffer against short term fluctuations in labor market conditions;

--creating more opportunities for social promotion; and

--providing a basis for more broadly shared decision-making power in economic enterprises.

The validity of such claims cannot be tested against simple GNP-indicators alone. Increasingly, questions are asked about the conditions under which individuals work. Traditionally, some minimum work conditions have been regarded as constraints upon the production process. Gradually, however, promoting the welfare of those involved becomes one of the objectives of such processes, in line with other outputs.

Working conditions also form part of the wider social climate in which production takes place, and may be as decisive for successful economic performance as any "internal" productivity factors. This wider context is essential to the understanding of work-education relationships.

Continuous updating of skills today belongs to the job requirements in many professional and semi-professional positions. On the other hand, a vast number of jobs "at the floor level" in industry do not require anything of this kind. On the contrary, they are organized in ways that directly discourage more basic insight in the production processes. Such fundamental differences in job content is a consequence of current patterns of organization in industrial production, including many service industries. Such organizational patterns have often been regarded as dictated by the necessity of modern technology. The implications of future technological developments in this respect have been the subject of major studies, with no decisive outcome.

But recent research and large-scale experimentation on alternative sociotechnical designs have shown, however, that the assumed tight relationship between production techniques and organizational patterns are at least partly fictitious. Industrial enterprises, ranging from simple mechanical engineering to complex process industries, can be organized according to principles breaking the traditional trend more towards specialization and division of labor. Similar results have been achieved in shipping and in service industries.

In all these experiments productivity in conventional terms has increased, as has the satisfaction of those involved with their working conditions. It is worth noting that when such experiments have been carried out in Norwegian industry, one of the basic conditions agreed upon by both employers and employees is that each job shall offer opportunities for personal development and learning. This is, in fact, one of the basic purposes of the reorganization.

We are thus not faced today with a situation where the question of updating of skills is relevant to certain jobs and not to others. So recurrent education for the continuous updating of labor skills depends upon what kind of production structure we want, not "objective" technological requirements.

One of the difficulties in skill updating and reschooling is that when organized by industry itself, educational programs tend to be too narrow in their definition of skills needed. Individual firms are interested in providing the specialized skills associated with their own particular task structure and processes; however, they are often reluctant to provide skills that might increase the general market value of the worker. They tend to prefer training of the latter kind to be provided by educational institutions.

However, attitudes may differ from country to country in this respect, depending upon national arrangements for encouraging training within industry and the size of individual firms and the general size structure of different branches of industry.

Educational institutions, on the other hand, fight a constant and often losing battle against obsolescence. Keeping teachers technically up to date is extremely difficult, and coping with technical developments in equipment is often prohibitively expensive. So the tendency is for educational institutions to concentrate more strongly on providing a fundamental knowledge base and to leave specific skill training to industry itself.

Thus, enterprises and educational institutions not only have somewhat different qualifications to offer for educational purposes, they also tend to represent different interests. Consequently, it is difficult to define a "proper" division of labor between the two types of institutions. Adding to this confusion is the growing uncertainty as to what is really relevant education for work-life. As indicated above, we must clearly look far beyond more technical training in this context. To quote the director general of the biggest industrial enterprise in Norway: "As it is inevitable that workers will have a say in the running of our business, it becomes a managerial interest to make sure that they acquire the necessary qualifications for it."

The irrelevance of a distinction between "vocational" and "professional" training on the one hand, and "general" education on the other, is clearly brought out if we take a closer look at what "updating of knowledge" or "retraining" really involves. We find that often the educational programs offered can serve a wide variety of purposes, some of them vocational, others not clearly connected with any particular job. Frequently the characterization of such a program as "vocational" or "general" can only be based on guesses about the subjective motivation of participants or the extent to which knowledge gained might come in handy in some future professional situation.[4] One of the real obstacles today to the development of recurrent education is the traditional belief that one can make a meaningful distinction of this kind. When we try to do so, what is measured is often only the limited stretch of our own imagination.

Possibilities for "social promotion" through recurrent education may be important to employees, and may offer enterprises better opportunities for talent utilization. Yet, recurrent education is in itself not likely to change the pyramid of social positions in society. To the extent recurrent education provides new criteria for social promotion, it may mainly serve as a substitute for other promotion criteria. Recurrent education may be a useful means for enterprises wishing to increase the social mobility among its employees. However, the net effects from a social point of view are more uncertain.

Work-relevant programs of recurrent education do not, however, necessarily result only from initiatives by firms or by educational institutions. The emergence of "industrial democracy" in a number of European countries, permitting part-taking in decision-making by employees through a representative system, has created training needs of a new kind. Agreements between employers' associations and trade unions about shared financing of the training of worker representatives are not uncommon in Europe. In Norway, for instance, employers and workers make compulsory contributions to a common training fund which contributes both to the general training program of a firm, and to the particular training needs as seen by the trade union.

In firms where the democratization includes reorganization permitting participation even by workers at the "floor level," other forms of training also come to the foreground. A striking side-effect of such reorganization is the increased demand for education among groups which normally have been beyond the reach of both educational institutions and adult education organizations. It seems doubtful whether such institutions are really prepared to meet this kind of demand. The education requested has to be immediately relevant to the worker's situation, and to be offered close to his work place. Quite often, such demand is closely related to the immediate tasks of the workers. Sometimes, however, work relationship is more indirect, and in quite a few cases the relationship between education demanded and work seems quite distant.

It appears that recurrent education in this form requires organization by the workers themselves. They have to work out their own

---

4. There is a clear parallel here with attempts to distinguish between "applied" and "basic" research. In this case also we have either to guess about the subjective motivation of researchers for undertaking projects or about what possibly could be useful in the future--both rather futile exercises.

education programs and to draw upon resources made available by educational institutions, adult education organizations, or by the firm itself. Such programs have to be kept quite apart from the general training policies of the firm, and the education asked for rarely provides a basis for "social promotion." Even the upper strata in the trade union hierarchy is looked upon with some scepticism in this context. The immediate purpose seems to be to make the jobs more meaningful, to provide better possibilities for collaboration with others, and to build a more solid basis for participation in decisions about one's own situation.

There is no doubt that if the necessary means are made available, educational programs of this kind can have a strong impact on work performance. Their main objectives, however, are related to the quest for equality, not only in economic terms, but in status as human beings.

To sum up, there is no doubt that recurrent education can effectively enhance economic performance by updating relevant skills and knowledge. It can also offer opportunities for more flexibility in relation to new job requirements. In a situation where the futility of "manpower requirements" as a basis for educational planning has been clearly demonstrated, recurrent education might offer an additional means for the necessary adaptation on the demand side to outputs from the educational system.

However, the usefulness of recurrent education in this context is dependent upon how relevant skills and knowledge are defined. A too narrow definition, as will often result from enterprise-dominated programs, may only have marginal effects, and may even be harmful in providing excuses for lacking programs of a more general nature.

To some extent recurrent education may be useful in reducing an assumed "mis-match" between supply and demand in the labor market. However, as such a "mis-match" is often only an expression of rigid conventional qualification requirements. Recurrent education used for this purpose may prevent more fundamental adaptation of job definitions and the corresponding work organization.

Recurrent education is potentially of fundamental importance in relation to major organizational changes in work-life which would make conditions for personal development and learning a part of the job description of more than a minority of positions. This also implies more general participation in decision-making in economic activities, both through representative arrangements at higher levels in decision-making hierarchies, and through organizations insuring more autonomy lower down in the hierarchy.

If a development in this direction is thought desirable--or at least unavoidable--large scale recurrent education programs may be a necessary condition for such systems to function. It is not, however, so much a question of internal educational programs or promotion schemes of firms, as programs emerging from needs felt by the majority of the clients themselves, workers and employees low down in the traditional hierarchy. Viewed in this light, the enterprise might become another essential institutional framework for educational activities, a parallel to educational institutions and organizations with predominant educational purposes. The latter, however, may have to provide much of the qualified personnel needed for such new educational tasks.

The economic performance of a country is not, however, solely dependent upon what happens inside firms and enterprises. The question also is whether a country as a whole is able to handle its own affairs in a sensible way, which again depends on the ability of the population at large to contribute to wise decisions. This points towards recurrent education programs far beyond what might be thought of as directly useful for vocational purposes. It becomes a matter of providing all adults with the means by which they can achieve a minimum of control over their own fate, without going too far in exploiting that of others.

Viewed in this light, it is obvious that evaluating recurrent education in terms of increases in personal income is a rather meaningless exercise. The same applies to other simplistic cost-benefit operations assuming that economic performance can be measured in productivity terms. The interplay between work and education is far more complex; the potential contribution of recurrent education to this interplay is far more basic.

Effects On Equality

The idea that the introduction of a system of recurrent education in itself will contribute to more equality of opportunity is widespread, but hardly well founded. Groups with much previous educational attainment are demanding and obtaining most postwork education. If no specific precaution is taken, a recurrent education system is likely to have exactly the same effect. It will primarily be oriented towards, and utilized by groups with much previous education, and thus increase inequality in educational attainment.[5]

It is certainly valuable to avoid dead ends in the educational system, and to provide opportunities for return to the school by those who have left at an early stage. Yet, we know very well that the school losers concerned will rarely use such opportunities, while similar opportunities will be grabbed with enthusiasm by those who have always succeeded at school.

---

5. This is, incidently, the same effect as we achieve by a general, unselective expansion of preschool education, in spite of the frequent attempts to sell it as an equalizing device.

The total effect can hardly be a contribution to equality, unless we directly prevent individuals with a high level of school attainment from access to postwork education. Some countries, such as Scandinavia, however, may be prepared to give priority to educational programs aimed at entire groups with low educational attainments. No country, however, seems prepared to prevent high attainment groups from getting what they want, even if it has to be supplied by private institutions.[6]

This general conclusion may, however, be somewhat modified if we look at individual dimensions of inequality. Inequality concerning age is an area where literally per definition quite a lot could be achieved by recurrent education. In many countries, and perhaps more in Sweden than elsewhere, "equality between generations" has been an essential argument for the introduction of recurrent education. It is possible, however, that we may end up in "the late-comers dilemma."[7] When those lagging behind have achieved a level previously held by others, the other groups have moved further ahead. Yet clearly the opportunity to compete in educational terms will be felt as a right by many adults, and serves as a strong argument for extended recurrent education programs.

Groups fighting for equality between the two sexes have seen recurrent education as a means by which current discrimination against women can be remedied. From the experience we have already, we know that refresher or retraining courses for housewives wanting to re-enter the labor market may significantly facilitate such re-entry. Yet in many countries, housewives staying at home still represent a large part, perhaps even a majority, of adult women. Their average level of educational attainment is much lower than that of women active in the economy. Yet there is little pressure on behalf of women for major recurrent education schemes aimed at housewives, to improve skills needed for their tasks, to enhance their participation in civic and social affairs, to bridge the generation gap between them and their children, and to break their social isolation. Such aims would be essential if recurrent education were to be used seriously as a means of counteracting discrimination against women.

In most European countries recurrent education programs aiming specifically at groups with low social status are not too easy to

---

6. The idea that each individual should have the right to a "quota" of education breaks down, in fact, because no country seems willing to prevent the establishment of a "black market" for education beyond the free quota. The implication is then that access to educational levels higher than the average will be even more dependent than before upon the individual's ability to pay his way.

7. Cf. Thomas Green, "The Dismal Future of Equal Educational Opportunity," in Educational Planning in Perspective (London: Futures, 1971).

achieve on a large scale, though some of the same effects could be achieved by concentrating on groups with little formal schooling. Correspondingly, paid leave or other special rights connected with recurrent education cannot easily be reserved for special groups. Until now, it has been more easily achieved by groups with high social status and long previous training.

It is certainly valuable to develop forms of "second-chance education," but evidence shows that early school leavers are rarely tempted to return to formal education. A few may change their mind, but "second-chance education" will usually serve as a safety valve satisfying a limited number of exceptional cases.

However, if we should succeed in developing a kind of work-life in which even the majority of low-level positions provide incentives and opportunities for personal development and learning, an established pattern of "second-chance education" may be of decisive importance, and could contribute substantially to social equality. A vision of this kind may underlie many of the future perspectives in which recurrent education plays a major role. However, for the moment we may not be able to count upon large scale developments of this kind.

Recurrent education for special ethnic or cultural groups may be politically feasible in quite a few countries. It may help bring such groups into the "cultural main-stream" of the country in question. Thus, from one point of view, recurrent education could be an effective means of reducing inequality. The main problem here is the extent to which we are willing to accept cultural predominance of specific subgroups in society.[8] Equality may also mean the right to be measured by one's peer group, yet the typical approach to equality is to measure all subgroups by the values of the economic or culturally predominant groups. We do not want here to go further into those really tricky aspects of the equality issue. It is sufficient to point out that recurrent education may be an even more effective means of achieving equality within the framework of a "different but equal" policy.[9] We then leave unanswered, however, the fundamental question of whether such policies are reconcilable with the predominant reward structures of our societies.

---

8. The same actually applies, though usually not to the same extent, to the other subgroups we have dealt with, according to age, sex, social status, etc.

9. "Black studies" and their equivalents in other countries, various forms of "counter-expertise," etc. are examples.

In sum, when developing a system of recurrent education, one would have to make considerable efforts to avoid an increase in its contribution to inequality in society at large. Whether one can get beyond that point, and make recurrent education a means of achieving greater equality, is an open question. It seems feasible under certain circumstances in relation to some minority groups. In general it may require overly restrictive measures towards currently privileged groups to make such policies very likely.

Transfer Of Values

The stated goals of our policies for education usually include assumptions about the transfer of political, social and cultural values, as part of the socialization process for the young. It is very debatable to what extent our traditional school systems are able to achieve this, and it may be especially doubtful in cases where the values to be transferred by the school are questioned by other parts of society. The same applies to values preached by the school, but not practiced by it, such as the virtue of democratic procedures, tolerance towards the less successful and appreciation of effective features of individuals. In such areas the schools can achieve little more than ritualistic behavior apparently in accordance with such values. Yet the school obligingly continues to attempt such value transfers on behalf of society, which may be one of the main reasons for the current authority crisis in education.

Postwork education differs from this pattern in several ways. When noncompulsory, the only way it can recruit students is by making the teaching relevant to them as they see it. It is often said that postwork education gets more motivated students. This may simply be a reflection of the fact that the educational programs offered have to meet the interests of the participants.

Furthermore, quite frequently the students in postwork education will jointly know more about the subjects taught than the teachers. The task of the latter is primarily to create a situation in which the actual knowledge and experience of the participants are brought out to the benefit of them all. This calls for a completely different authority relationship between "teachers" and "students" than in more traditional education, and for a different institutional role for the school itself. This educational situation is likely to bring out the importance of values held by individual participants for the conclusions reached, but will rarely lead to the transfer of specific values from the school to all the participants. They may learn to respect the values of others, and thus have a practical exercise in tolerance and techniques of joint problem solving, but that is all.[10]

If large scale recurrent education programs are developed by educational institutions, it seems inevitable that some of the experience from such programs will affect the more traditional programs of those institutions. One may obtain a more realistic understanding of the possibilities and conditions for transfer of values even to children, including some minimal consistency between theory and institutional practice.

Such repercussions of recurrent education for the traditional part of the educational system may be the most important consequence of such a policy. Yet it presupposes a central role for educational institutions even in postwork education, and genuine integration within such institutions between educational programs for different age groups. The typical pattern today of establishing separate departments for adult education is one way of preventing repercussions which would force the older parts of the system to reconsider its current practices.

Contributions To Personal Development

Underlying the whole philosophy of recurrent education is the fundamental assumption that individuals have the potential of developing aspects of their personality throughout their lives. Genuine political commitment to this goal would have revolutionary consequences for our societies. We would have to face the fact that most adults today are put in situations which offer very little stimulus for learning or development. We would also have to face the consequences of overwhelming evidence showing that dehumanizing and personality contracting work situations cannot be compensated for by more leisure time or money. The spill-over effects from the work situation predominate and prevent the development of a separate "leisure-time personality." Human beings may play different roles, but basically they are individuals. Reduced to nearly nothing in their most essential life situations, humans cannot suddenly become significant in other contexts.

The contribution of recurrent education to personal development is thus decisively dependent upon the life situation of individuals in other areas. Yet recurrent education may have an independent contribution to make, provided it is not used to reinforce the dehumanizing effects of other aspects of modern societies. One can

---

10. Even adults will adopt ritual behavior, however, when incentives are strong enough. I vividly recollect the repulsive sight of a group of research institute leaders subject to a course in research salesmanship. As the course was arranged by the research council financing most of the institutes, most "students" adopted the required advertising manners.

envisage a system of recurrent education which provides individuals with means of growing out of current limitations and gaining more control of their own fate.

I should like to quote the former Norwegian Minister of Education who commented upon the education-work relationships in those terms: "Job requirements are not something given according to which people should be trained. We should rather think in terms of jobs as they ought to be in order to satisfy human beings, and then train people for such jobs. Maybe that is the most effective means of making jobs become what they ought to be."

This idea is valid also for training for purposes outside work-life. We have gradually recognized that our economy is a means by which we can achieve the things we really want. Education is often a means by which such objectives can be reached without going through the long process of production. It would be utterly irrational to treat education as if it were just an auxiliary activity to the economy, when in many cases educational measures seem a safer way of achieving many aspects of the quality of life to which we all pay lip-service.

This also should serve as a strong warning against the idea of distinguishing between work-relevant and other programs of recurrent education. In welfare terms, many people do need recurrent education of a kind not closely related to work performance. Furthermore, that need may be even greater for many groups not actively engaged in the economy. Any system of financial or other measures to facilitate individual access to recurrent education should not discriminate against those not registered as employees.

In practical terms this means that agreements within the labor market organizations can never solve entirely the question of financing individual participation in postwork education. This also applies to legal measures defining obligations and rights only for employers and employees. Recurrent education policies stopping at that would reveal a rather narrow conception of the goals of modern societies.

Ends And Means

Many of the objectives which can be set for recurrent education policy could, at least in principle, be achieved by changes within the framework of the traditional educational system. There may be an element of over-optimism in the assumption that so much which we tend to regard as not really feasible within the traditional system will suddenly become feasible if only we establish a system of recurrent education. The political forces which prevent feasibility in the first case may well be as operational in the latter. The fact that it has not yet become an established system may have some advantages.

Even more important, however, is the relation between potential objectives and specific implementations. In terms of achievement of objectives, the central point may not be whether we introduce a system of recurrent education, but how we do it.

General objectives of economic policy add to the rationale for introducing a recurrent education system. It is rather important, however, to define responsibility for organizing such education. If the aim is to improve the overall capacity for economic performance of the adult population, the main responsibility for developing recurrent education programs may have to rest with the educational institutions. Otherwise, the narrow interests of individual enterprises or professional organizations may work counter to policies beneficial for society as a whole.

The potential impact of recurrent education upon work-life increases when seen as a means for providing increased access to central decision-making for those involved in economic activities, and also for increasing control over work conditions by "floor level" employees. Education programs of this kind could be a major lever for policies that would change the dismal trends of functional specialization that make work more and more meaningless to the individual. Recurrent education could serve to counteract current inequality in education. Experience indicates, however, that this would imply very restrictive measures, limiting the rights of the groups benefiting most from the present educational system. If such policies are unrealistic, recurrent education may eventually increase inequality in education.

There is also a serious danger of discrimination between those who might want postwork education to increase their economic performance (or simply to earn more), and those who have other aims. A one-dimensional set of economic objectives for society might justify such an approach, though it might imply an over-estimation of our ability to distinguish what is economically relevant. However, if we accept political commitments to broader social goals, distinctions of this kind are unnecessary.

Correspondingly, there would be no rational arguments for discriminating against those not economically active. Criteria related to the need for postwork education are necessarily based on value judgments. Yet it seems likely that criteria could be agreed upon that would identify the needs of nonemployees.

Postwork education implies an educational situation different from traditional programs for the young. It differs in terms of relevance as seen from the point of view of participants, motivation and authority relationships. Potentially, experience gained in adult education may lead to significant changes in more traditional education. This presupposes, however, that educational institutions play a major role in postwork education, and that no institutional walls are permitted to safeguard the traditional functions from spill-over effects from the new to the old ones.

Whatever we want, real access to recurrent education is likely to be a strategic point in its implementation. It seems likely that we shall need legally defined rights to leave from work during postwork education. Otherwise, the specific interests of employers will become too dominant in deciding the main direction of recurrent education programs.

The question of financial compensation for income foregone during postwork education will have to be raised at a relatively early stage. How far one would want to go with such compensation would depend upon the training capacity available and the scale of education desired.

I doubt whether there would be much point in establishing priorities for different kinds of recurrent education. It might be more meaningful to attach priorities to specific target populations, bearing in mind, however, that programs designed for a specific group do not necessarily reach their target.

It is quite conceivable that rights to paid leave during postwork education will be obtained first through labor-management negotiations. This is how many other social benefits have emerged,[11] to be later replaced by legislation insuring more comprehensive coverage. This could also be the strategy for development of recurrent education programs. The risk would be, however, that groups with less bargaining power, or with no access to bargaining positions at all, would be discriminated against for a long time.

Covering a major part of income foregone during postwork education is often held to be economically prohibitive. Yet the costs to society are not substantially greater than by a corresponding prolongation of prework education. In the latter case the income foregone does not only correspond to salaries for beginners, one also has to include a lasting delay in salary increases due to practical experience. The total loss of salary will not be substantially different from the corresponding loss in the case of postwork education leave. Bearing in mind that salaries are bad measures of actual social costs anyway, the difference here is hardly significant.

What is significant is the difference in the form of financing. While we still rely mainly upon income foregone during prework education to be financed by individuals and their families, financing must at least partly come from other sources during postwork education. To some extent the source could be industry, but a more general system would need public financing. For countries with a comprehensive system of social security, it may offer a convenient mechanism for the gradual development of a system for financing individual participation in recurrent education.

---

11. Such as sick leave, old age pensions, etc.

On the supply side, two main alternatives are expanding the regular school system (including public mass-media) to take care of a major part of organized recurrent education programs, or subsidizing private activities. The latter will leave very little possibility for control over priorities; social biases and predominance by economic interests would be unavoidable. The former alternative would maintain a certain control, at least in principle, and may also help develop a system responsive to the potential students.

The future role of recurrent education will first of all depend upon the extent to which we are willing to accept that human beings both can and should develop and learn throughout their lives. If we decide to face the far-reaching political consequences of such a decision, recurrent education will be a key instrument in the social changes that follow.

If, however, we are more concerned with conserving social institutions as we know them today, and the established power structures of current society, recurrent education is unlikely to introduce fundamental new developments. Its main function will then be to reinforce the conserving nature of traditional school systems and the control by interests predominant in contemporary society.

supply and demand factors

532-819 O - 74 - 4

restructuring education and its timing

VIRGINIA SMITH

For some, recurrent education is a form of adult or further education; to others, it is an educational approach that relates to the whole of postcompulsory education.

Clearly, the exact type of recurrent education sought will largely dictate the desirable structures and timing by which it will be accomplished and will also determine the extent to which the basic structures of higher education themselves will be changed.

In the United States, a substantial part of the impetus for recurrent education has come not so much from the direct desire to alleviate inter- or intra-generational gaps but rather from the desire to bring about a qualitative improvement in higher education itself and to make it more beneficial to those who had gained and are continuing to gain access to it.

In 1900 only about six of each 100 persons 17 years old in the United States graduated from high school. By 1970 over 70 out of each 100 graduated from high school and over 50 percent of these went on to college.

By the beginning of the 1970's mass higher education was a fact in the U.S. and universal access to higher education was a reality in many states. More than a thousand two-year community colleges, most of them operating under open admissions policies, offered education beyond high school to young and old alike.

While most policy makers were agreed upon the benefits of universal access to higher education, by the 1970's several were questioning the wisdom of universal attendance in higher education as the best way to meet the postcompulsory needs of all. And several were questioning whether traditionally organized collegiate programs were necessarily the best vehicles for educating the nation.

In its report, Less Time, More Options, the Carnegie Commission on Higher Education observed that:

> society would gain if work and study were mixed throughout a lifetime, thus reducing the sense of sharply compartmentalized roles of isolated students v. workers and of youth v. isolated age. The sense of isolation would be reduced if more students were also workers and if more workers could also be students; if the ages mixed on the job and in the classrooms in a more normally structured type of community; if all members of the community valued both study and work and had a better chance to understand the flow of life from youth to age. Society would be more integrated across the lines that now separate students and workers, youth and age.[1]

The Carnegie report did not use the term "recurrent education" but the above quotation and many of the recommendations in the report were clearly directed to the achievement of those elements central to the concept of recurrent education--the distribution of education over the total life-span of the individual in alternation with work and with leisure and retirement.

The Carnegie Commission was not alone in the U.S. in expressing this need. The Report on Higher Education,[2] issued by a task force appointed by the Secretary of Health, Education, and Welfare, was concerned with this problem and some of the same concerns were expressed in the first report of the Assembly on Goals and Governance sponsored by the American Academy of Arts and Sciences.[3]

Consensus among these groups does not, however, reflect unanimous endorsement, either in theory or practice, of this principle within the system of higher education nor within the general society. There are formidable barriers to recurrent education. These barriers are present to some extent in all colleges and universities, and their impacts continue to affect large numbers of potential learners. While the present structure of American higher education permits a high degree of mobility among institutions and substantial flexibility in patterns of attendance, the system still to some extent is characterized by elements that favor the full-time student working without interruption toward a degree.

---

1. Carnegie Commission on Higher Education, Less Time, More Options (New York: McGraw-Hill, 1971), p. 2.

2. Frank Newman, Report on Higher Education (Washington, D.C.: Government Printing Office, 1971), p. 7.

3. American Academy of Arts and Sciences, The Assembly on University Goals and Governance (Boston: American Academy of Arts and Sciences, January 1971).

When qualified applicants have to be narrowed for admission, the part-time student may be denied entrance.

Most college curricula are planned with the degree in mind as the terminal point, thus little attention is given to the development of shorter, educationally cohesive modules, except in nondegree extension programs or in certain occupational certificate programs in community colleges and in some experimental colleges.

Both the scheduling of courses and course load limitations have generally been designed with the full-time young student in mind. While scheduling is based on the assumption that students are available on a full-time basis, course-load limits appear to be based on the assumption that students are really only devoting a part of their time to study activity. This is probably appropriate for the young full-time student who is expected to engage in considerable extracurricular activity, but it is not necessarily appropriate for an adult who may have a shorter block of time available, and who may want to use it more intensively.

Both financial subsidies to students and direct institutional support in many states are based on sharp distinctions between students enrolled for degrees and those simply taking courses. In some states, it has been proposed that a student taking work not required for his degree should pay the full instructional cost of such work. In many states, substantial institutional support is given for day-time classes and regular residence programs, but extension and continuing education programs are required to be fully self-supporting.

In some institutions, even in the recent past, the in loco parentis approach of the institution was entirely inappropriate for an adult learner. Although this has largely disappeared from many institutions, some organizational and physical vestiges of it remain in many colleges.

Faculties, by and large, have not generally given the same recognition to off-campus instruction or to lower division instruction in institutions limited to lower division courses as they have given to courses offered in their own residence programs.

Interaction between the learner and educational institutions can be characterized as a discontinuous series of interactions with progressively higher levels of institutions. Although it has always been possible for a person to work for a while before going on to the next institutional level, until recently this has been considered a disadvantage, rather than an advantage. The break in educational progress, for instance, can handicap an applicant in the area of gaining the necessary letters of recommendation from past instructors.

In the U.S., conscious efforts are currently being made to modify these structural barriers:

1. The "stop-out" is gaining new acceptance. The Carnegie Commission recommended that:

> service and other employment opportunities be created for students between high school and college and at stop-out points in college through national, state, and municipal youth programs, through short-term jobs with private and public employers, and through apprenticeship programs in the student's field of interest; and that students be actively encouraged to participate.[4]

In supporting this recommendation, the Commission noted that in a study of 1961 college graduates, over three-fifths of those responding felt that there should be some stopping-out either between high school and college or during college.[5]

In its supplement to the report, Quality and Equality, the Commission recommended that students earn educational benefits while participating in service activities similar to those earned in military service.[6] In a recent report of a higher education task force established by the Department of Health, Education, and Welfare, the task force proposed that legislation be introduced to provide:

> limited education benefits to those people who voluntarily choose to step out of formal education in order to participate in select national, regional and local programs of community service. The benefits, modelled after those of the G.I. Bill, would accrue during the period of service and would be used later whenever the volunteer chose to enroll in a postsecondary education institution.[7]

Some colleges have changed admission policies or have more actively publicized traditional policies that enable students to delay entry.

2. The sharp line between high school and college is being modified by a variety of techniques:

College admission at the end of the sophomore or junior year, always possible for a selected few, is being expanded.

---

4. Less Time, More Options, p. 13.

5. Joe H. Spaeth and Andrew M. Greeley, Recent Alumni and Higher Education (New York: McGraw-Hill, 1970).

6. Carnegie Commission on Higher Education, Quality and Equality Revised Recommendations (New York: McGraw-Hill, February 1972).

7. Chronicle of Higher Education, 7, 23 (March 12, 1973): 22.

One midwestern liberal arts college now admits a quarter of its freshmen on this basis.

Through the advanced placement testing program, college entrants become instant sophomores at some institutions if they perform satisfactorily on the examinations.

In some areas, cooperative arrangements have been worked out under which high school students are permitted to enroll in some college courses while still attending high school.

3. Recent federal legislation has recognized to a greater extent than previously the need for extending certain types of financial aid to part-time students and to students enrolled in short-cycle vocational courses at noncollegiate institutions.

4. Colleges and universities are experimenting with new delivery systems, with external degree programs, with alternate scheduling systems in order to expand educational options.

Many of these experiments will make education more accessible to the adult learner and facilitate a system of recurrent education. They are far from adequate in themselves, however, to assure that a system of recurrent education will come about. If recurrent education is to be fostered, the structure of postcompulsory education must accommodate the educational goals of the adult learner. The concept of recurrent education and its necessity in a post-industrial society is frequently tied to rapidly changing technology and the need for job retraining in response to job obsolescence. While this is clearly a critical individual and social need, as Professor Halsey, in his paper presented at this conference, pointed out, "beyond the need to build an antidote to the obsolescence of productive skill," a powerful productive system also "generates what might be termed the need to educate for consumption. Consumption in this context means the passing on and renewal of all those elements in a culture which relate to every aspect of life other than economic production."[8]

A recent survey on what adults would like to study in the U.S. provides evidence for this conclusion. See table 1.

In their study of educational activities of persons over 20, Johnstone and Rivera in 1962 found a similar pattern among those reporting educational activities, as shown in table 2.

---

8. A. H. Halsey, "Recurrent Education: More Equity or Less," see p. 89.

Table 1. What Adults Would Like To Study.

Subjects	Total Choices	First Choices
Vocational subjects (architecture, business skills, commercial art, computer science, cosmetology, education and teacher training, engineering, industrial trades, journalism, law, management skills, medicine and dentistry, nursing, salesmanship, technical skills)	78.2%	43.0%
Hobbies and recreation (crafts, fine and visual arts, flight training, performing arts, safety, sports and games, travel and living in foreign countries)	62.8	13.4
Home and family life (child development, gardening and flower arranging, home repairs, sewing and cooking)	56.0	12.0
Personal development (investment, occult sciences, personal psychology, physical fitness and self-development, public speaking)	54.3	6.8
General education (basic education, biological sciences, creative writing, English-language training, great books, humanities, languages, physical sciences, social sciences)	47.9	12.6
Public affairs (citizenship, community problems and organizations, consumer education, environmental studies, public affairs)	36.3	4.5
Religious studies	15.4	3.0
Agriculture and farming	10.9	2.9

Source: The Chronicle of Higher Education, 7 (February 5, 1973): 7.

Table 2. Educational Activities Of Adults.

Vocational	32%
Hobbies and recreation	19
General education	12
Religion	12
Home and family life	12
Personal development	5
Public affairs and current events	3
Agriculture	1
Miscellaneous	3
Total	99%

Source: John W. C. Johnstone and Ramon J. Rivera, Volunteers for Learning (Chicago: Aldine Publishing Co., 1965), p. 51, table 3:10.

Examination of these tables leads to a variety of questions:

1. To what extent has the U.S. already achieved some degree of recurrent education without systematizing it?

2. Given the nature of the educational interests, is it appropriate to put a large share of the responsibility for meeting these educational needs on colleges and universities?

3. To what extent would we want to provide public subsidy for each of these types of educational activity?

4. Is it necessary to have a planned educational system of recurrent education encompassing all of these educational goals, or is it only necessary for certain goals?

5. Are we presently making optimal use of existing non-collegiate postcompulsory educational institutions and agencies?

Answers to many of these questions are impossible at this stage because of a lack of adequate data. Only for collegiate education are there readily available, relatively reliable figures on such matters as total enrollment, expenditures, information on programs, and number of graduates. There is enough information, however, to demonstrate that substantial numbers of adults in the U.S. are enrolled in education and that much of this education takes place in noncollegiate institutions. One of the few studies that provide estimates of total learning force involvement based on an intensive study of a sample is that reported in Volunteers for Learning.[9] In that study, the researchers estimated that over 13.5 million adults were engaged in some type of educational activity in 1962 and that another almost 9 million were engaged in independent self education in 1962. The following table is a breakdown by type of sponsoring institution of the number of adults attending classes, lectures, talks, or discussion groups.

Table 3. Estimated Number of Persons Who Attended Formal Education Programs at Different Sponsoring Institutions.

Sponsoring Institution	Estimated Number of Persons	Percent of Total
Churches and synagogues	3,260,000	22.3%
Colleges and universities	2,640,000	18.0
Community organizations	2,240,000	15.3
Business and industry	1,860,000	12.7
Elementary and high school	1,740,000	11.9
Private schools	1,120,000	7.7
Government (all levels)	1,050,000	7.2
Armed Forces	480,000	3.3
All other sponsors	240,000	1.6
Total	14,630,000*	100.0%

Source: Adapted from Johnstone and Rivera, Volunteers for Learning, p. 61, table 3:14.

* There is double counting in this figure to the extent of 1,270,000 persons since that many persons reported taking courses from two or more sponsoring institutions.

9. Johnstone and Rivera, Volunteers for Learning.

While these figures do not include postsecondary learners who are under 20, it does provide substantial evidence that, for the adult learner, noncollegiate postsecondary institutions and agencies provide a significant portion of postsecondary educational experience.

It is interesting to compare this universe of postsecondary education with that reflected in the recent survey of adult learning sponsored by the Commission on Non-Traditional Study.[10] Unfortunately, the data in the two studies are not completely compatible, but they are roughly designed to measure the same type of educational activity. A comparison suggests certain shifts that warrant a more careful examination of the data. The 1972 study shows a relative drop in the importance of churches and synagogues. While these accounted for 22.3 percent of the educational activities of individuals over age 20 in 1962, they had dropped to 6.3 percent in the 1972 study. Private schools, which enrolled 7.7 percent of these persons in 1962, dropped to 2.9 percent in 1972. The importance of business and industry as an educational enterprise seems to have increased, as evidenced by the figure of 12.7 in 1962 and 18.4 in 1972. And, even though there has been a tremendous increase in the number of community colleges with their emphasis on adult education, the importance of colleges and universities in the total postsecondary educational complex has dropped from 18 percent to approximately 11 percent.[11]

Overall, Johnstone and Rivera estimated one in five persons over 20 was involved in some type of postsecondary educational activity. A recent estimate of the learning force by the Educational Policy Research Center at Syracuse University (SURC) came up with an even higher participation rate. Table 4 summarizes SURC's estimates.

Table 4. Adults Participating in Postsecondary Education, by Type of Participation, 1970 (in millions of people).

College and university	7.3
Business, government, military	21.7
Proprietary	9.6
Correspondence	5.7
Television	7.5
Other adult	10.7
Total	62.5

10. The Chronicle of Higher Education, 7 (February 5, 1973): 7.

11. Many of these shifts may be explained by differences in definitions of educational activities and in the questions asked in the two studies. Since the full 1972 study has not yet been published, this detailed comparison was not possible at this time.

Double counting for students engaged in more than one type of postsecondary educational activity may inflate the SURC estimates to some extent. Nonetheless, it is interesting to note that college and university enrollment as a part of the total postsecondary educational complex accounts roughly for only 12 percent of the total number of persons participating in postsecondary education, which is within the range suggested by the other two studies. On the other hand, the relative importance of business, government and military, and proprietary schools appears to be substantially greater in the SURC estimates than in the other two studies.

As mentioned earlier, information concerning noncollegiate postsecondary education is fragmentary and incomplete. There is, however, some information available on particular segments of that universe:

In 1962 it was estimated that about $17 billion would be devoted to education by business that year.[12]

A later study, with a more restricted definition of education, estimated that nearly $20 billion was spent by approximately 85 percent of the major industries in America in 1967 for scientific, management, and technology educational programs within industry--an amount greater than the expenditures of all private and public colleges and universities in the nation for all types of college level education that year.[13]

In 1968 the United States Armed Forces Institute offered over 8,814 courses to members of the armed forces and in 1967 it was estimated that almost $2 million was obligated for armed services education in that year.[14]

By 1970 there were over 275,000 apprentices who registered in some 350 formal occupational apprentice programs.[15]

---

12. Sally J. Olean, Changing Patterns and Continuing Education for Business (Syracuse, N.Y.: Syracuse University Press, 1967), p. 8.

13. William G. Torpey, "Company Investment in Continuing Education for Scientists and Engineers," Educational Record, 45, 4 (Fall 1964): 408.

14. Amiel T. Sharon, College Credit for Off-Campus Study, Report 8 (Washington, D.C.: ERIC Clearinghouse on Higher Education), p. 15.

15. Manpower Report of the President (Washington, D.C.: Government Printing Office, 1972), p. 271, table F-11.

There are various estimates of the number of private specialty schools and the number of students enrolled in them. Johnstone and Rivera estimated that over one million students were enrolled in private noncollegiate postsecondary schools in 1962.[16] In 1964 Clark and Sloane estimated that there were 35,000 specialty schools with more than five million students enrolled.[17] The Educational Policy Research Center at Syracuse University estimated that there were 9.6 million students in such schools in 1970 (see table 4). Including only those specialty schools that offer primarily vocational education, Belitsky estimated that there were 7,000 such schools in 1966 serving about 1.5 million students.[18] In 1971 almost 5,000 specialty vocational schools enrolled one or more students receiving veterans' educational benefits.

In addition, adults were also enrolled in a variety of educational activities sponsored by community organizations, churches, labor unions, museums and libraries, professional associations, and in government-sponsored programs.

Unfortunately, we lack information concerning the characteristics of the learners in these various programs. Only for very limited parts of this universe do we have information on age, economic status, and past educational experience of the learners. Such information would seem to be essential for intelligent planning of recurrent education structures in this nation.

This lack of information combined with other factors lead many of those in postcompulsory education to operate as though all educational needs subsequent to high school must be provided within the framework of colleges and universities, or if not provided, at least validated by such institutions. This is probably a natural outgrowth of the following factors:

--The importance given to college degrees as a symbol of educational achievement and of social status.

---

16. Johnstone and Rivera, Volunteers for Learning, p. 61.

17. Harold S. Clark and Harold S. Sloane, Classrooms on Mainstreet (New York: Teachers College Press, 1966), p. 4.

18. Harvey A. Belitsky, Private Vocational Schools and Their Students (Cambridge, Mass.: Schenkman Publishing Company Inc., 1969), p. 8.

--The widely disseminated research findings that college graduates enjoy higher earnings.

--The more favorable treatment given to colleges and universities for direct and indirect financial subsidies.

--The increasingly accepted requirement for a college degree for employment, even though the work leading to the degree is not directly related to job performance.

As pointed out by Sir Eric Ashby, in the U.S. traditional higher education and other kinds of postsecondary education are not segregated. No sharp distinction is made between further education and higher education. This failure to make a sharp distinction between further education and higher education may make it more possible and also more likely that colleges and universities will be the primary vehicle for all forms of recurrent education. It is not at all clear, however, that this would be a desirable use of resources. Sir Eric suggests two other possible disadvantages--that it would be difficult to protect that "thin stream of intellectual excellence on which the society depends for innovation, for wise judgment in unforeseen crisis, for management of highly complex systems," and that vocational education might well be given short shrift.[19]

There are some counter forces that are operating to shift attention to the noncollegiate segment of the postcompulsory educational system:

1. Evidence is growing that a significant number of the eight million students now attending college are "reluctant college attenders." The most recent evidence comes from a study of student attitudes sponsored by the Carnegie Commission. The results of that study suggest that one out of every 10 students would prefer to be doing something other than going to college. An additional two out of every 10 students who indicated their disagreement with the statement: "I would rather be going to college than doing anything else," did so with reservations. Thus, in the eight million students, somewhere between 800,000 and 2.4 million students would prefer not to be attending college.[20]

2. Colleges and universities, with the exception of their professional schools, have not seen vocational or occupational education as their central mission. For many college students, however, the

---

19. Eric Ashby, Any Person, Any Study (New York: McGraw Hill, 1971), p. 30.

20. See Carnegie Commission on Higher Education, Reform on Campus (New York: McGraw-Hill, 1972), pp. 98-99, Appendix A, table A-28.

primary motivation for attending college is its use as a path to employment. Both the growing signs of an oversupply of college graduates in the job market and several studies demonstrating lack of relationship between college success and job performance are reducing the attractiveness of college as a path to employment in certain fields. Moreover, colleges are becoming concerned about the misfit between what they view as their limited vocational functions and student expectations.

3. The widespread use by employers of degrees or diplomas as a prerequisite for employment is increasingly under attack in job discrimination litigation. In the recent case of Griggs v. Duke Power Company, the Supreme Court referred to the "infirmity of using diplomas or degrees as fixed measures of capability" and commented that "history is filled with examples of men and women who rendered highly effective performance without the conventional badges of accomplishment in terms of certificates, diplomas, or degrees."[21]

4. Many of the nation's heaviest manpower needs in the future will be for those skills which have not been considered important elements of most college programs and for which many colleges would lack the appropriate human and physical resources even if they chose to redefine their educational missions to include them.

5. While most colleges have been primarily concerned with the cognitive development of their students, many students are becoming concerned with the affective domain, with personal growth and development. Other types of activities, such as service, travel, or work experience, may prove as effective or more effective than traditional colleges for this type of learning.

6. The rising cost of college education and the growing competing demands on public budgets have led many to call for fresh and more careful consideration of the alternatives to college attendance for educational activities beyond high school.

7. Growing public concern, motivated by recognition of a shift in manpower needs and the rising costs of higher education, about the possible mismatch between needs of the economy and expenditures on education beyond high school has led to some pressure for new emphasis on vocational education in the allocation of funds.

The use of the whole range of institutions and agencies within the postcompulsory educational universe may provide the array of resources required to implement a system of recurrent education but their use raises some formidable problems which may require new structures.

---

21. 401 U.S. 424, 91 S. Ct. 849, 28 L. Ed. 2d 158.

In the past, the relationship between the individual learner and the institution has been essentially a closed system. The goals of the learner are delineated in institutional terms, and educational services to meet those goals are supplied by the institution. This arrangement has been possible where the major postsecondary educational experience is concentrated largely in one block of time and at one institution.[22] But with a shifting emphasis to education over lifetime and to individual determination of educational objectives, this type of relationship is not possible. The type of agency with which the individual learner might need to have his closest and most continuing relationship would be the educational consultant or broker. In a recent report, The Campus and the City, the Carnegie Commission calls for establishment of an agency of this type--the Metropolitan Educational Opportunity Counseling Center. The report states that the center would be designed to encourage more effective use of the educational resources in the area by the educational consumer. Specifically, the center would advise the citizens of the metropolitan area, regardless of their age or past educational preparation, as well as advise the Higher Education Council on the need for new facilities and on discernable shifts in student educational demands.

It was anticipated that centers be established in metropolitan areas and would have available complete resource lists of educational institutions and agencies in their areas. The Commission suggested that the centers be located in existing facilities such as libraries, community colleges and available space in other colleges and universities.[23] The Commission on Post-Secondary Education in Ontario recently made a similar recommendation calling for the establishment of counseling and guidance services available to all adults and located at public libraries.[24]

A major deterrent to recurrent education will be cost to the learner and cost to the government for student space in public institutions. Selma J. Mushkin has suggested that a system of recurrent education requires an educational leave program in which the cost is financed by a social security type scheme and in which the leave from work operates similarly to the faculty sabbatical leave.[25] In the U.S. the cost of a recurrent education system is further complicated by our mixed public/private system. If the educational security system is designed to

---

22. This has been changing and present college attendance patterns include substantial mobility among institutions, but in many institutions the transferring student is still at a disadvantage.

23. Carnegie Commission on Higher Education, The Campus and the City (New York: McGraw-Hill, December 1972).

24. Commission on Post-Secondary Education in Ontario, Draft Report, W. Kenmond (Toronto: The Queens Printer, 1972), p. 10.

25. Selma J. Mushkin, "Resource Requirements and Educational Obsolescence," in E. A. Robinson and J. E. Vaizey, eds., The Economics of Education (New York: St. Martin's Press, 1966).

cover only subsistence, then most learners would feel compelled to attend lower tuition public institutions. Access to such institutions would be partly conditioned by the state in which he happened to reside. States are now beginning to provide partial tuition grants to students, thus permitting a larger number to attend private institutions. These tuition grants are typically based on demonstrated financial need by reference to a prior year's earnings. If this system were to have any benefit for those foregoing current income to participate in education, this technique would need to be modified. Private institutions, given the present dollar gap between tuition at public and private institutions, might fare even less well in the market place in a recurrent education system than they now do.

The benefits of alternative timing for postcompulsory education have not been subjected to systematic analysis, but many have questioned the assumption that the present system is necessarily the best. The Ontario Commission asserts that there is "little logic in the assumption that one more year of schooling at the age of 20 is more beneficial than at the age of 30, 40, or 60."[26] Indeed, if one listens to faculty members' nostalgic references to the returning G.I.'s after World War II, it would seem that there is more evidence that the reverse is true.

Over half of those responding to a Carnegie Commission survey of 1961 graduates indicated that they wished they had learned more about literature, art, music, and philosophy while in college. It is quite likely that courses on these subjects were available and that these students could have taken them. But it was only after they became somewhat settled in their work and gained their independence that they felt the need and interest in them. This may also be true of those high school graduates who choose to take short, intensive technical or trade courses at a private school rather than attend longer courses at a community college where they might also include some general education courses. There are some at that age who do not feel sufficiently relaxed to study poetry or consider philosophy. They have an urgent need to accomplish their financial and human independence, and they should have the option to do so without foregoing their right to later broaden their educational interests.

As noted earlier, the U.S. has already introduced and is expanding structural changes in higher education that will facilitate the development of a system of recurrent education. We have a rich array of noncollegiate postcompulsory educational institutions and activities that can supply some of the educational services needed in such a system. But the full utilization of these changes and resources to accomplish recurrent education awaits careful consideration and action on the following:

1. Stop-outs, particularly between high school and college, will not be a real alternative to immediate entrance to college until there

---

26. Commission on Post-Secondary Education, Draft Report, p. 11.

532-819 O - 74 - 5

are available employment opportunities, service programs, and knowledge about noncollegiate educational channels. Job opportunities will have little value unless the high school graduate has already acquired a marketable skill by the time he graduates from high school. This requires a careful reexamination of the career education and vocational education and training available in secondary schools for all secondary school students, regardless of whether they eventually plan to undertake studies at the collegiate level.

2. Colleges and universities have not only supplied educational services but also have evaluated student performance on work taken in the institution, and, to varying extents, have validated work taken in noncollegiate institutions, and, in some instances, have validated experience acquired in noneducational settings. This type of credentialing function is normally exercised as a part of the institution's degree granting authority, and the degree requirements usually include provision that a certain proportion of the degree work be taken at the institution granting the degree. This practice would not be consistent with certain recurrent education models permitting greater mobility among institutions and shorter blocks of time than in the current educational system. It may be that new structures will be required to certify competencies more specific than those expressed by the baccalaureate degree. It is not yet clear that colleges and universities constitute the best agencies to perform this type of credentialing function. These several factors may gradually move colleges and universities out of the credentialing business.

3. The development of shorter than degree length, internally cohesive, collegiate educational modules requires a substantial rethinking and reworking of present collegiate curricula. The integration of general and specialized education within such modules, ascertaining the background skills and knowledge needed for entry level for each such module, and the relevance of the module to broader educational goals are all essential elements in a program of education that permits re-entry for short periods of time.

4. Better information must be obtained about the educational activities and students of noncollegiate postcompulsory education institutions so that the availability of these resources might be taken into consideration in planning the college and university system. At the present time in the U.S., the agencies that have responsibility for planning public higher education have inadequate information on the scope and quality of educational programs at these institutions.

5. An effective liaison must be formed between employers and educational institutions for the purpose of planning to greater purpose the educational services that each type of institution is best able to supply for current and projected manpower needs.

More important than any of these is the necessity for analyzing educational goals in terms of the appropriate mix of study and experience to achieve those goals. That blending, as well as the educational structure, will not be the same for all goals.

Although the U.S. has many features in its postcompulsory educational system that facilitate movement toward a system of recurrent education, it has certain structural problems which will make it harder to move in that direction. Expansion of some of the structural changes already underway and new developments along the lines described above may require different staffing patterns than those now in existence in higher education institutions. At the present time, however, several factors are operating which tend to freeze existing patterns of staffing: (1) the spread of collective bargaining; (2) increasing proportions of faculty with tenure; and (3) a lack of growth of enrollment in many institutions making it difficult to change staffing patterns through expansion.

The optimal use of all educational resources would suggest differentiation of functions among institutions. But declining enrollments with their impact on financial problems may lead many institutions to expand their offerings to attract more students. Rarely would the new programs replace old ones.

Finally, because the majority of the post-high school age group in the U.S. now attend college, and because college is generally accepted as the most desirable form of postcompulsory education, it may be difficult to obtain necessary acceptance for noncollegiate institutions and activities. Recent collegiate enrollment figures provide some hope that this might be possible, but it is too early to determine the meaning of shifts in enrollment trends. If the lockstep in collegiate education can be broken, if a shift toward a genuine system of recurrent education can be made, then within such a revised context it might be possible to develop a new mix of postcompulsory educational services within the U.S. that would more nearly meet the diverse educational needs of the post-high school population over their life spans.

the further education and training scheme

H. and H.M. PESTON

The Second World War was the breeding ground for a great many social experiments that led to many important advances in the provision of social welfare.[1] One such experiment which does not appear to have been studied in great depth and is now largely forgotten is the provision of higher education for ex-servicemen and ex-servicewomen. Curiously enough, the origins of this experiment go back to the First World War at the end of which provision was made for the return to higher education of ex-servicemen. Arrangements after the Second World War, however, were much more extensive and elaborate. They represent a distinct advance over some three previous decades. In fact, they comprised an extremely interesting experiment on the issues now typically discussed under the headings of "adult education" and "recurrent education."

Essentially, the British government decided as early as 1941 that a scheme similar to that introduced after the First World War must be initiated. It was called the Further Education and Training Scheme (FETS). The purpose was by no means narrowly academic--not even for those recipients of awards who went to universities. According to the Ministry of Education, the scheme had the twofold purpose of

---

1. R. Titmus, <u>Problems of Social Policy</u> (London: Her Majesty's Stationery Office, 1947). It is curious to note that despite the success of the FETS, it has not received the acclaim it deserves. It is not mentioned in the standard histories of the war nor in the memoirs, autobiographies, and biographies of leading figures such as Churchill or Bevin. Not much importance is attached to it in histories of education and no account of it is given in the literature of educational planning. Finally, it does not appear to have been referred to in the Robbin's Report on Higher Education.

enabling those whose postschool education or training had been interrupted by their military service and insuring a supply of men and women trained to occupy in the future posts of responsibility in the professions, industry, and commerce.[2]

It showed an explicit concern with manpower considerations and also the willingness of the state to bear the cost. Broadly speaking, anybody who could gain entrance to a full time course would receive an award. The awards were not in return for success in a competitive examination (as were state and local scholarships). If the entrance standards for universities, technical colleges, and the like were met, the award was available. Since those entrance standards were de facto much lower than subsequently, it is clear that FETS represented a distinct change compared with previous peace time provision. It was flexibly administered to enable people who were part-time external students before call-up to become full-time internal students after demobilization. Of all applicants for awards, only four percent were rejected. In this connection, a further quotation is apposite, showing how generous the approach was.

> The scheme, though it was comprehensive, did not aim generally at providing those who were in settled occupations before their service with fresh opportunities of enjoying the benefits of a university education, and candidates were at least expected to show that their service had deprived them of educational opportunities which they would otherwise have enjoyed. There was, however, a special provision which allowed awards to be made to those who had had little opportunity of advanced education after leaving school but who had shown in the course of their service that they had high capabilities.[3]

Another significant change over the First World War scheme was that ex-servicewomen and everyone who had done work of national importance were included. In fact, comparatively few women did benefit. Of the total number of awards made up to the end of 1955, only 7 percent were to women, i.e., 6,278 out of 86,425.

The scheme was explicitly intended to prepare people for future employment and that was what the large majority of recipients wanted. It was operated to meet their wishes as much as possible and was not

---

2. Ministry of Education, Education in 1949 (London: Her Majesty's Stationery Office, 1950), p. 66. This edition of the annual report of the Ministry of Education contains the fullest account of the scheme available, and the authors have relied on it to a considerable extent in the writing of this paper.

3. Ibid., p. 68.

restricted to any special kind of course or institution.[4] Table 1 shows the intended destination of students.

Table 1. Intended Vocation of Students Who Applied for An Award.[5]

	Men	Women
	Percentage	
Architecture	6.0%	2.1%
Art	4.5	13.4
Chemistry	3.0	0.7
Civil Service	5.8	3.0
Commerce	3.1	14.2
Dentistry	1.6	0.3
Engineering	14.6	0.0
Law	2.9	0.4
Medicine	6.3	3.2
Music and Drama	2.3	10.0
Pharmacy	1.4	0.3
Religion	5.9	0.0
Teaching	27.3	23.5
Welfare	1.0	9.6
Remainder	14.3	19.3

---

4. In all, awards were held in more than 700 institutes, including some overseas.

5. Ministry of Education, Education in 1955 (London: Her Majesty's Stationery Office, 1956), p. 225. This information derives from the fact that when the students applied for an award, they were asked to state the general area in which eventually they hoped to work.

Although these figures do not give a full economic picture, and the ultimate destination of many of these people will have been different from their initial destination, it is noteworthy what a comparatively small fraction of these people intended to go into the ordinary world of industry and trade. The maximum that this could have been was about 35 percent, and that assumes most of the "remainder" category had this as their destination.

The women's column is significantly different from that of the men. Although they were eligible for awards, they were not treated equally. The low percentage entering engineering schools and the high percentage in art, music and drama may have been due to personal predilections, but the figures for various forms of medicine and the law indicate the usual discrimination. Figures on those who completed their courses satisfactorily are set out in table 2.

Table 2. Percentage of Students Completing their Course Satisfactorily.[6]

	Men	Women
Architecture	68%	61%
Art	77	63
Chemistry	65	59
Civil Service	91	87
Commerce	80	85
Dentistry	80	70
Engineering	74	100*
Law	87	86
Medicine	76	74
Music and drama	85	79
Pharmacy	59	65
Religion	86	100*
Teaching	91	88
Welfare	86	83
Remainder	78	77
Total Average	81	79

* n.b. only tiny numbers were involved.

6. Ministry of Education, Education in 1949, p. 130.

The overall dropout rate was about 20 percent. There was no significant difference between women and men. If we assume that broadly speaking intended areas of work correspond to subject choice, it may be assumed that arts and social studies took 50 percent of the places as did science and engineering. These figures have a margin of error of 10 percent. Within that margin, therefore, the subject mix appears to have been no different from the present day, as shown in table 3.[7]

Since precise figures on the courses followed are unavailable, it is impossible to relate the numbers on FETS to the total numbers of students, subject by subject. In the six to seven years after the war when the pressure was greatest, the total number of students enrolled in universities was as follows:

Table 3. Full-Time Students Enrolled in Universities.[8]

(1938 - 9)	(50,246)
1946 - 7	68,452
1947 - 8	78,507
1948 - 9	83,690
1949 - 50	85,421
1950 - 1	85,314
1951 - 2	83,458

Precise figures are not available on which institutions the FETS students went to or on the length of their courses. It is apparent that the overwhelming majority of awards were made by 1952, and

7. Department of Education and Science, Statistics of Education (England and Wales), Vol. 6, University (London: Her Majesty's Stationery Office, 1972).

8. University Grants Committee, Annual Report, 1953. It is worth remarking that numbers increased from 38,000 at the end of the war to 85,000 five years later. This is the fastest rate of expansion in the history of higher education in the U.K. up to the present time. The figure remained at 85,000 up to the mid-1950's when the second phase of post-war expansion began to get under way. It is reasonable to suggest, therefore, that the effect of the war and FETS was to increase the size of the university sector by 70 percent. We comment further on this below.

virtually everybody had worked through the system by 1955.[9] In the peak years up to 1951, the fraction of FETS entrants was altogether about 55 percent of total entrants. In 1948 some 10,000 entrants were ex-service on FETS. By 1951 this was down to 110.[10] New awards to university students from public funds are given in the following table.

Table 4. Type of Award.[11]

Academic Year	FETS	State Scholarship	L.E.A. Major	L.E.A. Minor	Total
1948 - 49	8,960	1,152	4,026	1,206	15,344
1949 - 50	4,376	1,784	5,880	1,251	13,291
1950 - 51	803	1,974	7,346	1,509	11,632
1951 - 52	110	2,640	8,830	1,435	13,015

In this period, university departments were oversubscribed, but the pressure on them was not as great as it might have been because compulsory military service persisted throughout this period acting as a temporary offset.

Nonetheless, an effect of the war and the FETS was an expansion in the number of university places. It was already agreed during the war that universities should be given a high degree of priority in demobilization and the redeployment of manpower. In fact, a class B priority release from the services was given to university staff and to 3,000 students.

The number of entrants increased after the war by some 10,000 students, an expansion of nearly 70 percent. This build up took

---

9. It is amusing to note that 14 years after the war in 1959 three medical students were still left in the scheme not having yet successfully taken their finals. Ministry of Education, Education in 1959 (London: Her Majesty's Stationery Office, 1960), p. 87.

10. Ministry of Education, Education in 1951 (London: Her Majesty's Stationery Office, 1952), p. 45.

11. Ministry of Education, Education in 1952 (London: Her Majesty's Stationery Office, 1953), p. 40.

place essentially over some three to four years at a faster expansion rate than achieved subsequently, although, of course, starting from a lower base figure. The universities were sufficiently adaptable to deal with this kind of development.

Fairly soon after the war, once the bulge had been dealt with, it was assumed that the problem was going to be one of dealing with a diminished demand for places.[12] This assumption ran counter to the fact that higher education in comparable foreign countries at that time took relatively more students than the U.K.[13] The realities of the immediate postwar period undermined that assumption. Decision makers were slow to respond but realized eventually the need for social and educational equality and a better supply of higher educated manpower. By the early 1950's, however, it was increasingly recognized that rapid university expansion would be required almost indefinitely to meet national needs. Yet it was not until the early 1960's that the Robbins' Committee was set up and its recommendations for fast expansion to meet student demand, albeit at a high academic entrance standard, was accepted.

It is virtually impossible, however, to say anything valid about the entry standards of the universities at this time, but it appears that part of the postwar expansion was met by eliminating a large number of the extremely weak students who used to gain entry before the war.[14] In that sense, the marginal entry qualifications rose. Ignoring this weakest group who may be said to have entered university for nonacademic purposes, and considering only those who went to universities for largely academic reasons, the evidence is less clear that there was an increase in the marginal entry qualifications. The U.G.C. was also worried that the number of very bright students was not rising at the same rate as the total student body. This fear grew stronger in the early 1950's when the FETS was coming to an end, and when it was felt that maintaining universities at their new scale, let alone moving to a larger one, would mean a decline in the relative numbers of those getting first or second class honors degrees.[15] The Ministry of Education itself was worried about all this. They remarked in 1949, "It remains also to be seen how large a number of students can attend universities and other higher institutions without depressing the general intellectual standard."[16]

---

12. University Grants Committee, Post-War Development and Problems 1947 (London: Her Majesty's Stationery Office, 1947), p. 33.

13. Ibid., p. 21.

14. University Grants Committee, University Development 1953 (London: Her Majesty's Stationery Office, 1953), p. 25.

15. University Grants Committee, Post-War Development and Problems 1947 (London: Her Majesty's Stationery Office, 1947), p. 15.

16. Ministry of Education, Education in 1949, p. 71.

This fear of declining standards was not shared by all universities. Reports from some individual universities do not indicate that the entry of ex-servicemen and women led to a lowering of standards.[17] In many, if not most, cases the older students seemed to take their studies more seriously, and it was widely recognized that their influence was altogether beneficial. Many of them were not at university just for love of learning. They mainly wanted a professional qualification, but they had a practical approach.[18] In that sense they hardly differed from their successors. One wonders if they really differed from their predecessors except, of course, in age and maturity.

Turning now to the specific value of the grants, they were intended to maintain the student together with meeting tuition, fees, and all ancillary and incidental expenses, including books and instruments. Also included were allowances for dependents, i.e., wives and children. These were available even to students who married during their course of study. It does not appear that women received dependents' allowances for husbands and children.

The grants themselves varied in tuition and maintenance according to the institution; the average value being £250 per annum tax free.[19] To appreciate the generosity of these awards, it should be recalled that the average earnings of men manual workers in all industries at that time was about £330 per annum and of women about £180 per annum.[20] The average grant was, therefore, about three quarters of the average wage.

Today the average grant is less than a quarter the average wage--which is scarcely above the old FETS level.[21]

For students under 21, a parental contribution was required although there cannot have been a great many in this category. Here too, the scheme was generous in two particular ways. First, the parental contribution ended as soon as the student became 21. With

---

17. Annual reports of the University of London, _seriatim_.

18. J. Dent, _Growth in English Education_ (London: English Universities Press, 1962).

19. Ministry of Education, _Education in 1947_ (London: Her Majesty's Stationery Office, 1948), p. 260.

20. Department of Employment, _British Labour Statistics_ (London: Her Majesty's Stationery Office, 1971), p. 99.

21. Department of Education and Science, _Statistics of Education_, Vol. 5, 1972 (London: Her Majesty's Stationery Office, 1972). A curiosity of educational finance in recent years has been the decline in the average grant per student. In 1970-1971 it was about £300 which in real terms was over 10 percent less than in 1963, and almost 50 percent less than the average FETS grant.

other awards at the time the parental contribution was expected to continue once it had begun. Second, the starting income for parental contribution was £800 per annum. Then that was two and a half times average earnings. Today the starting point for required contribution is £1100 which is somewhat below average earnings.

The Ministry of Education claimed to be most responsive to special cases and the need to revise grants. They claimed, "For many months on end grants were recalculated at the rate of at least 500 a week."[22] In addition, a system was developed whereby grants were payable immediately when the term began.[23]

The administration of the scheme was altogether of some interest in that apart from the education departments, the Ministry of Labour and National Service and the Ministry of Agriculture and Fisheries were also involved. While the Ministry of Education dealt directly with grants for courses of an essentially educational nature, the Ministry of Labour concentrated on those devoted chiefly to training (professional or otherwise).[24] In fact, all nonagricultural applications were made initially to the regional offices of the Ministry of Labour and were sifted there before being sent on to the Awards Branch of the Ministry of Education.[25]

FETS paved the way for the present situation in which broadly speaking anyone gaining entrance to higher education is eligible for an award. This was simply not so before the war. Postwar progress by 1949 can be measured by the Ministry of Education remark that, "It can hardly yet be maintained that the system of admissions to universities is so nicely adjusted that the fact of a candidate's admission alone justifies spending public money on him."[26] This implies that up to then FETS was still regarded to some extent as a reward for national service and a means of meeting a possible one-time shortage in the supply of higher educated manpower. Nonetheless, as table 4 shows, there was a considerable expansion in central and local government awards by 1951. The impetus came initially from FETS, but the need was actually to replace FETS. It was only some six or seven years later that the first recognition of Britain's lagging growth appeared and it was suggested that the expansion of governmental award was connected with a shortage of higher educated

---

22. Ministry of Education, Education in 1949, p. 70.

23. Ibid., p. 71.

24. Ibid., p. 66.

25. Ibid., p. 67.

26. Ibid., p. 72.

manpower, notably scientists and engineers.[27]

As for the economic consequences of the scheme, it is impossible to pronounce with any confidence on the basis of the published information. The scheme was intended to affect the economy by anticipating and removing a shortage of qualified manpower. True, the Ministry of Education in its review of the scheme indicated it would try to discover its effects,[28] but as far as we can see, no follow-up study was undertaken, or, at least if it were, nothing was published.

It is possible at this late date, however, to devise a followup study which could shed light on the Ministry's questions. This information could be compared with two other sorts of career patterns. One of people who attended university at the same time as the FETS students, and another of people who attended university after the FETS was substantially over. It would, of course, be a biased comparison, but would enable us to place the FETS students into some sort of perspective. The problem with either comparison is that the non-FETS people would most likely have contained a larger fraction of the more intelligent students since they would have received their grants on a competitive basis. They would have been younger, and some would have done their national service--compulsory in those days--while others would be doing national service after graduation. It could well have been that the FETS group was physically more healthy than the university population as a whole. It is also true that it contained relatively fewer women.

A particular question that arises is whether we ought to compare people by chronological age or years since graduation. Is FETS to be deemed successful if a person with certain relevant characteristics reaches the same position at various ages whether or not he was in the scheme? Or is the base line to be the date of gaining a degree? The former view means that, up to a point at least, when a degree is taken eventually becomes irrelevant. The latter view would be that pre-degree experience is totally irrelevant.

An area in which such a comparison could be made is the civil service, where jobs are standardized. Careers could be compared more easily. Promotion is a function of age, time elapsed since entry,

---

27. All of this dates back to the Barlow Committee Report, Scientific Man Power (London: Her Majesty's Stationery Office, 1946). In 1956 there appeared a survey on the scientific and engineering personnel employed in Britain together with a projection of future demands. Advisory Council on Scientific Policy, Scientific and Engineering Manpower in Great Britain (London: Her Majesty's Stationery Office, 1956). This was followed by a great many similar reports.

28. Ministry of Education, Education in 1949, p. 71.

and ability. The administrative staff is largely graduate and the entry qualification of its members are well documented. What is more, much of the relevant information has already been collected by the Royal Commission on the Civil Service and could well be available in future researches.

We turn last to a brief comment on the U.S. experience.[29] In the Second World War the U.S. was mobilized to a much smaller extent and for a much shorter period of time than the U.K. Higher education also covered a much larger fraction of the age group as it continues to do. Equally what was provided for veterans went on much longer in time because of the Korean War.

The U.S. provision appeared to have differed from the U.K. chiefly in the following ways. To begin with, the U.S. provision was restricted to veterans, and was on an altogether larger scale. It is alleged to have involved over 50 percent of all relevant World War II ex-servicemen. In the U.K., the various schemes covered some 25 percent of the relevant population.

The U.S., however, concerned itself explicitly with the problem of the ex-servicemen's adjustment to civilian life, which was rather taken for granted in the U.K.

Because of the greater heterogeneity of the U.S. education system, there were serious difficulties preventing abuse and deciding which institutions were to be approved of for grant purposes. Complications arose because some universities were private and others were in the public sector but financed by the individual states. The grants themselves were from the federal government.

A number of U.S. universities introduced special schemes for veterans and a few separated them from the general body of students for much of their courses. This too was different from the British experience.

There were serious staff shortages in U.S. universities which does not appear to have been the case in the U.K. There were also serious housing difficulties.

Considering the differences in the standards of living and grant practices in the two countries, it is difficult to say whether the U.S. scheme was more or less generous than the U.K. But it did not lead--as it did in Britain--to a state financed system of maintenance, fees and tuition grants for all students subject to their admission to university.

---

29. The President's Commission on Veterans' Pensions, Readjustment Benefits: General Survey and Appraisal, and Education and Training, and Employment and Unemployment (Washington, D.C.: Government Printing Office, 1956).

To summarize, FETS in the U.K. and its related scheme in the U.S. did achieve their immediate social aims of assisting people to resume higher education or start it. The economic aim of supplying higher level personnel was met as well. In addition, insofar as that was important, ex-servicemen were helped to adjust once more to civilian life. At the supply end, the universities did expand--although not without some initial difficulty in the U.S.--without a decline in standards. Indeed, those standards rose despite continuous doubts and headshakings by the pessimists.

Major unexpected benefits followed in the U.K. A narrow elitist system which had hardly advanced at all in the inter-war period developed rapidly in size and improved in quality. In that respect and in many others, the scheme contributed positively to the higher education boom of the past 25 years.

The success of the scheme provides hope that a similar scheme of recurrent education could succeed as well.

some thoughts on adult education and the public library

HOMER D. BABBIDGE, JR.

At the busiest intersection in downtown New Haven, Connecticut, a tarnished brass plaque calls attention to a virtually unnoticed establishment. Located above a vacant store is "The Young Men's Institute, Founded 1826." A vestige of America's earliest efforts in adult, or continuing education, its history reflects much of the ebb and flow of such efforts over a century and a half. The Young Men's Institute was originally the "Apprentices' Literary Association" and was founded by eight young mechanics who saw their association as the means for self-improvement and vocational advancement. Courses included natural philosophy, chemistry and bookkeeping; visiting lecturers and library reading rooms played a prominent role in the instruction.

The New Haven Mechanics' Association was part of a larger, more general development in the cities of the new nation. Mercantile and mechanics' libraries appeared almost simultaneously in cities throughout the Northeast. The mechanics' and merchants' libraries were class libraries directed not only to the readers' edification, but to "keeping them out of mischief" as well. The readers' ages ranged from 12 upward. An 1820 regulation of the Massachusetts Mechanics' Association directed that all books in its library be "gratuitously loaned to all mechanics and apprentices who shall produce to the librarian certificates from their masters that they are worthy of confidence ...."[1] Many of these libraries gained local citizen support. In 1823, in Brooklyn, New York prominent citizens pushed wheelbarrows through the streets collecting books for the apprentices' library of the Village of Brooklyn.

---

1. C. Seymour Thompson, Evolution of the American Public Library (Washington, D.C.: Scarecrow Press, 1952), p. 82.

532-819 O - 74 - 6

The mercantile libraries were also directed to a specific group of young boys, those entering a mercantile career. While the mechanics' libraries were charitable organizations, largely dependent upon philanthropic support, the Boston Mercantile Library set the pattern for its kind in the regulation of 1820 that the facilities be made available to any young man over 15 who "was in the employment of some respectable merchant." Admission was conditional as well upon the payment of two dollars and the donation of "one or more volumes of books to be approved by the directors."[2]

The 18th Century also saw the beginnings of social libraries that were not aimed at one particular profession. The social library, or library company, was an organized group whose members had united through the purchases of stock to form and maintain a library for their own benefit. The Book Company of Durham, North Carolina, for example, was founded in 1733. Each member paid 20 shillings for stock for the purchase of books. Members agreed that "we will each of us so often as we shall agree by our major vote bear our equal parts in advancing any sum of money at any time as a common stock to be laid out for such books as shall be agreed upon by the majority vote of the company... which books shall be kept as a common stock library by some person whom we shall choose, each member having an equal right in said Library."[3] Originally only Durham residents were admitted to membership, but this rule was later rescinded. The leadership of the company was to ensure that all books purchased were "not only entertaining, but instructive, and tending to advance useful knowledge extensively, and especially to promote the true principles of Christian piety, virtue, and good manners among all...."[4]

Within six years after the Book Company of Durham was organized, three other libraries were formed in Connecticut. Libraries were organized in Germantown, Pennsylvania in 1745, at Charleston in 1748, at Trenton in 1752. No fewer than 64 were formed before American independence was declared.[5] After the war, as the liberated colonies began to feel more unity as a nation, thought began to turn more to books. Westward migration was accompanied by a transplanting of social libraries to the Northwest Territory and beyond.

Membership in a library was usually granted only with the approval of the directors. The price of a share was seldom more than

---

2. Thompson, <u>Public Library</u>, p. 98.

3. <u>The History and Records of the Book Company of Durham, Founded AD 1733</u> (manuscript owned by Mrs. Howard B. Field of Durham).

4. <u>Ibid</u>.

5. Thompson, <u>Public Library</u>, p. 55.

$5 or $6, and often only $1 or $2. To preserve democracy in administration, most libraries permitted no proprietor to own more than one share, or ruled that additional shares should not confer additional voting privileges. The books were kept at the home of the librarian and were accessible on a weekly or monthly "Library Day."

Many social libraries emphasized their potential value to people of all vocations. The catalog of the Juliana Library stated in 1766: "It is by no means intended that all persons should sit down in a library and become studious. All men are not born nor fitted for such employment; but each man has leisure to read some...he may view the schemes of millions that have gone before him in the same art, compare them with his own, and put into practice that which he thinks best."[6] This supported the more general idea of equality of educational opportunity and its advantages for preserving liberty. "A general diffusion of knowledge, to every class in society," said the Worcester Associate Library Company in 1793, "has the greatest tendency to meliorate our natures and forms the best security of equal liberty to all members of a free independent community."[7]

After 1820 subscription libraries, which required only an annual membership fee, began to be more popular than the idea of the common stock library. They made books available to many who would have been unable or unwilling to purchase stock, and they were better suited to less homogeneous and more rapidly changing communities. But for nearly a century, the social library was essentially the only agency endeavoring to meet the popular demand for books.

The history of libraries is also closely associated with the lyceum movement. The lyceum was an association providing public lectures, concerts, and entertainments. By the late 1820's nearly 2,000 lyceums had been established in New England, New York, and the Midwest.[8] Their main activities included lectures, musical programs and debates, but many lyceum constitutions stipulated the gathering of books for a library as one of their aims. Although these centers catered mostly to those interested in cultural rather than economic or social advancement, other groups used the lecture method. The mechanics' and apprentices' societies heard lectures in the 1820's on the practical applications of science. Mercantile Library Associations offered lecture courses to stimulate reading on subjects which otherwise might be ignored. They also realized that lectures were a good source of publicity and revenue.

---

6. Catalog of the Juliana Library Company (Philadelphia, 1766).

7. Worcester Associate Library Company Rules and Regulations (Worcester, 1793).

8. Carl Bode, The American Lyceum (New York: Oxford University Press, 1956), p. 244.

The Young Men's Associations were literally lyceums without the name. A flourishing example was the Young Men's Association of Buffalo, which strongly supported both its library and lecture programs. For lectures as well as books, history was the most favored topic, followed by science, fiction, and travel. Common titles included "South Carolina in the Revolution," "Columbus," and "The Winds and the Sea."[9]

In the 1850's, political topics were popular. The Young Men's Institute in New Haven, for example, heard Henry Ward Beecher, Theodore Parker, and Wendell Phillips speak about the abolition of slavery.

Libraries and lyceums also merged because many lyceums left their books to the local libraries when they withered or died. Some lyceums actually became libraries when their lectures and other oral activities atrophied. A comment on The Chicago Public Library describes such a case: "In 1868 the Young Men's Association changed its name to the Chicago Library Association, an indication of the extent to which the conduct of the library had superseded all other activities."[10]

The movement for public, free-access libraries grew from objections that mercantile and mechanics' libraries, social libraries, lyceums and similar institutions restricted access at a time when mass access to books was deemed desirable.

During the early part of the 19th Century a belief was widely held among influential citizens that all men were endowed with unlimited rational capacity and that every human being had a natural right to knowledge. If suitable means could be found to develop their natural capacities, a continuing improvement of society would be assured. Free-access libraries could help with that development.

With the granting of male suffrage, it was recognized that unenlightened persons to whom the privilege of citizenship had been extended could not be expected to uphold democratic institutions unless they understood them. These persons, as well as new immigrants who had to be assimilated into the political and cultural patterns of America, needed a continuing source of information to help them contribute toward a sound, collective judgment on public affairs.

The steady development of public school education helped to produce an increased number of literate and inquisitive young people. But when these young people left school, all but those who could buy their own books were barred from further learning. The lyceum movement had stimulated an interest in cultural development. Here also the availability of books for self-education was indispensible.

---

9. Bode, The American Lyceum, p. 246.

10. Thompson, Public Library, p. 147.

In the same period, industrialization and increasing urbanization gave rise to new social and moral problems: crime, alcoholism, gambling, prostitution, and child delinquency. Leading citizens, convinced that the republic could not survive unless its people were virtuous as well as intelligent, were seeking ways of suppressing vice and implanting good morals. They perceived the public library as a potential enemy of crime, and as a continuing means of moral elevation for the working adult--a tool much less expensive to maintain than a prison or reformatory.

Although societal forces created a need for the public library, certain conditions had to be met before a library could be established: a community needed the financial ability to set up and maintain a library, and progressive leaders who recognized the need and could persuade their fellow citizens to tax themselves to support a public library.

In 1833, the citizens of Peterborough, New Hampshire, without the sanction of state legislation, voted to set aside for the purchase of library books a portion of the state bank tax which was distributed among New Hampshire towns for "purposes of education."[11] Thus the first American town library, open to the public and continuously supported by tax funds, was begun. This was significant in that it set a precedent for the use of public funds. The organization of free public libraries was slow, however, until 1854 when the City of Boston established a public library. This marked the turning point in the history of the public library movement in the United States. The organization of a public library by a major metropolitan community and the formulation by its founders of a rationale for free public library service provided the impetus needed to set the public library concept in motion.

The immediate inspiration for the Boston library came from an emissary of the French government, M. Nicholas Marie Alexandre Vattemare, who came to America in 1841 to establish a system for the international exchange of books. A corollary of his plan involved the establishment of a free public library. Although his ideas were greeted with enthusiasm, no official action was taken. In 1850, Senator Edward Everett of Massachusetts became interested in the public library idea. He was joined in his efforts by George Ticknor of Harvard. These two men were largely responsible for defining the purposes and responsibilities of the new library. They reasoned that: "...a free public library is the next natural step to be taken for the intellectual advancement of this whole community...it is of paramount importance that the means of general information should be so diffused that the largest possible number of persons should be induced to read and understand questions

---

11. Robert E. Lee, Continuing Education for Adults Through the American Public Library, 1833-1964 (Chicago: American Library Association, 1966), p. 6.

going down to the very foundations of the social order, which we as a people are constantly required to decide either ignorantly or wisely."[12] In 1854, after four years of careful planning, the library opened its doors.

The Boston Public Library came into existence not because the people demanded a library but because a small number of learned influential citizens decided it was a good idea. They were motivated by effective leadership and benevolent philanthropy, and a firm belief in the social value of education as a permanent means of moral improvement and political progress. Historians remind us, however, that a belief in Jacksonian democracy was not among the motives of the Boston intellectuals in their efforts to establish a public library. As a group they believed in the persistence of natural inequities, the necessity of aristocracy, the importance of religion and morality, the sanctity of property, the nonwisdom of majority rule, the urgency of constitutionalism, and the folly of attempts at social and economic leveling. They wanted to inculcate others with the same beliefs, and a public library system seemed the best way to reach the masses.[13] Similar motives led to the establishment of public libraries all over New England soon after Boston set the example.

During the first period of public library development, librarians were concerned chiefly with collecting books. They undertook this work with a clear understanding of the library's educational function--to inform and enlighten. They thus selected only books of intellectual and literary value and refused to circulate popular novels.[14] Some library historians view this period as one of authoritarianism and elitism during which books were chosen with the specific purpose of "molding" the character of the "dangerous" classes to make them carbon copies of their benefactors.[15]

During the 1880's and 1890's, the library's role was broadened to include the public library not as a supplement, but a complement to the work of the public school. Three major services--personal assistance to readers, recreational reading, and informational

---

12. Robert E. Lee, Continuing Education, p. 8.

13. M. Harris, "The Purpose of the American Public Library," Library Journal, 98, 16 (September 12, 1973): 2512.

14. An interesting controversy arose in the 1870's when many librarians refused to put Horatio Alger novels on the shelves because the Alger hero's overweening self-reliance threatened family discipline and social order. See Dee Garrison, "Cultural Custodians of the Gilded Age: The Public Library and Horatio Alger," Journal of Library History, 6, 4 (October 1971): 331-2.

15. Harris, "American Public Library."

reference service--were added to the library's responsibilities. Multipurpose book collections replaced the standard erudite and literary works. Librarians stressed the library's specific role of encouraging self-education of adults in an atmosphere of freedom unlike the rigid disciplined atmosphere of the public school.

A more substantial contribution to the movement came later from a man originally excluded from one of the "working-boy libraries." Colonel James Anderson of Pittsburgh in 1850 opened his personal library of some 400 volumes to "working boys," by which he meant boys with a trade. A 15-year-old telegraph messenger boy, in a letter to the Pittsburgh Dispatch, urged that the Colonel's library be opened to "messenger boys and clerks" as well. He signed his letter "A working boy, though without a trade." A day or two later the Dispatch carried a notice on its editorial page asking the "working boy, though without a trade" to call at its offices. The doors of the library were opened to him. It was from this early experience, Andrew Carnegie later wrote, "that I decided there was no use to which money could be applied so productive of good to boys and girls who have good within them and ambition to develop it, as the founding of a public library in a community which is willing to support it as a municipal institution."[16]

Carnegie was convinced that of all benevolences the public library was the most significant because it gave nothing without demanding something in return and helped only those who were willing to help themselves. He never gave funds for the purchasing of library books or for the operation of libraries. The ownership, control, administration, and support of public libraries he erected were always the responsibility of the community.

Carnegie's motives were also related to his attachment to the socioeconomic climate which had brought him much success. "The result of knowledge," Carnegie claimed, "is to make men not violent revolutionists, but cautious evolutionists; not destroyers, but careful improvers."[17]

The concept of the lecture circuit grew concurrently with the development of the public library movement. The lyceum circuit became commercialized (e.g., the Redpath Lyceum Bureau of Boston) and the famed Chatauqua Movement emerged.

The Chatauqua Movement was founded in 1874 by Lewis Miller (a clergyman) and John Heyl Vincent (a former circuit rider), as a study

---

16. Andrew Carnegie, Autobiography (Boston: Houghton Mifflin Co., 1920), p. 45.

17. J. F. Wall, Andrew Carnegie (Oxford: Oxford University Press, 1970), p. 821.

group to embark on a four-year program of guided reading. Originally for the training of Sunday School teachers, it eventually expanded to include pioneering correspondence courses, lecture study groups and reading circles.

The movement was further spurred on by William Rainey Harper (later the first President of the University of Chicago) who, by 1883, had opened summer schools in Worcester, Massachusetts, New Haven, and Pennsylvania. The bible study central to his summer schools became a keystone of the Chatauqua Movement. The ultimate format of the movement emerged in 1907 with the introduction of 22 "tent circuits" spread throughout the U.S.

The tradition of professional oratory so begun, has lingered. It produced such great "circuit speakers" as William Jennings Bryan who delivered his famous "Cross of Gold" speech more than 600 times. The champion Chatauqua speaker, the Reverend Russell Herman Conwell delivered an address entitled "Acres of Diamonds" not less than 6,000 times.

Conwell's "Acres of Diamonds" address--with the theme that the man who roams the world searching for diamonds returns home to find they have been in his own back yard--is relevant to those seeking a structural framework for contemporary out-of-school education.

If educational "innovators" were asked to list the characteristics of the ideal educational institution, the list would probably constitute a fairly accurate description of the American public library: (1) open admission, (2) low cost threshold, (3) proximity to people, (4) emphasis on independent study, (5) emphasis on individually paced progress, (6) absence of requirements and restrictions, (7) absence of examinations and grades, (8) ready access to a wide range of teaching materials, and (9) nonresidential.

Thus, it is conceivable that the vast system of public libraries spawned in the 19th Century might become a foundation for a 21st Century system of education for adults.

However, our public libraries are not now effective education centers. One finds them serving a limited clientele of a few serious students, recreational readers and school children--a far cry from the experience that led Andrew Carnegie to bestow a fortune on the ideal. The librarians themselves recognize their weaknesses. The American Library Association recently issued the report of a special committee which reviewed the past with frankness and set forth a bold program for the future. This document makes four sets of recommendations designed to (1) achieve a better understanding of the public library in the community, (2) stimulate a broad program of research which will undergird effective performance, (3) support continued efforts to disseminate this research and embody its results in prototype programs, and (4) mount an extensive educational effort to help librarians learn how to accomplish new goals by non-traditional means.[18]

It may be argued that the basic functions of the early library have been preempted by the public school system. Others contend that Americans no longer have good within them and ambition to develop it. But if we assume that adults have educational needs not met by the formal school system, and that Americans are still ambitious, public libraries still have two major deficiencies.

The first shortcoming is the absence of teachers. The circuit-riding lecturers who rode off independently found books were not essential to fees, but left the library devoid of their stimulating rhetoric and the lively discussions that followed. Ever since, the libraries have said, as it was once said of a great 20th Century venture in adult education: "The new school does not pretend to teach; it offers all the facilities in its power to those who wish to learn." But for most of us one of the essential "facilities" for learning is encounter. The library could once again regain its teaching function with the simple addition of formal encounters with more knowledgeable minds.

The second, and equally important, missing ingedient in the library-as-a-learning-center touches on Carnegie's reference to ambition: People don't study seriously in public libraries because they don't get credit for it. In a credential-oriented society, study and knowledge count for little if they are not certified in sheepskin. Andrew Carnegie lived and worked in a world that gave one a chance to demonstrate what he knew. Today one's chances are greatly enhanced if he comes bearing beribboned and embossed assurances that he is prepared. Our public libraries offer no such credentialling. Even if they were to teach, they would not view themselves as freight-forwarders. Nor should they, lest they lose their genius. Librarians must have the means to motivate the user who knows that he has to have something concrete to show for his independent study.

There is a device that holds the promise of encouraging library use--a new set of nationally-administered examinations to assess educational competence--however and whenever attained. The College Level Examination Program (CLEP) of the Educational Testing Service is designed to certify for the benefit of individuals and for degree-granting institutions, levels of knowledge and skill achieved by anyone. The General Examinations of the CLEP are objective tests that measure achievement in five basic areas of liberal arts: English Composition, Humanities, Mathematics, Natural Sciences, and Social and Science History. Each has a time limit of one

---

18. Commission on Non-Traditional Study, Diversity By Design (Washington, D.C.: Jossey-Bass, 1973), p. 84.

hour. One to five General Examinations may be taken in one day. The Subject Examinations measure achievement in specific college courses. Each includes a 90-minute objective test and a 90-minute essay section. It is now possible for the independent student, the library user, the book reader to test himself, privately and at his leisure. If he discovers he has mastered introductory chemistry, or college level English, he can obtain proof of it. He can even, if he aspires to ultimate status, claim credit or advanced standing in his progress toward a degree.

To meet the needs of the independent student interested in the CLEP, a two-year pilot program, the Independent Study Project (ISP), was instituted in the Dallas Public Library in 1971. Funds for the project were provided by the National Endowment for the Humanities, the Council on Library Resources and the College Entrance Examination Board. Five branches of the library system were selected as model public libraries, geographically situated to reach a maximum number of neighborhood residents. Educators from Southern Methodist University developed study programs and tools such as reading lists and study questions. College Entrance Examination Board tests were used to give participants the opportunity to earn up to two years of college credit at one of 500 participating colleges or universities. The result was the independent study concept, designed not to replace but to complement formal and traditional on-campus college studies.

In September 1973, a final report was submitted by the ISP.[19] Statistics compiled by the five branch libraries show that approximately 3,300 persons showed interest in the ISP over the past two years. A total of 6,000 study guides/reading lists were distributed; English Literature, American History, English Composition and Grammar, American Government, and General Psychology were the most popular subjects; 114 workshops of about nine persons each were conducted. Those attending had a myriad of interests, levels of experience with independent study, and motivation to continue. The average attendee was a 35 to 40 year old working woman seeking information or college credits to update job requirements. Others included housewives wanting self-improvement, formal students looking for curriculum enrichment, retired persons seeking academic stimulation or a new career, and families interested in cultural enrichment. Secretarial, accounting and clerical positions were the most common occupations represented.

At the close of August 1973, 88 of those involved in ISP, 41 men and 47 women, had taken CLEP examinations. The total number of potential credits earned was 943, the equivalent of 31 years of college at a cost of only $3,015.

---

19. Jean Brooks and Betty Maynard, Final Report to the National Interest Council (Dallas: Independent Study Project, 1973).

On the basis of telephone interviews, conclusions were drawn about student attitudes toward ISP. General comments were highly favorable, though the interviews reveal some weaknesses. Less than 10 percent of those who showed initial interest in ISP were still participating at the end of two years. Reasons given included: too busy to participate, lost interest, now a full-time student, and no advanced course offered. Another major problem was with self confidence and motivation--many students found they needed more direct supervision and instruction than offered by ISP.

Perhaps the most significant comment by the librarians in their interviews was that even though a large number of persons requested information about ISP and CLEP, few ever returned or were seen engaged in independent study. Thus the new role of the librarian implied by ISP, that of an academic counselor, was rarely used. Some librarians felt this was because many were attracted to the program because they thought it was a quick and easy way to get college credit. Once disabused of this notion, they did not return. Other patrons who had had college courses before were more capable of getting counseling outside the library.

Profiting from what had been learned with ISP, the Dallas Public Library System proposed a second phase to improve the weakness and expand the strengths of ISP. Those areas where ISP needed additional support were personal assurance and special materials. Librarians felt each participant should have one person to whom he could relate and who would be available to him each time he came to the library. Incentive, recognition and reward structures had to become an integral part of the program. The ISP revealed a need for experimentation with study materials, evaluative backups, and instructional packages which would present adult learning experiences in a paced format for returning learners. Existing commercial programmed materials were often too confusing to use independently.

In the second phase, the Dallas County Community College District would join the public library in an attempt to meet those needs identified by ISP. Two library learning centers, equipped with special audiovisual and print materials, and manned full-time by para-pro fessional college counselors have been proposed. Community impact programming and publicity would be explored. Accessibility to counseling and information would be maintained for all libraries in the Dallas System through a telephone hotline.

If the second project's effort is effective in expanding and strengthening the Dallas community's continuing learning interests, further expansion of the program would be recommended.

This new element of the American scene may spark a dramatic revival in out-of-school learning by adults. It may provide for independent study that element of practical value that, added to curiosity and ambition, seems essential to adequate motivation.

If it does, we might predict a renaissance of the American public library. With over a thousand such institutions in our population centers (25,000 persons or more), with their two hundred million volumes and 50,000 librarians, we might find within them the "Acres of Diamonds" we are seeking for adult education.

It might even be that the Young Men's Institute of New Haven would be rewarded for having sustained itself for a century and a half; it might once again become a vital gathering place for those who have "decided that more knowledge was necessary for them to advance in life."

demand for recurrent education

S.M. MILLER

The demand question in recurrent education[1] can be looked at from two basic perspectives--policy formulation and program planning. In the policy approach, we determine a need, then chart the "best" strategy. Alternative ways of meeting that particular need are considered along with the multiple objectives which are usually involved. In the planning approach, we take a program policy directive and try to estimate what kind of quantities and qualities are needed to accomplish this directive. For example, how many facilities must be added and where should facilities be located.

At this point questions about recurrent education are fundamentally at the policy level. Is there a need for recurrent education? Will people go to programs? To whom should programs be directed? What different kinds of educational goals should be met? What are the criteria for success? But planning or programming issues cannot be ignored. The planning and program issues center on such questions as what specific programs are to be developed? Will these specific programs be utilized? What are the most effective ways of organizing programs? What kind of curricula?

The question of "the demand for recurrent education" seems for many to mean what demand awaits any future recurrent education programs,

---

1. A definition of recurrent education is carefully eschewed in this paper. Obviously, the scope of the definition affects the magnitude of the demand. For a discussion of the role and experience of recurrent education in the U.S., see Bruno Stein and S. M. Miller, "Recurrent Education: An Alternative System?", New Generation 54 (1972): 1-8.

what would be in the English phrase, the "take-up" of programs if they were offered.

The unavoidable issues are which types and numbers of students should be in the program, and what can be done to produce the desired results. Value decisions about the purpose of recurrent education underlie all discussions about demand; they are inescapable, although often ignored.

The more important question has two parts, the first of which is a should issue, not an empirical one: what kind of demand should recurrent education seek, i.e., who should be in the program doing what? The second part then raises the operational question of what can be done (at what costs) to obtain the particular kind of demand that is desirable? If the dipper image is demand in the sense of discovery, this Galbraithian view is of created or achieved demand--how many of what kinds of students would involve themselves in recurrent education if this or that activity were engaged in?

It can be argued that the level of expenditure on recurrent education can be treated independently of the nature of students and curricula. Indeed, they can. But is it desirable to do so, for different objectives in terms of students and curricula might lead to different levels of expenditure. Even where a budget constraint is initially imposed, rather than largely emerging from experience, how funds are to be used depends on objectives about students and curricula.

Nevertheless, there is a fear that since it is mainly educational professionals and social reformers who espouse recurrent education, a great desire for it among its presumed beneficiaries and clientele does not exist. But budget officers fear the opposite problem. To allay those fears, we turn first to the issue of overall demand.

The "Need"

In determining need, a standard is set for a particular type of educational or social service and the number of people who would require such a service. It is then possible to move from need to program planning by estimating the number of units which are required to meet that "need." This concept parallels the economist's notion of "want." It is not a question of people having resources to purchase a particular good that they desire, but rather whether there is a desire which would be fulfilled by a particular commodity or service. The public health field abounds with measures of need and appropriate professional standards of services. Thus at various times it has been argued that one physician should be available to every 1,000 or 600 persons, or that every 1,000 students require one psychologist and one counselor.

Similarly, a need level for recurrent education could be computed by deciding on the requirements for improving the situation of disadvantaged workers who want to be upgraded into better jobs. A further need estimate would be derived by quantifying services to overcome educational inequalities associated with age. Such a measure of need is a Swedish concern. An additional estimate would be based on those needed to be trained to meet the skill requirements of a changing technology or to shift to new jobs because of displacement or because of a desire for a new work experience. On the basis of these and obviously other components, it would be possible to compute the basic need structure of recurrent education.[2]

The experience with need-standard estimates is that they are expert professional guesses and may be highly misleading. While they are conceptualized as a scientific estimate, they are actually based upon a compound of professional aggrandizements, humanistic aspirations, and specialized interpretations of difficulties to be overcome, as well as some notion of the effective distribution of manpower. These standards are obviously Utopian targets rather than practical guidelines for planning and programming.

Yet, I do think it is a largely ill-based fear that a program could be started, a facility built, and few clients attracted. It is my belief, based on the U.S. and to some extent the U.K. experience, that there is a <u>myth of under-utilization</u>.

In the mid-1950's in the U.S., the argument was that social service resources were being concentrated on multi-problem families. The charge was that a high percentage of all social service resources in a number of cities were being utilized by a small number of so-called "multi-problem families." In the Minneapolis study by Bradley Buell and Associates, estimates were made of the extraordinary concentration of activity upon this restricted number of troubled and, possibly more important, troubling families. The concern then was that a relatively small number of families were overly utilizing resources. By the late 1950's and early 1960's, the sentiment had changed very considerably. In the Cloward-Ohlin analysis of social services in the Lower East Side of Manhattan--which led to the formation of Mobilization for Youth, the first nationally funded community action program--the argument was the reverse. Social services, especially voluntary, had moved away from the poor. The launching of the poverty programs and the expansion of services made us realize that under-utilization was seldom a problem. Few programs had to close because an insufficient number of people desired them. The over-utilization of resources was much more common.

The experience in American manpower programs was similar. Few programs overall lacked sizeable numbers of clients.

The United Kingdom experience is also instructive and parallels the American. In the U.K., there is a great deal of concern about the under-utilization phenomenon. The concern is with the lack of "take-up" of the benefits of a particular public program since the figures for nontake-up are usually high. Sometimes 30 percent or more of the eligibles do not apply

---

2. One procedure for estimates along these lines would be to take short-run (five years or less) manpower requirement projections. How many people would have to get what kind of education in order to meet the skill demands? Then add to this figure the demands for recurrent education coming from other sources.

for aid to which they have a legal right. While the still predominating analyses of nontake-up stress the fear of stigma, the difficulty in filling out forms and the lack of information of the nonutilizer, there is a growing number of experts like Della Nevitt of the London School of Economics who now believe that nontake-up is a rational process. Some individuals do not take-up resources for which they are eligible such as rent rebates because of a "poverty trap;" they would have to forego other public resources which they currently receive because their increased income would end their eligibility for the other resource. Perhaps more important, the net gain in getting the public benefit is so small that it is not worth the effort or involves making public authorities aware of activities which they prefer to keep private.

The argument follows that take-up is not a function of the limited perspective and ignorance of the prospective client, but is a rational decision that the gain involved is not worth the cost. To increase take-up requires increasing the gains to be made by taking-up. Small-scale gains, rather than a tendency to ignorance, laziness and perversity, explain low utilization.

These experiences have led me to reformulate Say's Law. Say's Law is the assertion that supply creates its own demand. Keynesian economics contested the validity of this analysis. In a world of leaks and lags, of savings and consumer's preferences, it is clear that the production of supply by itself does not guarantee there will be effective demand for the product produced. But Say's Law, reformulated, does seem to operate in the social services. Useful programs produce their own demand.[3] Where people have doubts about the quality of the program, its relevance to their needs, or where it is difficult to obtain, they may not utilize the service.

Planning And Programming

There are two basic ways of thinking about how to increase the attractiveness of recurrent education programs. One deals with the internal structure; the other with the external environment.

More important than the question of total numbers in a recurrent education program is the issue of who would be in the program doing what. This issue leads to the question of the expenditures we are willing to make in order to attract particular "who's" into a program. Thus the demand for a program is a function of the nature of the supply and price. Obviously, both the supply and its costs can be manipulated in order to attract particular groups. Pathways can be built to attract and keep particular people in a program. A major issue is then how much should be spent in what ways to alter or expand the demand.

---

3. Cited in Alan Gartner's, "Consumers as Deliverers of Service," Social Work 16 (October 1971): 28. See also Catherine Kohler Riessman, "Birth Control, Culture and the Poor," American Journal of Orthopsychiatry 38 (July 1968): 696.

Demand questions are always very difficult. The question is demand under what conditions. And with recurrent education, as we shall see, there is an additional question of whose demand. In the perfect market of standardized goods, the "conditions" become only one condition--price. How much change in demand for recurrent education would occur as a result of a change in price is another way of putting it.

It is now common in analyses of the economics of education to emphasize rate of return as the basic variable affecting the demand for education. In the case of recurrent education, some of this thinking can be applied, thinking of price as the money cost to the individual in order to obtain the particular education.[4] This includes not only transportation expenses, tuition fees, but more importantly, foregone earnings. Money gains from education are calculated by estimating (a very difficult process) what the income gain from new education would be and then discounting these gains to allow for the lower satisfaction today of long-term gains. Sociological factors can also be brought in but they offer even graver difficulties in attempting to estimate how much they augment, offset or interact with the effects of the monetary return from education.[5]

If the investment returns for recurrent education cannot be improved, then demand might be improved through publicity, but how effective this would be is not clear.

To a large extent, a major issue in recurrent education is how to create demand of particular groups rather than how to discover or forecast what the aggregate demand might be. For example, the Open University in the U.K. attracted many students but has been criticized because of the characteristics of the students who joined. A high proportion of students are not those who never went beyond secondary school education, but rather are those in the so-called semi- or demi-professions (disproportionately female) like teaching, which in the U.K. requires postsecondary education but not up to the credential of a bachelor's degree. It is the educationally disadvantaged, post-college age, middle classes who are in the program, not manual workers.[6] The Open University's critics harp on the nature of its students, not their numbers. Thus the issue is not who would enter a recurrent education program, but who should

---

4. Estimating the non-money costs (loss of leisure--family time) and gains (cultural satisfaction) would make the analysis more realistic in scope but more treacherous in terms of reliability.

5. Richard Layard argues that sociological explanations are "stimulating but somewhat lacking in explanatory power." "Economic Theories of Educational Planning," in Maurice Peston and Bernard Corry, eds., Essays in Honour of Lord Robbins (London: Weidenfeld and Nicolson, 1972), pp. 119-120 and 141-147.

6. Naomi McIntosh has data showing that a high proportion of the Open University students in the white collar occupations come from lower social origins so that the criticism of the Open University on the basis of social class composition is not fully appropriate.

532-819 O - 74 - 7

be in the program?[7] Rates of return cannot answer _should_ questions. They even have particular difficulties in guessing at the returns for different groupings since it is probably misleading to assume that the income effects of increased education for different social groupings are similar over time and unaffected by numbers.

The inescapable question is demand under what conditions? What is a program willing to do in order to get a particular kind of student? If one starts from the assumption that a program does not face absolute inelasticity of demand of any particular group, the issue becomes what could be done and what is the program willing to do to enlarge the participation of this group? A basic policy question is who should be in recurrent education?

Demand can be thought of as of three types: derived, awakened, and backlog. Derived demand is external to programs and results, as we shall discuss later, from the operation of the expectations of business and government; awakened demand largely arises from the efforts of programs to stoke up interest from groups who are not readily committed to education. Backlog demand refers to the readily available clientele awaiting a program: establish a mental health clinic, and there is immediately a heavy demand for its services from those who have sensed for some time that they wanted such a service but found none easily available. Similarly, recurrent education programs will often find numbers who do not have to be persuaded or encouraged to join a program--as was the experience of the U.K. Open University--but are ready, willing and eager to participate.

Frequently, these backlog students are a "cream" population in that they are the least disadvantaged of a disadvantaged population. Indeed, many if not most, programs aimed at disadvantaged groups tend, unless they make deliberate contrary efforts, to deal with the least disadvantaged of their disadvantaged prospective clientele.[8] "Creaming" may be a useful short-run policy to facilitate the beginning of a program to win acceptance, but it should not be assumed that it is the most desirable policy, even in the short-run. Thus policy planners and program administrators cannot avoid the issue of what kind of students they wish to have in a program.

---

7. Since drop-out rates from recurrent education programs tend to be high, attention has to be given to the characteristics of those who finish as well as those who enter. For a useful discussion of the tasks and roles of recurrent education (which can be translated to the level of the choices of students), see Denis Kallen, Jarl Bengtsson, and Ake Dalin, _Recurrent Education: A Clarifying Report_ (Washington, D.C.: CERI/OECD, working draft, October 1972): 32. For the decisions which have been made by various nations, see the Centre for Educational Research and Innovation national series, _Recurrent Education: Policy and Development in OECD Countries_ (Washington, D.C.: CERI/OECD, 1972).

8. For an exposition of how this comes about, see S. M. Miller, Pamela Roby, and Alwine de Vos van Steenwijk, "Creaming the Poor," _Trans-Action_ 8 (June 1970): 38-45.

Choices have to be made on the basis of personal characteristics of students--age, sex, occupational level, work history--and in terms of the kinds of programs that are considered desirable--narrow, specific vocational, more broad but still vocational, to more culturally oriented, or various combinations of these foci.

Hopefully, the main ingredient in an enrollment decision will not be a simple program cost criterion--or even a social rate of return calculation--for then the chosen population is likely to be those who are amenable, flexible, least disadvantaged, easily fitted into on-going practices, rather than students who may be difficult to attract and to keep in a program.

Choices will vary from nation to nation. Assuming that such choices have been made, what can be done to attract the kind of clientele in the desired numbers? Affecting the demand of particular groups is the objective rather than only estimating their demand. Demand can be affected through cost, accessibility, relevance and attractiveness.

Cost has two essential elements in recurrent education. One is the actual outlays; the other, and much more important, is the value of lost work time and income of students.[9] Tuition-free programs obviously reduce the first cost to zero. The heavy lost income cost requires a subsidy to the individual if he is to be a student during normal working time. A variety of schemes have been recommended[10] along these lines and obviously if they were to be adopted, they could have considerable import for the program. They require either stipends or subsidies from employers or from the state to cover the income that would have been derived from employment.[11] The availability or absence of such aid is thus a basic characteristic of a program.

Stipends are not only expensive, but may be misdirected and fail to attract the kinds of students wanted for a balanced program. Without them, however, recurrent education is likely always to attract the better off and highly motivated.

Accessibility refers to the programming and location of courses. If programs are given at restricted times and located in places with negative features, demand is likely to be low. More accessible, locally oriented programs would be much more attractive.

---

9. A less easily monetized loss, and frequently more important, is the inroads on leisure time because of attending classes and studying.

10. Kallen, et al., A Clarifying Report.

11. "Lost time" income may not be the only or primary employment-related issue for many students. Leaving the work place for an extended period of education may interfere with the accumulation of seniority rights and may retard promotion opportunities when the education is not related to a specific career line within an enterprise.

As for relevance, programs should connect directly with jobs so that graduates benefit economically. The feeling that the program is improving the student's employability is also necessary. Not only is it important that there be economic value, the student must see that value as well. A feeling of accomplishment during the course of the program is thus highly significant.

Aside from the problems of developing a relevant program, there is the actual pursuit of that relevance. Many programs are designed to avoid too much vocationalism and strive for cultural and intellectual stimulation as well, for greater economic relevance frequently means a narrowing of programs to very limited and specific job niches. But programs then are in tension about the degree of specificity in objectives and constraints in broadness of curriculum.

The attractiveness of a program is affected both by curriculum and teaching. Difficult and uninteresting programs are obviously not particularly attractive and may sift out the "noncream" potential students. Smaller classes may be desirable not because they necessarily lead to more learning. There is considerable evidence that there is no clear-cut relationship between class size and learning, but smaller class size does engender more informality and spirit. The additional costs of smaller classes may pay off by being able to attract and keep students who are likely to drop out of cold and formal programs. But the additional costs of small classes may limit the possibility of doing other things which would be significant for providing an adequate program for many students.

Attractiveness involves, what Layard calls, "changing the taste for education." "Low motivation," the usual explanation of failure to attract the clientele appropriate to the policy objectives of a program, should be considered as a challenge rather than an epitaph. To change the taste for (formal) education, to awaken demand, may require seed activity. For example, Brendan Sexton, former education director of the United Automobile Workers, a large U.S.-Canadian trade union, has suggested utilizing brief periods during the work day for discussion of issues that are of current interest to workers (e.g., consumer issues, problems of admittance of children to college). Over time, many workers who would not ordinarily think of entering a formal educational program might become interested and/or confident enough to pursue such an activity. This suggested program is an example of constructing a road to a particular demand of a group that would not readily enlist in formal schooling.

External Factors

Two sets of external factors affect participation in recurrent education programs. One factor is employer demand for graduates. Does the program have a sizeable economic return for its graduates? Will there be a chance for higher income, or more satisfying jobs? Such considerations, which are largely external to the program itself, affect attractiveness of the program and its demand. From this it is obvious that employment policies have to be influenced so that the opportunities for recurrent education graduates are greatly enhanced, before participation in such programs will be attractive.

Many programs founder because their students are prepared for more demanding kinds of tasks and more rewarding jobs than employers offer them. This mismatch occurs because employers do not have a positive view toward the program or because there is an inadequate number of attractive jobs. In the former case, obviously some effort should be devoted to informing employers about the capabilities of students. Some manpower programs in the U.S. have financially rewarded employers for hiring or promoting employees whom they ordinarily would not hire. To attract particular groups to a program and find later that employers refuse to employ these graduates is disastrous. If the graduates of recurrent education programs become second class high school or college graduates with limited possibilities for improvement, these programs are unlikely to attract a diversity of students.

If the problem is an inadequate number of attractive jobs, then government policy may be necessary in order to affect the total number of decent and attractive jobs. When two-thirds of college and secondary school graduates work in public employment, as Layard contends is the case in the U.K. and other nations, the increase of appropriate places for more highly educated and trained people rests to a large extent upon the expansion of public employment or upon public financial inducements to affect the nature of jobs and tasks in the private employment sector.[12] Senator Edward Kennedy's 1973 Bill on research of job satisfaction[13] suggests that it may not be ridiculous to posit that government can try to affect the nature of the occupational structure and the possibilities of work satisfaction. If employees require more education in order to keep their current jobs, if there is increasing competition for the limited number of available jobs, then the achievement of recurrent education programs would be to enhance the relative position of its graduates in the competition for keeping a job. The question would then be not that of advancement, but of not being demoted or unemployed.

The second external factor is that of contagion or, what Layard terms, "snowball" effects.[14] A demand for education of the recurrent type may increase because one or two individuals getting it will attract others. This might be because of status reasons, economic competition, intellectual curiosity, greater awareness or other interactional effects. The idea here is that an "infection" of

---

12. Layard, "Economic Theories."

13. Senator Edward Kennedy, "Worker Alienation Research and Technical Assistance Act of 1973," Senate Committee on Labor and Public Welfare Bill No. S-736, February 1, 1973.

14. Layard, "Economic Theories."

recurrent education spreads.[15] For example, Opportunities Industrialization Center in Philadelphia set up "armchair" programs located in the homes of participants. These local citizen groups hopefully would attract other neighborhood people to organize similar groups. Snowball-contagion-infection effects are not easy to engineer, but they need not be left to chance.[16]

Forecasting

Recurrent education programs obviously differ in estimating the demand for particular groupings. They can follow existing programs and attempt to extrapolate from them to other kinds of programs and circumstances. While the usual practice is to forecast demand in terms of national aggregates, the more important figures may be for localities. The more appropriate but more difficult procedure is to build national aggregates up from the local estimates. More difficult still is to estimate the demand for particular kinds of programs on a local basis.

Five approaches are outlined below on forecasting demand:[17]

---

15. An opposing view is that instead of spread, a new program shrinks. Its initial demand arises from backlog and creaming, both of which will soon dry up as sources of students, and from the effect of excitement created--for only a short time--by a new program.

16. The difficult question is the extent to which client preferences should be determining the objectives and directions of programs and to what extent should there be a program effort to encourage prospective clients to be interested in particular kinds of programs. This is an endemic problem in the social policy field. It was the source of a controversy about medical care between the free-market Institute of Economic Affairs in London (which conducted a survey of class attitudes about choice in medical care) and Brian Abel-Smith of the Department of Social Administration at the LSE. Abel-Smith, in his Fabian pamphlet on health, attempts to reconcile the two perspectives by providing the information and circumstances which make consumer choice an informed decision.

17. It would be a useful exercise to estimate the three types of demand, derived, awakened, and backlog, on the basis of each of these forecasting approaches.

(1) Demographic approaches. What are populations at risk, e.g., post-30, low educated? Tables that cross-tabulate age-sex-education-occupation (on a locality basis) would be particularly useful.

(2) Recurrent education experiences. The demand for programs expanded beyond current recurrent education offerings could be projected by taking the characteristics of students and estimating enrollment when there are more programs available. A more refined approach might be to study the more successful programs in terms of attracting particular kinds of students and estimating future demand on the basis of other individuals with similar characteristics. A variant would be to take programs which have been successful in enrolling difficult-to-reach students, gauge the elements which led to their enrollment and then estimate what the demand would be if similar circumstances were offered in other programs.

(3) Elasticity approaches. What would be the demand for a particular program of recurrent education under some specified conditions? If stipends were provided for a program, for example, what would demand be compared to what it would be with no stipend? Or if the program were conducted in late afternoon compared to evening, or twice a week rather than four times? The effort here is to forecast demand under differing conditions rather than as a stable correlate of fixed conditions. One way to develop such schedules of demand would be to utilize the approach of (2) above on recurrent education experiences, comparing the results of programs with similar content but offered under different conditions.

(4) Institutional changes. What changes in other work, family or educational institutions would affect the demand for recurrent education? For example, what would be the effects of increasing emphasis on formal education and training rather than experience as the basis for promotion to first-line supervisory roles? Or, it could be assumed that industries with slow rates of technological-organizational change will move over time closer to the rates of high-change industries, then the recurrent education demand of the latter concerns could be projected for the former. Obviously, too, the high-change industries may slow up and approximate the recurrent education demand of the now low-change industries. A third area might be that of changes in individual work histories. For example, if it is assumed that employees will increasingly have work histories marked by changes in occupations and industries, then a projection could be based on the recurrent education demands of those who already have such work histories.

A variety of models could be developed. If work satisfaction issues become more important and new work arrangements or job rotation became institutionalized, what kind and amounts of recurrent education would be demanded?

(5) Attitudinal changes. These influences overlap with the institutional changes of (4). How do the younger generation's attitudes toward schooling and marriage affect their interest in recurrent education? What will be happening as they age? Are the work/educational attitudes of women changing? Will there be a spread of the post-30 crisis of occupational identity among men and what will be its effects on the demand for recurrent education?

These five approaches may yield widely varying results that may not be summable or averageable. Perhaps their major contribution is to provide a range of estimates of prospective demand.

Some are more speculative than others. Consequently, it is generally preferable to approach forecasting differently. One step is to study whether or not there are important trends that would support the policy initiative; e.g., is recurrent education bucking a tide which is moving against education and training of adults, or is there a swelling interest in adult postsecondary education? A second approach is to search out starter mechanisms as Frank Reissman calls them which can push programs and build demand, rather than trying to design large-scale blueprints.

Conclusion

The question of whose demand, for what, at which costs, is basically a value question of the objectives of policy. While it should not be assumed that any particular kind of demand can or should be engineered, the other side of the issue is to recognize that by omission or commission, a policy on demand is being pursued. If no special effort is made to affect demand, that is a (creaming, largely backlog) policy. While recurrent education programs have an uncertain demand, at least at their beginnings, and not a perfectly elastic one, they are not without possibilities to affect both the size and character of their demand. The basic perspective should be that "demand" (of particular groups) is a function of policy at least as much as program policy should be a function of (immediately available) demand. Demand is not pre-formed but results from the interaction of many forces, some of which are amenable to program and policy influences. Who should be in the program doing what is the issue. The character of recurrent education will affect the size and nature of the demand for it.

target group focus

recurrent education: more equity or less

A.H. HALSEY

The pendulum of hope for equality through education has swung violently towards despair since the mid-1960's with the apparent failure of higher educational expansion at one end and compensatory nursery provision at the other. This is the context in which a policy of recurrent education is being debated. Will it work or will it make egalitarian matters worse?

The Definition Of Recurrent Education

On the meaning of recurrent education, A Clarifying Report[1] was presented in November 1972 to the Governing Body of the Centre for Educational Research and Innovation by Denis Kallen and his colleagues in the Secretariat; and it is indeed clarifying. Kallen has described a long-run transformation of education in future society in a way which avoids the simplistic polarization of education as either omnipotent or impotent as an agent of social change. Recurrent education, as Kallen conceives of it, constitutes an alternative system of social learning that would be consonant with many of the features of post-industrial society on which most futurologists seem to agree.

The reference here is primarily to a society of advanced technological development, that is, to a society which is rich because its productive system is based on scientific knowledge. Such a society inevitably has a complex division of labor and a high rate of investment in human skill. At the same time, such a society is vulnerable to rapid obsolescence.

---

1. Centre for Educational Research and Innovation, Recurrent Education: A Clarifying Report (Paris: OECD/CERI, 1973).

But out of these technological conditions there arises also a problem beyond the need to build an antidote to the obsolescence of productive skill. Precisely because such a society produces so much, it generates what might be termed the need to educate for consumption. Consumption, in this context, means the passing on and renewal of all those elements in a culture which relate to every aspect of life other than economic production. The more powerful the system becomes the more necessary it is that education contributes to the capacity of populations to use and enjoy the abundant material environment which they thereby create.

The second problem relates to social order. If the social order is based on consent rather than force, educational systems, as transmitters of culture, play a central role. They distribute opportunities and indoctrinate individuals to accept the principles through which men are selected and certified for their places in society.

Kallen's definition takes meaning against this background. Recurrent education is a comprehensive educational strategy for all post-compulsory or postbasic education, the essential characteristic of which is the distribution of education over the total life-span of the individual in a recurring way, i.e., in alternation with other activities, with work in the first place, but also with leisure and retirement.

This definition of recurrent education contains two essential elements.

It offers an alternative to the conventional system concentrated on youth and spreads postcompulsory education over the full life-span.

It proposes a framework within which lifelong learning will be organized. This framework calls for interaction between education and other social activities during which incidental learning occurs.

This definition differs from L'Education Permanente which distinguishes between learning as a broad concept and education as a more narrow and formal one. Kallen's definition, on the other hand, focuses on alternation.

All situations are potentially educational. An educational system is, in reality, an abstraction of those settings which are specifically and primarily designed for learning from the totality of social relationships. The idea of alternation, though it may be new in the thinking of educational planners, is also a reflection of an old idea which was formulated by the American psychologist William James in the aphorism, "We learn to swim in winter and to skate in summer." The further implications of this psychological reality for the problem of an individual who, in modern and future society, must constantly adapt and re-adapt to a culture which itself changes rapidly is at the heart of the idea of recurrent education.

The concept of recurrent education is thus an exciting one. If realized, it could change the character of socially distributed opportunities and values. It could be an agent of reform and equality.

Equity, Equality And Post-Industrial Society

The origin of the problem of equality and education can be found, at least in Europe, in the struggles of the 19th Century to develop school systems responsive to the new industrial and urban conditions. For the ruling classes, the problem was the need to create a punctual, orderly, consensual, and more or less literate working force. For the emerging urban working class, the interest was different. Education was a possible means through which they attempted to come to terms with an environment dramatically different from the rural situations they and their ancestors had typically known.

The outcome, all over Europe, was compromise. There was a gradual introduction of compulsory schooling for children, but the curriculum was largely imposed by the national powers of church and state.

A separate system, explicitly designed for the needs of the upper and middle classes, leading through primary and secondary schools to the universities, was slowly developing in parallel. The equality issue was raised in Europe mainly in terms of providing access from the first to the second system. It was promoted by liberal thought as one or another strategy of equality of educational opportunity. Educationally, the first half of the 20th Century was a history of the ramifications of these strategies of access. Among them that of the simple expansion of more privileged and advanced forms of education has been the dominant one, especially since World War II. It brought an upward trend of secondary and postsecondary enrollments in all the progressive Organisation for Economic Cooperation and Development countries. Europe chased a California dream.

This strategy of expansion is in the mainstream of liberal thought. It can trace intellectual descent from Alfred Marshall's famous 1873 essay[2] which forecast that in 1973, "by occupation at least every man would be a gentleman." The argument was fashioned from the simplest of economic reasoning. Education determines skill; saleable skill determines wages; raise the supply of education and you will reduce the supply of unskilled labor. This argument was perhaps less persuasive for some than the repeated demonstration that, for individuals, the economic rate of return to higher education was 10 percent or more.

---

2. Alfred Marshall, "The Future of the Working Class," in A. C. Pigou, ed., Memorials of Alfred Marshall (London: MacMillan, 1925), pp. 101-118.

In the postwar years, a vague but widespread political sentiment in favor of education as a solution to economic sluggishness was enough to encourage governments to supply--and parents to demand--educational expansion to the extent of doubling university places every decade. National riches and economic quality, it was hoped, would result from the most amiable of social policies, that is, the encouragement of dons and schoolmistresses.

But the origin of the problem of equality and education can be found in the future rather than the past. Daniel Bell and the so-called "Eastern Liberal Establishment" write so brilliantly nowadays in The Public Interest[3] about the "post-industrial society" and the future role of education. Their eyes are on North America and the half-dozen countries which vie with one another to be the richest in the world. The outstanding attribute of such societies is abundance based on the exploitation of advanced technologies through a complex division of labor. The fact of abundance, generated by human skill, challenges traditional principles of distribution. At the same time, theories about how skill, intelligence, and marketable labor are acquired raise the equity issue in an urgent form against the background of traditional inequalities. Individual wealth is increasingly hard-pressed to defend itself on the grounds of productive efficiency. Poverty becomes a remediable scandal. Social ethics are focused less and less on the productive and more and more on the distributive institutions of society. Against the promise of a bounteous future, one can see the emergence of a new social ethic. The ideological foundations of industrial society in individualism and liberalism are rapidly being eroded. Inequalities of wealth, income, power and self-respect, though modified by political democracy and liberal promotion of opportunity, no longer command wide or firm adherence. Neither the claims of class nor the pretensions of merit can serve in the future to legitimate a hierarchy of power, advantage, and affluence.

A new socialist philosophy is in the making. One of its more distinguished architects, Professor John Rawls, has enunciated the underlying social ideal for post-industrial society: "All social primary goods - liberty and opportunity, income and wealth and the bases of self-respect - are to be distributed equally unless an unequal distribution of any or all of those goods is to the advantage of the least favored."[4]

---

3. Daniel Bell, "Meritocracy and Equality," The Public Interest, 29 (1972): 55.

4. John Rawls, A Theory of Justice (Cambridge, Mass.: Harvard University Press, 1971), p. 74.

That the realities do not accord with this ethical prescription is massively documented in social science.[5]

Given educational expansion and skill obsolescence, contemporary society has a special problem of educational equity between generations. In general, the advantage is with the rising generation. For example, Kallen[6] has pointed out that by 1980 nearly 75 percent of people over 40 will have had only elementary schooling in Sweden unless, in the meantime, resources are switched to adult education. This type of generational inequality has received relatively little attention until highlighted by the discussion of recurrent education.

Meanwhile, neither the old class order nor the newer meritocratic order are compatible with this new social ethic. Social policy must treat unequal distributions, whether they stem from social inheritance or genetic endowment, as arbitrary. Moreover, wealth and wit must be treated as social, not individual, assets. In Bell's[7] phrasing, the principles of production and distribution become "from each according to his ability, to each according to the needs of others." The relevance of all this to our assessment of the potentialities of recurrent education stems from the proposition that, in the post-industrial society, schools and colleges come to occupy a place as central as that previously held by the business enterprise. Educational institutions, in Bell's argument, manage the transmission of culture, determine through research the direction of technological and, therefore, social change, and select and form social personalities for places in the occupational structure. Thus, education becomes an arena of modern political and social conflict, since equity, or its reverse, is distributed through schools and colleges.

But, in advance, we should reassert that the ethic formulated by Rawls addresses itself directly to current theories of the determinants of educational attainment. Whether, or to what extent, educational success is the outcome of social or genetic influences, of inequalities of school provision, of the ethnic or racial composition of schools, or of the class, status and power structure of the surrounding community is in one sense irrelevant since all of these factors are regarded as arbitrary in relation to distributive justice. Nonetheless, their exact analysis is required so as to determine what institutional changes are required to redress their arbitrary effects on the distribution of life chances. Recurrent education has to be assessed here on the

---

5. See, for the U.S., James S. Coleman et al., Equality of Educational Opportunity (Washington, D.C.: Government Printing Office, 1966); for Sweden, T. Husen, Talent, Opportunity and Career (Stockholm: Almqvist and Wicksell, 1969); and for Britain, A. H. Halsey, ed., Trends in British Society Since 1900 (New York: Macmillan, Inc., 1972).

6. CERI, A Clarifying Report.

7. Bell, "Meritocracy and Equality."

hypothesis that it provides a structure of opportunity which will avoid or at least reduce the morally arbitrary character of existing educational arrangements.

As Bell puts it, in his discussion of meritocracy and equality,[8] "the liberal principle accepts the elimination of social differences in order to ensure an equal start, but it justifies unequal results on the basis of natural abilities and talents." For Rawls, however, natural advantages are as arbitrary or random as social ones.

> There is no more reason to permit the distribution of income and wealth to be settled by the distribution of natural assets than by historical and social misfortune....The extent to which natural capacity develops and reaches fruition is effected by all kinds of social conditions and class attitudes. Even the willingness to make an effort, to try, and so to be deserving in the ordinary sense, is itself dependent upon happy family and social circumstances. It is impossible in practice to secure equal chances of achievement and culture to those similarly endowed and therefore we may want to adopt a principle which recognises this fact and also mitigates the arbitrary effects of the natural lottery.[9]

Bell and the modern liberal theorists will not, of course, follow all the paths of policy which might lead from this type of socialist argument. While scarcity remains in the world--not even tomorrow's America can promise wholly to abolish it--it is still open to non-socialists to argue, for example, in favor of the use of greater incentives for those who can add more than the common man to the total output of the productive system, thereby yielding a larger abundance to be distributed according to agreed social priorities (which might include discrimination in favor of the disadvantaged). Thus, Bell points out that "it is quite striking that the one society in modern history which consciously began with the principle of almost complete equality--the Soviet Union--gradually abandoned that policy not because it was restoring capitalism, but because it found that differential wages and privileges served as incentives and were also a more rational rationing of time."[10] And, writing in the same issue of The Public

---

8. Bell, "Meritocracy and Equality," p. 55.

9. Rawls, A Theory of Justice, p. 303.

10. Bell, "Meritocracy and Equality."

Interest, Seymour Martin Lipset raises again the fundamental Platonic argument about the family and social equality:

> If one really wishes a society in which there is not merely formal equality of opportunity, but where class background has absolutely no relation to success, one must be willing to pay the necessary price. And that price would appear to be the practical abolition of the family, the suppression of varying cultural and ethnic influences and a rigorously imposed uniformity in the education of the young. As the Communist experience has shown, the abolition of capitalism, at least in itself, is by no means sufficient.[11]

We mention these difficulties as between a socialist and a liberal social ethic in order to make it clear that various kinds of inequality may be regarded as legitimate or necessary in the future. In the educational sphere, its most interesting ramifications appear in debates concerning the displacement of the older liberal conception of equality of opportunity (in the sense of access) by the socialist notion of equality of outcome (in the sense of equal average attainment between noneducationally defined social groups). The socialist ethic justifies going beyond liberal policies which attack inherited wealth towards those which alter the experience of upbringing and livelihood in favor of the disadvantaged. It justifies, inter alia, positive discriminatory policies in education. It indicates that where a social or ethnic group has unequal educational attainments compared with other groups, there has been social injustice. The moral argument for recurrent education is framed in much the same terms. It is put forward as a more effective means to the same end. We, therefore, have to compare its claims to efficacy alongside those of other policies.

Education And Distribution Of Life Chances

This much we do know. The simple demand, supply and price argument which descends in liberal thought from Alfred Marshall has not worked out in practice. For example, Lester Thurow[12] has shown for the United States that "while the distribution of education has moved in the direction of greater equality over the post-war period, the distribution of income has not." Of course, income distributions are limited operational definitions of the concept of life chances. Life chances include opportunities for all forms of legitimate satisfaction in society: the capacity to use income and wealth as well as to acquire it; the opportunity to acquire self-respect as well as the respect of others; the chance to live, learn, marry, play, and understand; and the opportunity to participate in the world around one. No single measure can capture this totality. But the statistics of income and occupation, when related to such distributions as health,

---

11. Seymour M. Lipset, The Public Interest, 29 (1972).

12. Lester C. Thurow, "Education and Economic Equality," The Public Interest, 28 (Summer 1972): 66-81.

532-819 O - 74 - 8

social honors, capital ownership, social connections, and membership of powerful or prestigious groups indicate a continuing inequality of the distribution of life chances. There is a fairly similar hierarchy of occupational strata in all countries in the sense that there is high consensus on the pyramid of the generally desirable characteristics associated with different jobs. The correlation between occupational strata so defined and measures of income, capital, longevity, health and status have been repetitiously over-demonstrated. Moreover, the evidence produced by Thurow on trends in American society give no encouragement to the view that educational reform has made an impact on the more general inequality of power and advantage. "In 1950 the bottom fifth of the white male population had 8.6 per cent of the total number of years of education while the top fifth had 31.1 per cent. By 1970 the share of the bottom fifth had risen to 10.7 per cent, while that of the top fifth had dropped to 29.3 per cent."[13]

Nevertheless, the place of education, as cause rather than consequence in the structure of inequality, is not so clear. That educational opportunity and educational attainment is fairly closely related to social origin (as measured by paternal occupation) is, of course, well established. But the linkage of education to subsequent life chances, and, therefore, the possibilities of education as an instrument for changing that social distribution is more debatable. On this crucial subject, a summarizing and synoptic view has recently been presented by Christopher Jencks.[14] It is a well-known and much-discussed interpretation of the famous study by Blau and Duncan[15] that the American (and presumably any other advanced industrial) occupational structure is open in the sense that a relatively loose relation between social origin and occupational destination is largely to be accounted for by factors which, so far as the individual is concerned, might be regarded as luck, even though some of them have a structural basis. Thus, in his formulation, largely derived from the Blau-Duncan findings, Christopher Jencks writes:

> While occupational status is more closely related to educational attainment than to any other thing we can measure, there are still enormous status differences among people with the same amount of education. This remains true when we compare people who had not only the same amount of schooling, but the same family background and the same test-scores. Anyone who thinks that a man's family background, test-scores, and educational credentials are the only things that

---

13. Thurow, "Economic Equality."

14. Christopher Jencks, Inequality: A Reassessment of the Effect of Family and Schooling in America (New York: Basic Books, 1972).

15. P. Blau and O. D. Duncan, The American Occupational Structure (New York: John Wiley, 1968).

> determine the kind of work he can do in America is fooling himself. At most, these characteristics explain about half the variations in men's occupational statuses. This leaves at least half the variation to be explained by factors which have nothing to do with family background, test-scores or educational attainment.[16]

Some of this unexplained variation, Jencks argues, seems to be attributable to intragenerational occupational mobility. There is obviously some appreciable movement up and down, especially among those in their 20's and 30's. And presumably a system of recurrent education would amplify such movements. But Jencks is concerned to stress a different set of causative factors:

> Some of this unexplained variation is presumably due to unmeasured character traits, like alcoholism, mental health, and drive to succeed, but we doubt if these explain very much. Much of the variation is probably due to chance (one steel-worker gets laid off and takes a temporary job as a painter, while another keeps his job because his plant happens to be busier). Some is due to choice (a business man decides to give up making underwear and becomes a clergyman).

And on income inequality, Jencks adds:

> Income also depends on luck: chance acquaintances who steer you to one line of work rather than another, the range of jobs that happens to be available in a particular community when you are job-hunting, the amount of overtime work in your particular plant, whether bad weather destroys your strawberry crop...and a hundred other unpredictable accidents. Those who are lucky tend, of course, to impute their success to skill, while those who are inept believe that they are merely unlucky....In general, we think luck has far more influence on income than successful people admit.[17]

It is not possible to say on the basis of existing research and knowledge whether the luck hypothesis has much validity. In a talent replication of both the Blau and Duncan study and the study undertaken by Glass and his associates in 1949 in Britain[18] we plan to produce a

---

16. Jencks, Inequality, p. 91.

17. Ibid., p. 227.

18. D. V. Glass, ed., Social Mobility in Britain (London: Routledge and Kegan Paul, 1954). This new study is being undertaken at Nuffield College, Oxford.

sociography of luck by the study of cases which deviate substantially from the regression plane of a path analysis using the key variables of social origin and educational experience which have been used by our predecessors. But, in advance of this analysis, we may surely expect that some of the factors to which Jencks points are, as the Marxists might say, "no accident" if looked at structurally rather than through the eyes of an individual. Nevertheless, it is certainly important to bear in mind that, in the regression analyses used by Blau and Duncan, the explanatory power of variations in educational experience is limited as a proportion of all the influences affecting the distribution of life chances.

It is within this limited context that we must consider alternative educational strategies designed to produce more equality. We may now, therefore, look back at the liberal policies, consider the recently-fashionable compensatory strategies, and finally assess the claims of recurrent education.

The Policy Of Positive Discrimination[19]

The history of 20th Century attempts to use education as a means towards the political and social end of equality may be divided into three phases. In the first phase, from the beginning of the century into the 1950's, the definition of policy was liberal. To provide eventually for equality of access to the more advanced stages of education for all children irrespective of their sex or social origin in classes, religious and ethnic groups or regions was the goal. In Britain it expressed itself in such measures as building the scholarship ladder, abolishing grammar school fees, doing away with the system of separate secondary education for the minority and elementary education for the majority and substituting a system of common schooling with secondary schools "end-on" to primary schools. In the later years of this phase it also meant expansion of higher education.

The logical end of this first phase, when equality of opportunity is combined with national efficiency, is meritocracy. In its most advanced educational expression, this essentially liberal principle is to be found in the preface to the Newsom report written by the then Minister of Education, Sir Edward (later Lord) Boyle: "The essential point is that all children should have an equal opportunity of acquiring intelligence, and of developing their talents and abilities to the full."[20] But what we have seen for America in Christopher

---

19. For an extended version of this section, see A. H. Halsey, Educational Priority: Problems and Policies (London: Her Majesty's Stationery Office, 1972).

20. Ministry of Education, Half Our Future (London: Her Majesty's Stationery Office, 1963).

Jencks' summary was also true for Britain and has prevented the emergence of an educationally-based meritocracy. There were and remain formal and substantive inequalities of educational opportunity as well as noneducational routes to social mobility.

Nevertheless, this liberal notion of equality of opportunity dominated discussion at least until the 1950's and the essential judgment on its policies must be that they failed even in their own terms. For example, when, in a large number of the richer countries during the 1950's, a considerable expansion of educational opportunity was provided, it was more or less assumed that, by making more facilities available, there would be a marked change in the social composition of student bodies and in the flow of people from the less favored classes into the secondary schools and higher educational institutions. This certainly did not happen to the degree expected. There was some increase in both the absolute numbers and the proportions of poor families who reached the higher levels and the more prestigious types of education, nevertheless progress towards greater equality of educational opportunity as traditionally defined was disappointing. It is now plain that the problem is more difficult than had been supposed and needs, in fact, to be posed in new terms.

But liberal notions were never unchallenged by those who wrote in the tradition of R. H. Tawney and the central idea of equality of opportunity was effectively lampooned in Michael Young's Rise of the Meritocracy.[21] Writers like Tawney and Raymond Williams[22] always sought for an educational system which would be egalitarian in the much broader sense of providing a common culture irrespective of the more or less inescapable functions of selection for different occupational destinies. There is a broad distinction of political and social aim here which, in the end, comes to the most fundamental issue of the purposes of education in an urban industrial society and about which judgments are explicitly or implicitly made in any policy. One way of putting the distinction is that the liberal goal of equality of opportunity is too restrictive: We have also to consider liberty and fraternity. Properly conceived recurrent education reflects the attribution of value to these other two great abstractions of the modern trilogy of political aims. But an alternative is the policy of positive discrimination combined with the idea of the community school which my colleagues and I have been developing by the methods of action-research in five "educational priority areas" (i.e., districts identified as suffering from multiple deprivation in employment, housing, income, civic amenities or some mixture of these).

---

21. Michael Young, Rise of the Meritocracy (New York: Random House, 1959).

22. See, for example, Raymond Williams, Culture and Society (New York: Penguin Books, 1966), and The Long Revolution (New York: Penguin Books, 1965).

Our starting point for these experiments in policy was recognition that the older liberal policies had failed basically on an inadequate theory of learning. They failed to notice that the major determinants of educational attainment were not schoolmasters but social situations, not curriculum but motivation, not formal access to the school but support in the family and the community.

So a second phase can be said to have begun in the 1960's with a new emphasis on the theory of noneducational determination of education. In consequence of the experience of the first phase, there had to be a change in the definition of equality of educational opportunity. Its earlier meaning was equality of access to education. In the second phase, this meaning gradually became equality of achievement. In this new interpretation, a society affords equality of educational opportunity if the proportion of people from different social, economic or ethnic categories at all levels and in all types of education are more or less the same as the proportion of these people in the population at large, i.e., the average woman or black or proletarian or rural dweller should have the same level of educational attainment as the average male, white, white collar suburbanite. In the language of mobility analysis, and assuming random distribution of the relevant genetic qualities as between social groups, there would be perfect mobility. If not, social injustice could be presumed.

This social-cum-educational principle, with its radical implications for both social and educational policies, was graphically illustrated in the findings of the American Coleman Report[23] where educational attainments were compared as between Northerners and Southerners of white and nonwhite race. Put graphically, the results showed a divergence of the mean attainment of the four categories of children who were not directly defined in educational terms. The radical goal of educational equality of opportunity would, if realized, produce converging as opposed to diverging lines.

The British Plowden Report[24] (which paralleled that of Coleman) and the beginning of our research in educational priority areas (EPA's) belong to this phase in the development of understanding of the egalitarian issues in education and related them to the social setting of the school. With Plowden the close relationship of social deprivation, in neighborhood and home, and educational attainment was well-founded in research. The corollary was that if social conditions and parental interest could be improved, achievement might be expected to rise. The two policies to this end which we took and developed from

---

23. Coleman, Equality of Educational Opportunity.

24. Central Advisory Council for Education, Children and Their Primary Schools (London: Her Majesty's Stationery Office, 1967).

Plowden were positive discrimination and the community school. But in the early months of our work we began to realize that there were unsolved issues behind the equality debate even in its advanced Colemanesque formulation and especially when applied to the children of the educational priority areas. The debate could be taken beyond equality of educational opportunity to a third phase which involved reappraisal of the functions of education in contemporary society. Education for what? The debate over equality as we saw it was essentially a discussion about education for whom. In planning our new intervention in schools, we were forced sooner or later to consider both questions and in doing so, to ask whether an EPA program is anything more than a new formula for fair competition in the educational selection race.

What assumptions could be made about the world into which our EPA children would enter after school? Were we concerned simply to introduce a greater measure of justice into an educational system which traditionally selected the minority for higher education and upward social mobility out of the EPA district, leaving the majority to be taught, mainly by a huge hidden curriculum, a sense of their own relative incompetence and impotence--a modern, humane and even relatively enjoyed form of gentling the masses? Or could we assume a wide program of economic and social reform which would democratize local power structures and diversify local employment opportunities so that society would look to its schools for a supply of young people educated for political and social responsibility and linked to their communities not by failure in the competition, but by ample opportunities for work and life. Even short of the assumption of extra-educational reform, how far should we concentrate on making recognition easier for the able minority and how far on the majority who were destined to live their lives in the EPA? And if the latter, did this not mean posing an alternative school organization and curriculum, realistically related to the EPA environment and designed to equip the rising generation with knowledge and skills to cope with, give power over, and in the end transform, the conditions of their local community?

On the basis of three years' research in the British EPA's, I would assert that current pessimism as to the potential of education is much exaggerated. The newer strategies of positive discrimination and the community school are instruments of considerable power as yet not fully exploited. Positive discrimination, that is, the allocation of resources in inverse proportion to their existing distribution, offers an educational base from which to attack the fundamental economic and social inequalities on which educational disparities of achievement rest. On the same experience I would also add that the idea of the community school is one which might well be assimilated into a strategy of recurrent education. It has two emphases congruent with the idea of recurrent education which can be stressed. First, it extends the influence of organized education both downwards to the under-fives and upwards into postsecondary and adult education. And second, it conceives of the total resources of the community as available for educative purposes.

Accordingly, in making our recommendations to the British Government,[25] we laid great emphasis, within the framework of a positively discriminatory financial formula, on support from central government to localities for the development of a program of nursery education. Preschooling in our view is par excellence a point of entry for the development of the community school. It is the point at which, properly understood, the networks of family and formal education can most easily be linked. It is, by the same token, the point at which innovative intervention can begin in order to break the barrier which, especially in EPA's, separates the influence of school and community; the point where the vested interests of organization and custom are most amenable to change.

We also concluded that the preschool is an effective educational instrument for applying the principle of positive discrimination and this conviction rests partly on the theory that primary and secondary educational attainment has its social foundations in the child's experience in the preschool years and partly on the evidence that positive discrimination at the preschool level can have a multiplying effect on the overwhelmingly important educative influences of the family and peer groups to which the child belongs.

Nevertheless, as we see it, there is no unique blueprint of either organization or content which can be applied mechanically as a national policy. On the contrary, the essential prerequisite is a correct diagnosis of the needs of individual children and of particular EPA conditions (which, it cannot be too often repeated, vary enormously) with all that this implies for a flexible provision of nursery education for the under-fives in disadvantaged districts.

The Plowden conception of the community school was rudimentary but, as our action-research program progressed, we gradually redefined it as a broad aspect of the community itself to cover the organization and process of learning through all of the social relationships into which an individual entered at any point in his lifetime. Thus, the community school seeks almost to obliterate the boundary between the school and the community, to turn the community into a school and the school into a community. It emphasizes both teaching and learning roles for all social positions so that the children may teach and the teachers learn, as well as vice versa, and parents may do both instead of neither. It insists on seeing the whole of the social organization of a locality from the point of view of its educational potential, whether positive or negative. Thus, the family, the school, the workplace, the WEA, the public bureaucracies, the public house, the holiday camp and the street are all potential resources and potential

---

25. These are under consideration now and have already been reflected (perhaps in muted colors) in the recent White Paper: Education - A Framework for Expansion, Cmnd. .5174 (London: Her Majesty's Stationery Office, December 1972).

barriers to the educational development of the child, and the educational maintenance of the adult. This conception of the community school, which we realized in many different ways in our research and action program, is obviously in many respects another way of stating some of the principles of recurrent education.

American Compensatory Education[26]

That "compensatory education" in the U.S. has failed is a well-established belief in both America and Europe. Indeed, for some people, it is almost the only thing that is known about American compensatory programs. Many refer to the failure of this large American venture without having any idea of the complex variety of its components and the innovations which have been associated with it.

From a British standpoint, the American movement began with what appeared to be a simple educational problem, the fact that certain social groups on average had a lower level of educational performance. Experience of tackling the problem then forced the programs to go further and further outside the educational system. In this process, the most basic questions were raised about the nature of social organization and the explanation of the correlation between social status and educational performance. As the program developed, it became more and more clear that a purely educational solution was impossible. Action programs, following this pattern of development, sought first to introduce changes in the child's experience in the formal school setting, and then increasingly to widen the approach so that larger areas of the child's experience were affected. Thus, educational under-achievement became merely one manifestation of a long series of social and economic disparities experienced by disadvantaged groups. The long-term solution gradually defined itself as a comprehensive policy which would strike at these political, social, and economic inequalities.

Nevertheless, while recognizing the need for widely-based economic and social reform, we saw no justification for the wholesale condemnation of the compensatory education programs. There have been limited successes in American experience where careful programs have sought more modest ends. And in any case it is possible that educational programs may make considerable impact on the political consciousness of the poor. That awakening certainly accompanied the development of many of the experiments in the U.S. Such political awakening may be the most effective means of insuring that the gross inequalities between social and ethnic groups are, in the end, eradicated.

---

26. For a comprehensive review of this program, see G. Smith and A. Little, Strategies of Compensation (Paris: OECD, 1971).

The Claims Of Recurrent Education

In the light of this analysis, we may now assess the claims of recurrent education. We must begin by repeating that the potentiality of any form of education as an instrument of social change is limited. In part, education systems reflect the power structure and values of the society in which they exist. Recurrent education does not escape constraints; however, it can contribute to greater social equality.

There are claims other than equity to be made on behalf of recurrent education. For example, it can assist in cultural transmission.

But from the point of view of equity, we have two types of inequality to consider--the intragenerational and the intergenerational.

With regard to intragenerational inequalities of class, race, ethnicity, etc., recurrent education has no special claims compared with the EPA policy of positive discrimination and community schooling which I have sketched. Kallen has, in my view, written judiciously on this point.

> An equality policy in which high priority would be given to strategies for compensation in a much more systematic manner than at present is widely advocated. But in order to produce durable results, a more profound renewal of education is probably needed, bearing on the nature of the educational experience, on the relations between school and community, on an overhaul of the curricula of compulsory education, and on a re-evaluating in particular of the role of observation, experience and sense for a practical, problem-solving approach. Moreover, co-ordination between educational policy and socio-economic policies would be needed, which would in turn require the creation of administrative conditions for such a co-ordination. If all this can be achieved, compensatory education in the sense of special programmes might not be needed, as it is now, for the majority of children, but only for a small group of severely handicapped....In order to succeed, compensation programmes need more and other resources than have hitherto been allocated to them and they must go hand in hand with socio-cultural and economic measures.[27]

These are precisely the conclusions reached in our study of the British EPA's and our action-research programs of positive discrimination, preschooling and community schooling. Of course, such programs could be readily incorporated into a system of recurrent education.

---

27. CERI, A Clarifying Report, p. 31.

Indeed, the community school in the form now developed is a principal component of recurrent education as Kallen defines it. As he points out, "A 'compensation' task, i.e., to compensate for the inequalities of the present and near future"[28] would have to be undertaken by a recurrent education system.

However, with respect to the other main type of inequality, the intergenerational, the claims of recurrent education are powerful and convincing. They are based essentially on the principle of spreading educational opportunity over a longer period of the individual's lifetime and thus releasing him, at least to some degree, from the rigidities of social uniformity and the constraints of social origin. Recurrent education may be expected to motivate students to enter the labor market and to return, as of right, under the impulse of direct experience. In this way, reliance on pressures from home, which are known to favor those from advantaged socioeconomic background, is reduced. The second, third and 'nth chance is institutionalized and the fate of the man is thus less closely determined by the influences of birth and early childhood.

These are strong arguments but there has to be caution. The educational character of work experience must insure a reinforcement of educational motivation and society would have to invest in high quality information services. These would be necessary prerequisites to institutionalizing multiple chances through recurrent education. Without these preconditions, it could all too easily turn out that the manipulation of the recurrent education system would once again follow the traditional and familiar lines so that motivation and choices would remain essentially determined by social background and the arbitrary inequalities which these policies are designed to eradicate. As Kallen has wistfully observed, "Recurrent education could thus lead to an increase in inequality that would be much more difficult to counter than the present inequality."[29]

---

28. CERI, A Clarifying Report, p. 31.

29. Ibid., p. 33.

intergenerational inequality and recurrent education: the case of sweden

J. BENGTSSON

Educational Equality: Some Introductory Remarks

Social equality has been a well-discussed and major political issue for a long time in most countries. The scope and meaning of this concept have changed from time to time and from culture to culture. To begin with, the main political goal was to obtain equal formal rights for every member of society to take part in voting procedures and to employ the resources that society makes available. A second development was to equalize the opportunities for everyone to make real use of these rights, irrespective of role, sex, religion, social, economic, and geographic backgrounds. When and where such an attempt was evaluated, the results often showed a low degree of achieved equalization. Consequently, a third and current political issue in many countries today is to see that social equality really is attained in terms of results. This is a goal that goes beyond the mere removal of obstacles to positive political measures of compensation and support aiming at equal social outcomes.

Educational equality has developed similarly to the more general concept of social equality. Formal right to education is no longer a political issue in most countries, as is also the case of equal educational opportunities, but the different practical, philosophical, and political questions related to a policy of equal educational outcomes is now the focus of the debate. Bell[1] recently presented a challenging view on this issue and seems to be rather sceptical as to the rationale of a policy of equal outcomes in an emerging post-industrial society. However, even if this new and basically philosophical thinking is essential for the future debate on social and educational

---

1. D. Bell, "Meritocracy and Equality," The Public Interest, 29 (Autumn 1972): 29-68.

equality, it seems to explicitly and implicitly deal primarily with the intragenerational aspects of equality. The other important political issue of intergenerational inequality is paid little attention.

This problem is a specific one in the field of educational equality, and it is sometimes argued that it is only a short-term problem. The present and future youth generations will be given an education such that the problem will disappear within one generation. But this is debatable.

Firstly, there is the fact that in many countries a large part of the present youth generation has only basic and compulsory education. Secondly, even for the young who have a more extensive education, much of this will certainly become obsolete in a rapidly changing society. Therefore, intergenerational inequality should rather be seen as both a permanent and a short-term problem. It is also significant that the problem has been linked especially to the new thinking on lifelong learning and recurrent education that often has been considered as the potential educational strategy to deal with it.

How this problem has been perceived and discussed in Sweden, and how it has been related to the idea of recurrent education is the aim of this paper.

The Educational Gap

As in most countries, the educational reforms in Sweden have been geared primarily towards providing a good education for the young. This has found expression in extensive reforms in the last two decades. Briefly, the result is that compulsory schooling covers nine years and, through optional and further studies, about 80-90 percent of the young get an 11-12 year basic education. This educational expansion gives today's young people a far better chance of coping with changes in the labor market and society at large than any earlier generation.

However, the situation of the older generations is made relatively worse, as it must compete with well-trained younger people in the same labor market. At present, between 70 and 75 percent of the population aged 15-65 years have only six-seven years of elementary schooling. In absolute figures, this means that about 3.5 million people, or nearly half the population of Sweden, have a very short basic elementary education.

The crucial problem is that this educational gap will persist for a long time.

Figure 1 shows a prediction of the educational composition of different age groups of the Swedish population between 1970 and 1990.

Figure 1. **Predicted Educational Background of the Swedish Population, 1970 – 1990**

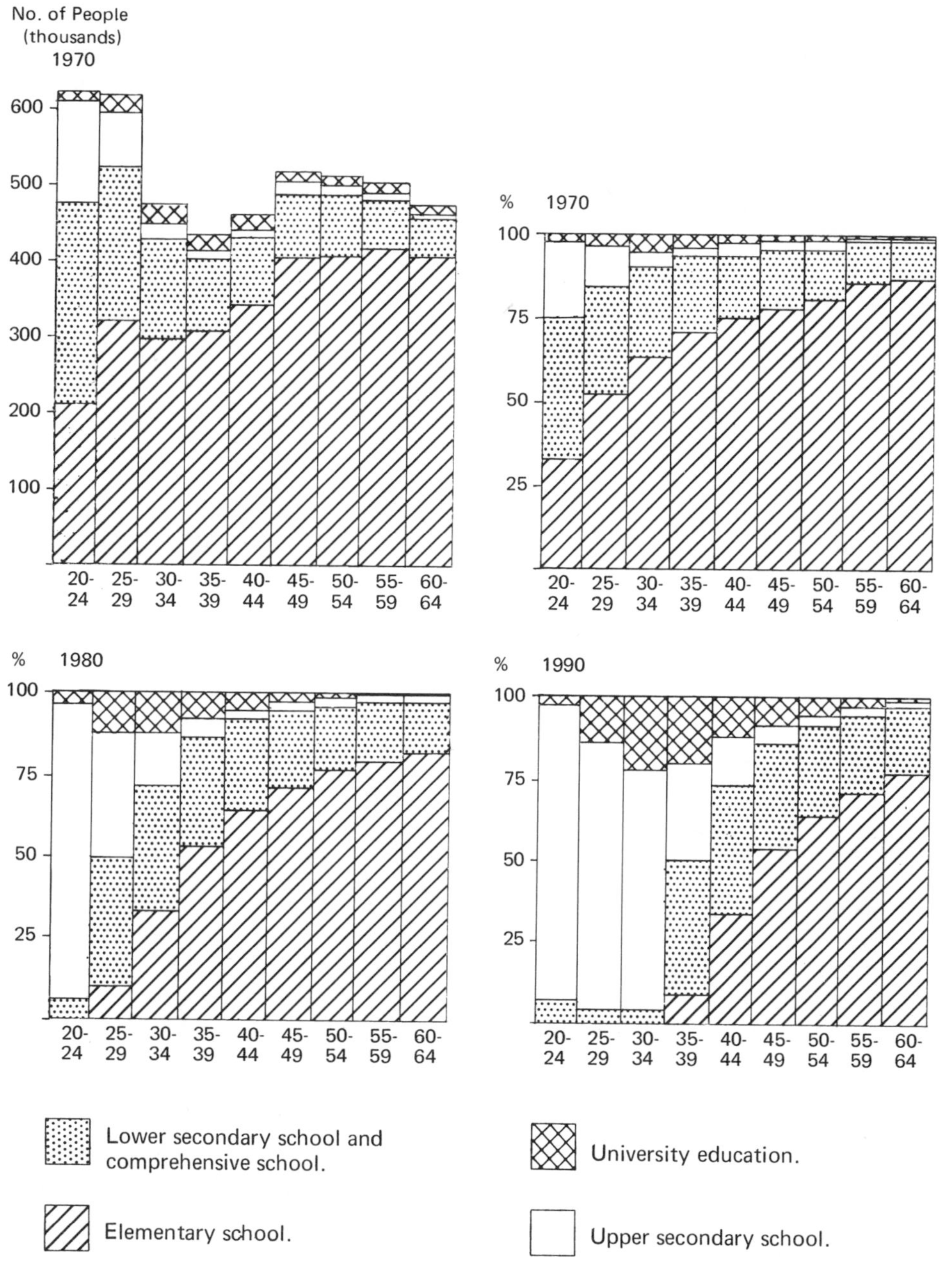

Source: From "Uppsökande verksamhet for cirkelstudier inom vuxenutbildningen," FOVUX, *Sou* (Stockholm: Ministry of Education, 1972), p. 19.

The figure shows that if the present resource distribution between youth and adult education continues, about 50 percent of the population aged 35-40 will have received only elementary schooling in 1980.

It is clear from such forecasts that with an ongoing expansion of youth education, the educational gap between the generations creates a serious political problem. The Confederation of Trade Unions has especially emphasized this gap as a topic of high priority in policy discussions relating to equality.

The existence of this educational gap raises at least three major policy questions:

(a) First, should one continue the expansion of youth education and obtain larger and larger groups with longer and longer education, or should this expansion slow down in favor of an expansion of adult education? In the latter case, what kind of strategy would be used in order to attain a better balance between resources for youth and adult education and how would such a strategy be related to recurrent education?

(b) Secondly, what kind of adult education should be given priority? Should it be mainly a replica of youth education and somewhat institutionalized, or one that is basically new and takes as its starting point the specific needs of adults, including those needs that they themselves consider important.

(c) Thirdly, of what kind and amount are the actual and potential demand of individuals for adult education, and what obstacles stand in the way of those who wish to participate in education as adults?

The Educational Gap And Recurrent Education

The present educational policy in Sweden attempts to reach a better and more equal balance between youth and adult education. Such a policy aims at making possible a considerable expansion of adult education during the coming decades, and consequently also creates the need for an overall planning strategy that simultaneously encompasses both youth and adult education.

It is in this perspective that the idea of recurrent education has come into the debate. It was launched by a Royal Commission (U.68)[2] in 1969 and immediately stimulated an intensive educational debate as it put many of the old problems into a new and challenging framework.

---

2. U.68 Debatt, Hogre utbildning - funktion och struktur (Stockholm: Ministry of Education, 1969).

As with all new concepts, recurrent education has been difficult to define in an unambiguous way. Two different interpretations emerged in the general debate. First, recurrent education was seen primarily in a short-term perspective and as a new reform for adult education, giving the adults a second chance by a rapid and extensive expansion of present and new forms of adult education provisions. Implicitly or explicitly, it took the present system of youth education for granted, and did not anticipate any changes in it.

In the second interpretation of the concept, which was more long-term oriented, radical changes in the whole system of education were envisaged. Recurrent education was seen as a strategy for the whole postcompulsory system, including secondary and higher education as well as adult education. One of its basic principles was alternation between study and work or other activities.

It is the second of these two interpretations that has been more extensively discussed in Sweden. New and tentative definitions of youth and adult education have emerged in the course of the debate.

Some people consider that "youth education" should be defined as education given up to the age at which a pupil today normally leaves upper-secondary school in Sweden, and "adult education" as all education after roughly the age of 18. The latter thus comprises a number of different kinds of education: on the one hand, popular education, municipal adult education, and labor market education; on the other, higher education in all its different forms. Two main categories of adult students can be seen here: those with a long period of earlier education (i.e., those who have completed upper-secondary school), and those who have only basic or elementary education. It is obvious that the latter group is of specific importance as far as the educational gap and the goal of equality, in the shorter-term perspective, are concerned.

The term "overbridging education"[3] has been introduced in this respect, meaning education geared especially towards those adults with only a short education. In the debate, the difference between this concept and that of recurrent education has perhaps not always been very clear. But, according to present thinking, one should see the two concepts in relation to the two target groups mentioned above. Overbridging education, then, refers to the large group of adults with only a short education, while recurrent education stands for a more comprehensive planning strategy that will permit individuals belonging to the other target group to choose an education based on the principle of alternation between study and work or other activities.[4]

---

3. See footnote 2.

4. Jarl Bengtsson, "The Swedish View of Recurrent Education," in Recurrent Education: Policy and Development in OECD Countries (Paris: OECD/CERI, 1972).

In other words, overbridging education should be seen as a short-term strategy related to present intergenerational inequality, while recurrent education is a more long-term oriented strategy. However, both concepts are related to the problem of an educational gap, the former being a strategy to tackle the present gap, the latter, in this respect, a strategy to counteract future gaps both within and between the generations.

Hence, the experience gained from overbridging education will be of great importance in the gradual implementation of a system of recurrent education, especially as regards the different obstacles faced by the individuals who intend re-entering the educational system. An important problem is, of course, the distribution of resources between the two areas, in particular at those times when money is scarce. For example, a major endeavor to provide overbridging education would certainly result in less resources being available for recurrent education for those who already had a longer education.

If present policies are pursued, it can be anticipated that overbridging education will indeed be given a very high priority in the late 1970's in Sweden.

Types Of Overbridging Education

A discussion of future developments in overbridging education is not only a question of quantitative problems. Content and organization are equally important.

At present, many different types of adult education exist. This education has not been the result of a coherent policy for adult education but has rather developed out of different pressures and in different settings, without any overall central planning.

Broadly speaking, the present adult education provisions in Sweden can be divided into three major parts: municipal adult education, labor market training, and popular education.

Municipal adult education

Adult education arranged at the municipal level has been carried out since the beginning of the 1950's, but the major breakthrough came with the adult education reform of 1967. The state, as part of this reform, provided generous resources to the municipalities. It was not compulsory. The government assumed that the municipalities would voluntarily fulfill the existing need for adult education in their districts. The basic intention was that the municipalities would arrange adult education in accordance with the syllabuses for the last part of the comprehensive school and the upper-secondary school.

The 1967 reform caused a considerable expansion of this municipal adult education, as table 1 shows.

Table 1. Development of Municipal Adult Education in the Years 1967/68 - 1970/71 (figures are approximate).

	1967/68	1968/69	1969/70	1970/71	1971/72
Number of municipalities with courses on special subjects in local adult education	30	225	280	300	N.A.
Number of adults (higher stage of comprehensive school, technical school, high school)	12,300	37,000	62,000	87,000*	N.A.
State contributions in millions of SKr	11	52	83	98	130

* About 80,000 pupils attending vocationally-oriented courses are not included here.

Source: From "The Development of Adult Education in Sweden in the 1960s" (Stockholm: Ministry of Education, Swedish National Commission for UNESCO).

The most recent development in this adult education is increased governmental support for comprehensive school courses, and more restricted support and supervision as to the expansion of upper-secondary education courses. As from 1971, the expansion relating to adult upper-secondary education was fixed at 10 percent; previously, it was possible for all municipal adult education to expand freely. The decision was based on investigations showing that those enrolling in municipal adult education are rather young, and already relatively well-educated. In other words, the decision should be seen in the perspective of the educational gap, i.e., the government wishes to give priority to the adult with a short education.

Labor market training and education

This training or education, especially related to employment policies, aims to facilitate transition to new occupational tasks for unemployed persons or persons who risk becoming unemployed. In order to take part in this training, the individual must satisfy the following conditions:

(a) He or she must be unemployed (registered as unemployed), be threatened with unemployment, or be difficult to place in the labor market.

(b) He or she must have reached the age of 20 years.

(c) He or she must be in need of this education in order to find a permanent occupation.

(d) If not fulfilling condition (a), applicants must be aiming at an occupation in which there is a shortage of skilled labor.

This labor market training has expanded considerably during the last 10 years or so. In 1959-1960, approximately 14,000 were involved, in 1965-1966, approximately 46,000, and in 1970-1971, approximately 100,000.

Until recently, most of this training has consisted largely of purely occupational training. However, as most of the people receiving the training have had only a very short basic education, experiments were started in 1969 to include some general education. The results have been quite encouraging, and further experiments in this direction will be carried out in the future.

Popular education

Of all the different forms of adult education in Sweden, that known as "popular education" has existed the longest. The most important organizers of this activity are the educational associations and the folk high schools, which generally have no counterpart outside Scandinavia. The most important and predominant branch of activity in this field is the study circle. The average number of participants is about 10, but there may be as few as five. The members meet and together study a subject or a problem area that they themselves have chosen.

During the 1960's, this activity expanded considerably. In the years 1959-1960, about 81,000 study circles were arranged, with about 800,000 participants. Ten years later, there were some 180,000 study circles, with approximately 1.8 million participants. During this period, the state contribution to these activities rose from 13 million to 130 million SKr. Also, during this period, there has been an extensive debate on the role of this specific adult education in relation to municipal adult education. In particular, the debate has focused on the question of what type of adult education had the best chance of reaching educationally underprivileged adults, and, accordingly, how the communities' resources should be divided between different forms of adult education. The different associations in charge of popular education have often claimed that they have particularly good possibilities of working in this direction, as the participants in the study circles are relatively older than the participants in municipal adult education.

Apart from these three major forms of adult education, we should also mention the considerable amount of correspondence education, education on radio and TV, and also a vast and expanding type of on-the-job training. Taking all the different types of adult education together, one finds that at present more pupils are involved in adult education than in youth education.

However, even if the quantitative expansion during the last decade has been impressive, there are still many problems to be solved for better coordination of the different types of adult education. Especially important is which of the different types of adult education has the best chance of reaching the educationally underprivileged? Investigations carried out on recruiting--regarding age, sex, educational background, etc.--have revealed, for instance, that municipal adult education has attracted primarily younger adults with relatively recent study experiences and physically less demanding occupations. Such participants have concrete educational motives linked to the future. Of the adults attending this education, approximately 60 percent are 30 years old or younger, while only about 35 percent are over 35 years old. As to school background, about 75 percent have more than elementary school education. The general picture that emerges shows that municipal adult education attracts a younger and better-educated group of adults in comparison with the larger part of popular adult education.

The folk high school students also have lower average ages. About 90 percent are under 30 (the total number of pupils receiving this kind of education was about 14,000 in 1970, plus some 10,000 attending shorter courses). However, the school background of these pupils is somewhat lower than those attending municipal education. Over 50 percent have had only elementary education. All this shows quite clearly that unless special measures are adopted in terms of strengthening a type of overbridging education that reaches those with the poorest education, the already relatively well-educated adults will profit most from extended programs.

Obstacles To Overbridging Education

If the political intentions connected with overbridging education are to be realized, it is quite obvious that the present hindrances for the short-term educated must be eliminated. Roughly speaking, these hindrances are psychosocial, economic, and geographic. The obstacles are naturally not the same for all. Whereas, some fear their lack of study experience as the greatest obstacle, others fear the economic factor. From the investigations so far carried out in Sweden, it is not yet possible to say what most prevents the poorly educated from taking up adult education.

The psychological obstacles seem for the most part to be constituted by lack of both self-confidence and experience of study. The fear of revealing gaps in general education is great. Vast changes are taking place in the social environment and previous knowledge very quickly becomes obsolete. Other factors, such as heavy physical labor, working in shifts, home and family life, can hinder the student. Another important fact is that the educational courses now offered do not adequately deal with those problems faced by the individuals. In general, greater public participation in educational planning is needed to overcome many of the psychological and social problems.

As regards economic obstacles, one can distinguish to some extent between adult education given in the participants' spare time and that given full time. In Sweden study loans for adults are the same as for young people, and are, therefore, inadequate for an adult person with a family having high regular fixed costs. This must be changed if day tuition is to be a realistic proposition for adults. A Royal Commission[5] has been appointed to make an inquiry and propose measures insuring that adults are provided with the economic means to study full time. However, even spare-time studies entail economic commitments.

Geographical obstacles are for many the most concrete hindrance. It is, of course, more convenient to have the educational facilities in one's own district. Adult education must be given in many forms if it is to reach all parts of the country. The use of different mass media has not been very promising in this respect; it has attracted mainly the better-educated adults.

In the light of this very summary account of obstacles to overbridging education, it will be realized that this education must be designed with strongly selective measures. This selectivity applies both to the organizers of adult education and to measures adopted by the state, the municipalities, and the county councils. Some interesting experiments have been carried out in this respect in Sweden. They have been labeled, "outreach activities," meaning more active information to the potential students.

It is quite obvious that the information hitherto given to would-be adult students has not been entirely successful in recruiting more to adult education. It is, therefore, necessary to develop untraditional means if the political targets inherent in the aims of overbridging education are to be attained. As discussed in Sweden, information on possibilities of education should be given through direct visits to the places of work and via the trade union organizations. The idea is that the representative in question should consider the actual job situation of the individual, and be able to overcome eventual obstacles to study and recommend what type of studies should be undertaken and choice of subjects.

In the last two years, a number of initiatives have been taken, in particular by local sections of the Workers' Educational Association

---

5. "Vuxna Utbildning Studiefinansiering," Sou (Stockholm: Ministry of Education, 1971), p. 80.

(ABF) and various local trade unions, in visiting places of work. This activity has also been carried out by various organizations for the handicapped, in collaboration with the Workers' Educational Association. In a few cases, collaboration is between the enterprise in question and municipal adult education.

In order to evaluate these personal visits by trade union representatives or educational consultants, in 1969, the Swedish Confederation of Trade Unions and the Workers' Educational Association began experimental activities with visits to places of work. The state gave economic support to the proposal, which is being implemented by a committee (FOVUX)[6] consisting of representatives of the educational associations, the employees' and the employers' organizations.

Experiments are being carried out in about 10 districts representing different types of industry-heavy industry, industries with predominantly female labor, enterprises with day work, shifts, and irregular working hours. They concentrated on the groups with the poorest educational background, and on a few important subjects, such as Swedish, mathematics, civics, English, and also in some cases, some vocational subjects.

In most cases, the form of study was the study circle supplemented sometimes by short courses in special subjects at a folk high school. Before experiments began, the leaders of the study circles were given a week's training in which much attention was paid to the functions of the leaders in directing and stimulating the studies.

At each place of work, there is at least one organizer of studies who can give information about the possibilities of study during working hours. Recruiting for the studies has in the main taken the form of effective personal contact at the place of work. The organizers of the studies receive full compensation for wages lost because of these visits. They have all been given at least a week's training beforehand to equip them for giving advice and so forth.

In accordance with the recommendation, a number of measures intended to stimulate the studies have been implemented, e.g., studies during working hours, incentive grants, free textbooks, etc., care of children, traveling expenses, meals in connection with the studies, and so forth. No charges are made for participation.

The first experiences gained from these experiments are now available and have been published.[7] Of the 3,962 people contacted during

---

6. Kommitten for forsoksverksomhet med vuxenutbildning, Proposition (Stockholm: Ministry of Education, 1970), p. 35.

7. See footnote 2.

the first trial year, 2,074 or 52 percent wished to participate. The Committee has summarized some of its findings as follows:

> In the Committee's opinion, the recruitment result - 52 per cent of those contacted - is remarkably good, especially considering that two-thirds of the participants have not pursued studies since leaving the elementary school. It should also be borne in mind that the FOVUX courses on offer embraced only four subjects and that certain participants, owing to the experimental situation, had to study another subject than the one of first choice. If the range of offerings had been broader, it is likely that even more persons would have been interested in participating.
>
> Reaching out therefore makes an effective method of recruiting enrollments in FOVUX courses from the ranks of lowly educated adults. However, the results achieved by outreach depend upon a host of various factors whose significance in relation to one another has not been fully explained in the experimental scheme. Several such factors will be mentioned here. According to the study organizers, they should have a background similar to that of the persons sought out, as well as understanding of their situation, if they are to succeed in their mission. Obviously, thoroughgoing familiarity with the subject workplace makes an added plus for the study organizers, since that makes it easier for them to judge the right time and place to establish contact. And if the study organizers are themselves employed at the establishment, they are in a position to contribute solutions to the problems which may arise when a study circle starts or while a course is in progress. Moreover, it appears that reaching out is a relatively time-demanding activity. It may be necessary to pay several visits to each prospect before an appropriate conversational opportunity arises. Many of those contacted are hesitant and need time to think things over before they apply for enrollment. At establishments with irregular working hours each department has to be visited several times to permit contacting all the employees. The consequence of these factors during the first trial year was to make the study organizers work under severe time pressure, which precluded their giving everyone as much detailed information as would have been desirable, for instance, about the special program of financial assistance to studies. Another very important point: when engaged in outreach activity, the study organizers should be enabled to offer the contacted persons favorable terms as regards study periods, financial

assistance, travels in connection with the courses, and the like. The fact that course materials are brought along and demonstrated also appears to be conducive to recruitment.

Concluding Remarks

From the preceding analysis, it becomes clear that the problem of intergenerational inequality is looked upon as a serious matter in Swedish educational policy today. In a short-term perspective, many problems have to be solved as to priority and development of nontraditional overbridging education. The basic problem is that if only an extension of conventional education is provided, i.e., a replica of youth education, then this seems to attract primarily the already better-educated adults. The very poorly-educated adults are unresponsive.

In a long-term perspective, moreover, there is the problem of merging the different types of overbridging education with a newly developing policy for recurrent education encompassing postcompulsory education.

We started this paper with the notion that the problem of intergenerational inequality has often been overlooked in the general debate on educational equality. The reason is either that it is a short-term problem, or that the adult has little motivation to re-enter the educational system.

Furthermore, what we have called "overbridging education" is only one policy measure in connection with the broader concept of social equality. Consequently, if one is concerned about a more equal distribution of resources between the generations, the less privileged groups should perhaps be given forms of compensation other than just education. Educational efforts alone will not suffice.

But the chief question remaining relates to the growing importance of knowledge in an emerging post-industrial society. The post-industrial society is often labeled as the "knowledge society," where the "knowledge industries" that produce and distribute ideas and information will be more important than the goods and service industries. If this is a realistic feature of such a society, access to knowledge becomes an even more crucial issue than today in terms of equality.

In this respect, it is not only the problem of knowledge becoming more rapidly obsolete in our present and the emerging society, but rather the inability of individuals to get access to this new knowledge. The lack of access to knowledge diminishes the possibilities for a participatory society and increases the risk of alienation of the individual in his working and living environment.

However, education alone is certainly not the panacea for this problem, but the fact that knowledge more and more becomes the key to power and influence implies a responsibility for the educational system, in all its variety, to provide real access to knowledge, its creation, and its use.

In such a perspective, the concern for greater social equality between generations is not only a question of letting adults choose between more education or leisure or economic subsidiaries, it is also a question of the role of education in building a more participatory society. The educational system has still to prove its contribution to such a task, but it has at least the potential.

equity and efficiency considerations in recurrent education

THOMAS I. RIBICH

This paper attempts to describe and analyze the efficiency and equity principles relevant to the issue of recurrent education. After a brief description of the range and character of the activity to be discussed, the efficiency aspects of recurrent education are treated with special attention to the non-monetary (psychic) returns to education. This is followed by an analysis of the equity issues most germane to recurrent education and a final section dealing with the question of systematizing efficiency concerns.

Recurrent Education: Scope And Prospects

For at least some writers, recurrent education is a broad term used to describe the present network of programs available for those who wish to return to the classroom some time after leaving the regular education sequence.[1] Others associate the term with further systematizing of present programs, to more frequent or more purposeful return trips to school, to more formal certification of program graduates, to more abundant government financing, and/or to the reduction in government financial support for formal sequential education.[2] No one seems to suggest seriously that we abolish present

---

1. See Francis A. Fay, "Adult Education and Public Policy," Adult Education, 23, 4 (1972): 152.

2. See Organisation for Economic Co-operation and Development, Recurrent Education: Policy Implications and Issues (Paris: OECD/Education Committee, 1972).

arrangements for "nonsequential" education and start from scratch. This being the case, this paper concentrates on the present system and the equity and efficiency justifications for reform or nonreform of that system. And, since the reforms presently under discussion are many and multifaceted, the emphasis will be on general principles rather than specific proposals. Comments on particular programs and research results are limited to United States experience.

Before discussing specific varieties of recurrent education, it might be well to probe briefly the related issues of why interest in the topic seems to be on the upswing. To put the question somewhat differently and more specifically: why is it generally thought that enrollments in recurrent education are due to increase by large amounts?[3] It might all be attributed to the old standby of accelerating technological change. But other important forces are surely at work; not all of these can be traced back, in turn, to technological change sources, nor do all have the same promise of continuing indefinitely into the future. Among the most obvious developments are: the coming of age of the baby-boom generation; the unusually rapid increase in formal education experienced in the last decade; general unhappiness with the performance of formal schooling; rising aspirations of blacks and women; changing patterns of government sector demand; and lifestyles and life-expectancies that involve more leisure time.

These multiple sources of growth in enrollments not only indicate that predicting future demand may be difficult; they also suggest that recurrent education is a heterogeneous concept, the composition of which is subject to considerable change. Conclusions about recurrent education, from either an efficiency or equity standpoint, might be swiftly outdated. Moreover, even if the relative importance of various forms of recurrent education does not change appreciably, the current batch is sufficiently diverse as to defy easy generalization. The spectrum in the U.S. includes:

1. literacy training (e.g., the Adult Basic Education Program);

2. job training and retraining of the relatively unskilled (e.g., MDTA);

3. technical education for career advancement (e.g., night school accounting);

4. reschooling the unemployed professional (e.g., the Technology Mobilization and Re-employment Program);

---

3. See, for instance, U.S. Office of Education, Perspectives of Adult Education in the United States and a Projection for the Future (Washington, D.C.: Government Printing Office, 1972), pp. 72-181.

5. rounding out the education for the recent dropout from formal schooling (e.g., the Neighborhood Youth Corps);

6. helping the transition of returning veterans (e.g., the GI Bill);

7. education for general "self-improvement" (e.g., YMCA programs);

8. education for undertaking "second careers" (e.g., women with grown-up children);

9. executive institutes (and union institutes);

10. special extension services for farmers;

11. on-the-job training of various types;

12. retirement preparation; and

13. sabbatical leaves.

This taxonomy is not exhaustive. Even within the same education program, enrollees might differ a great deal in their motives for involvement and the use they make of the experience. One recent survey identified 5,733 reasons why people enroll in adult education courses.[4] A condensed version of that list of some 80 reasons could easily be faulted as incomplete--for instance, there was no item referring directly to the motive of wanting to earn more income.

In addition to the concerns already mentioned, this diversity raises doubts about whether it is even appropriate to attempt efficiency or equity comparisons among programs and among individuals in different programs, or even among all those within a given program. Moreover, many of the programs would seem to have more in common with "formal" education or other kinds of human resource programs, than they do with other recurrent education programs. This, in turn, creates conflicting tendencies to contract the range of considerations to some group of reasonably comparable programs or individuals, or to expand the analysis to include human resource investments that are not part of a recurrent education system.

Despite these problems, there is some precedent for treating the whole range together and in isolation (more or less) from other types

---

4. Paul Burgess, "Reasons for Participation in Group Educational Activities," Adult Education Journal, 22, 1 (1971): 3-29.

of human investments.[5] The remainder of this paper will follow that precedent.

Efficiency

It is difficult to talk about equity without reference to efficiency. To someone who asserts that equity in education would be best served if everyone got a Harvard Ph.D., the proper reply is not through the niceties of equity debate. It is rather the spelling out of the large resource costs this would entail, what this would mean in terms of goods and services sacrificed, and the diminishing returns implications of producing vast amounts of very highly trained manpower. Frequently, a trade-off between efficiency and equity will exist, and maximizing both simultaneously will be impossible.

Efficiency connotes very different things to different people. To some it suggests cost cutting; to others it means maximizing Gross National Product. To most economists it means something considerably broader than this, and it is this broader notion that seems most appropriate in the present context.

On the most abstract plane, complete efficiency to an economist means that it is impossible to rearrange things such that some individuals will consider themselves better off while no one feels worse off.[6] Since, in practice, it is extremely difficult for any large social change to leave no one feeling less well off, this very pure version of efficiency requires some modification lest it be used as a justification for even the most arbitrary status quo situation. The most widely accepted modification is that efficiency exists when those who benefit by any change would not be willing to compensate completely (by "side" payment) those who lose as a result of the change, or, alternatively, that the gainers fail to gain as much by the change as the losers lose. As a corollary, it can be said that efficiency is improved if a given change is such that gainers gain more than is lost by the losers--that the gainers would be willing to fully compensate the losers for their loss.

Still a briefer (and somewhat looser) way of saying this is that an efficient change is one where all benefits outweigh all costs. Many or most of the benefits of a particular change may be non-monetary,

---

5. See Melvin Levin and Joseph Slavet, Continuing Education (Lexington, Mass.: Heath Lexington, 1970); also Fay, "Adult Education and Public Policy," pp. 150-157, and OECD, Recurrent Education.

6. For a recent and precise statement by a noneconomist, see John Rawls, A Theory of Justice (Cambridge, Mass.: Belknap Press, 1972), pp. 66-70.

and the same might be true of the costs. Hence, the broader economic efficiency notion is not synonymous with Gross National Product, economic growth, or any of the other easily observed financial magnitudes. Nonetheless, any non-monetary aspect can be assigned a monetary value--a "shadow price," as some call it. Most commonly, this is thought of as the amount someone would be willing to pay for the non-monetary benefit, or the amount that would have to be paid to willingly accept a non-monetary cost.

In the transition from the pure definition of efficiency to the pragmatic benefit-cost standard, the question of who gets what tends to blur. The pure definition of an efficient change involves a guarantee that no one feels less well off. The impure version, though still rooted in individual preferences, only requires that the sum of perceived benefits outweighs the sum of perceived costs, without any restrictive requirements about the distribution among individuals of benefits and costs. That such distributional concerns are not imbedded in this modified version of efficiency does not imply that they must be neglected. What it calls for instead is an extra dimension--equity --which will be the topic of later sections.

For now, a brief exploration of specific efficiency concerns is in order. The discussion concentrates on two aspects: (1) the special human capital complications involved in recurrent education and (2) the problem of what is variously called psychic or non-monetary returns.

Human capital

While the first section of this paper noted some reasons for the growth of recurrent education, it seems well to outline the theoretical reasons why acquiring all of one's classroom learning early in life and prior to entry into the labor market is frequently not sufficient. Starting with the other side of the coin, it is true that absorbing education as early as possible has some distinct efficiency advantages. First, since child labor is thought to be relatively ineffective and is usually illegal, opportunity costs in terms of foregone earnings of children run from nonexistent to low; and the frequent surplus of young and unskilled labor keeps opportunity costs at low levels through early adulthood. A second advantage is the fact that the earlier one acquires his education the longer time he has to reap its rewards. Third, there is the general belief that young and resilent minds learn at a more rapid rate. These advantages may largely explain why the bulk of our classroom education takes place early in life. But recurrent education has advantages also, and some of the most prominent are almost direct refutations of the advantages for "early" education listed above. First, the existence of unemployment among mature workers means that foregone earnings costs of recurrent education may be negligible for at least some individuals. Second, obsolescence of learned skills may mean that it is economically inconsequential whether one gets his training at (say) age 18 or age 30 since changing technology may require re-education in a decade or so anyway. Third, certain types of learning may be quicker and more thorough if preceded by ample work and life experiences.

This kind of argumentation says little about whether we have too little or too much recurrent education presently, nor does it offer many clues for how relative emphasis among recurrent education programs might be altered. Not much can be said either on the basis of the degree of public subsidization presently enjoyed by recurrent education. By most relevant standards, recurrent education is subsidized less generously than is regular sequential education, but this may be entirely appropriate given the "economic maturity" of adults and depending on the quantitative balance of the arguments stated above.

Psychic (non-monetary) aspects

A case can be made that non-monetary returns is the most neglected of the important issues involved in educational choice. Since recurrent education involves considerable choice problems by individuals--more so than standard public education--these problems become more intense.

(1) Psychic returns, first of all, complicates the market knowledge problem of the private educational investor. The average financial return associated with many types of education is a widely reported number, but no one, to my knowledge, has attempted to specify some average valuation of psychic benefits for any type of education. Though psychic returns from education may be characterized as merely another consumption service, special problems interfere with a straightforward estimate of value. One frequently mentioned difficulty is the joint product problem: consumption and investment components are frequently combined in the same educational package. But even more troublesome is that education is itself often designed to change tastes and preferences. Is the valuation we are looking for ex ante or ex post? If the taste change is considered wholesome--the acquisition of "better" preferences rather than a neutral shift or a perverse "indoctrination"--the investment decision of individuals, necessarily made ex ante, must be considered incorrect and inefficient. The "superior" ex post tastes would have been a better basis for choice, yet these tastes are not developed until after the choice is made. It may, then, be said that some systematic underestimate of non-monetary returns takes place.

(2) The capital market imperfection often noted in human investment discussions also worsens when the psychic returns component of education is recognized. Increased earnings potential serves as a weak and insecure form of collateral. Increased learning purely for the sake of its non-monetary joys constitutes even weaker collateral.

(3) Even if capital markets and market knowledge are perfect, consumption elements in education mean that individuals of equal learning ability and similar preferences will not acquire similar amounts of education if their initial wealth and income positions are unequal. That perfect capital markets would yield an "equal educational attainment"

result among those of equal ability and tastes, regardless of the initial degree of affluence, is a repeated deduction in the neo-classical writings in the economics of education.[7] But those deductions fail to deal adequately with the implications of psychic returns. If the returns to be measured are purely financial and capital markets are perfect, both rich and poor would indeed continue their education until the rate of return falls to the market rate of interest; this should occur at the same point for all those of equal ability. But, in the more common case of a substantial consumption component, the already affluent individual can be expected to continue his education longer. He will consume more of this consumption service just the same as any other goods.

(4) The psychic satisfaction of a relatively high income or status may be a strong force pushing some individuals into overinvestment in education from a social point of view. Even if the anticipated rate of financial return for additional education is demonstrably below the market rate of interest, and no intrinsic joy is experienced from acquiring additional knowledge, the investment may still be made by the status-seeking individual or by parents anxious about the future status of their children. The additional relative status that is gained by way of the investment is, however, a relative status loss for others. The individual who undertakes the education may feel much better off, but this may be nearly counterbalanced by psychic pain felt by those who lose relative status. The net benefit of these two effects may exceed the direct cost of the investment, yet the investment might nevertheless be undertaken since the status loser has no say in the decision.

(5) Related more exclusively to the issue of recurrent education, and related also to point (4), is the problem of loss of occupational status. The psyche pain associated with such loss is undeniably severe and is unlikely to be measured adequately by the mere dollar loss of income that is involved.

Several conclusions can be drawn from the above in relation to recurrent education. First, and most obvious, is that psychic returns can have quite different implications for different types of education and people. The diversity of programs that are part of a recurrent education system makes it (once again) difficult to generalize. A second, and more specific, conclusion is that the existence of psychic returns has some potential for encouraging overinvestment and should not be considered merely as some hard to measure "plus" item to be added to the more tangible monetary returns from education. A third conclusion is that the efficiency argument for substantial public subsidization of recurrent education is strongest with respect to

---

7. Gary Becker and Barry Chiswick, "Education and the Distribution of Earnings," American Economic Review, 56, 2 (May 1966): 362.

532-819 O - 74 - 10

low-status adults. Low-status adults may have an overly low regard for the psychic components of education, and their low income position makes it predictable that they will purchase less than affluent individuals even if they become as convinced as the affluent of the nonmonetary rewards of education. Add to this the more severe capital market problem and the generally weak market knowledge of low-status persons, and a fairly convincing theoretical case results for subsidizing recurrent education for the relatively poor, independent of equity considerations.

Still, theory is not at all a substitute for actual benefit-cost estimates. For the bulk of recurrent education programs, no such estimates are available. The ones that are available relate mainly to low-status workers involved in job-training programs. These indicate benefit-cost ratios in excess of unity when only the financial returns to trainees are considered.[8] This tends to buttress some of the theorizing above. But numerous technical problems still exist for these kinds of estimates, and extension of the analysis into nonmonetary and externalities considerations is still a backward art. Nonetheless, I see no easy recourse but to use what we have in the way of benefit-cost estimates, improving upon them technically and judgmentally, and making informed guesses when the data are sketchy.

Formal choice criteria

Assuming one has in hand a detailed set of formal or informal benefit-cost estimates, efficiency rules for public policy could proceed the following way: (1) rank potential candidates for recurrent education according to the estimated benefit-cost ratio associated with undertaking the educational investment they are most interested in, (2) within existing budget constraints, maximize the difference between benefits and costs by subsidizing those individuals who would not go on otherwise by the minimum amount necessary to encourage their continuance, choosing first those individuals with the highest benefit-cost ratios and continuing in that manner until the budget is exhausted, and (3) expand the available budget at the earliest opportunity if the budget fails to reach all individuals where benefit-cost ratios are greater than one, and contract the budget if it is so large as to encourage the education of some whose benefit-cost ratio is less than one.

Further qualifications can be added to this. It would seem wise to make sure that capital markets be made as free-functioning as

---

8. For a good current summary, see Jon Goldstein, The Effectiveness of Manpower Training Programs: A Review of Research on the Impact on the Poor (Washington, D.C.: Government Printing Office, November 1972).

possible and that information be made widely available to individuals on recurrent education opportunities, and an expanded system of subsidies. It is advisable also to be conscious of diminishing returns as workers of advanced skill are available in greater numbers. And the likelihood that some individuals will be potential candidates for more than one type of education should also be kept in mind.

Equity Considerations

The most general and flexible equity ideas relevant to the question at hand are the economists' notions of horizontal and vertical equity. Horizontal equity prescribes that individuals in similar economic and/or social circumstances should be treated equally by public policies; vertical equity states that those in unequal circumstances should be treated unequally--more specifically, that public policy should be relatively more generous to those in relatively less well-off situations. A number of governmental tax and expenditure policies have been analyzed in these terms, and formal sequential education has been one of the areas where ambitious recent efforts have been made.[9] Recurrent education has so far escaped such attention.

In the specific area of educational policy, an even more widely used equity standard is equality of opportunity. Two distinct versions of this idea have emerged in recent years: equality in terms of equal inputs and equality in terms of equal average outcomes.[10] These have been much elaborated on, but, once again, specific application to recurrent education seems to be missing.

In addition to transplanting these standards to recurrent education, some further relevant equity considerations also deserve discussion. One such standard is the idea of education as reward--the practice, for instance, of providing generous educational subsidies to individuals who risked their lives in time of war. A second, and probably more important consideration, is the aim of fulfilling "legitimate expectations" threatened by forces outside the control of the individual--the most typical case of this being to restore or preserve occupational status lost or endangered by technological or supply-demand changes. Additional equity problems distinctively associated with recurrent education might also be listed at this point, but most, I would argue, fit legitimately under the principles already discussed.

---

9. Lee Hansen and Burton Weisbrod, Benefits, Costs, and Finance of Higher Education (Chicago: Markham, 1969), and John Coons, William Clune, and Stephan Sugerman, Private Wealth and Public Education (Cambridge, Mass.: Belknap Press, 1970).

10. Thomas Ribich, "The Problem of Equal Opportunity: A Review Article," Journal of Human Resources, 7, 4 (Fall 1972): 518-526.

Horizontal and vertical equity

Two individuals in the same socioeconomic circumstances should, it seems, be given the same opportunity to advance their education, i.e., the same degree of implicit or explicit financial subsidization--though other policy factors may enter in as well. Individuals similar in socioeconomic position may, of course, be very different in other characteristics. Some of these may be just as relevant as a socioeconomic position in specifying "equals" for purposes of recurrent education policy. Hence, being a woman or having experienced very low quality formal education may possibly be regarded as evidence of prior unfair treatment; and recurrent education subsidies might be made more generous to such persons than to others without these characteristics but in similar socioeconomic circumstances defined along the usual dimensions. By at least partially compensating for past inequities in this fashion, the phrase "equity through recurrent education" would begin to take on some quite specific meaning.

A related application of the horizontal equity idea is the notion of improving the education of older workers because their educational opportunities were not as great as those newly entering the labor force. This differs slightly from the suggestion made above that prior educational experience might be made part of the criteria for policy choice. Age is suggested here as a relevant dimension of its own, so that of two individuals with precisely the same education background and equal in all other respects except for age, the older might receive favored treatment on equity grounds alone, the idea being that he would have had a better educational background already if he had not had the bad luck to be born so soon.

It is apparent that juggling of equity notions in this way is limitless, and some arbitrary line must eventually be drawn as to what characteristics are to be taken into account and which ignored. It should also be noted that vertical equity merely amounts to gradating the degree of subsidization (and other means of opportunity provision) between individuals who are unequal along any of the relevant dimensions. Needless to say, specifying the appropriate gradation of advantages is a good deal more difficult than specifying when individuals are merely equal or unequal. Finally, it should be said that some of the more persuasive equity distinctions will be reinforcing to efficiency, at least up to a point, but some might run exactly counter.

Equality of opportunity

Equal opportunity can be thought of as a more aggressive form of vertical equity. Applied to the recurrent education case, it would seem to suggest the following: individuals of relatively low socioeconomic status should be subsidized to a degree sufficient to assure that they participate in recurrent education programs at the same rate as those of higher status. A more demanding criteria might insist additionally that the benefits received by the lower status participants be at least as great as those experienced by higher status individuals, probably suggesting that costs for recurrent education for the low status individuals be greater and the programs be longer and more intensive. A still more ambitious approach would be to assign recurrent education the role of making up for all the "bad breaks" of the past, so that presently low status individuals have just as great an opportunity of reaching high status as do those of present high status.

Even the most modest of these criteria are likely to be unattainable in full. Surely too massive a part of competitive advantage is determined prior to the coming of recurrent education, and too high a proportion of total classroom education will continue to occur in the early years, to be confident that "complete" equality of opportunity can be achieved solely through recurrent education. And even assuring equal rates of participation seems unlikely given the strong positive relation that exists between status and participation.[11] But while full attainment of equal opportunity goals may be prohibitively difficult, partial fulfillment may be relatively easy and very worthwhile.

Reward

Outside of policies towards returning veterans, there seem to be few examples of recurrent education used as a reward for services rendered or a job especially well done. Employers may finance the continuing education of an employee who has performed well on the job, but this presumably is mainly in the belief that such an individual will perform even better on the job with the education, with past on-the-job performance as a guide to selection of who to finance. If, however, the practice of interrupting one's education after high school becomes a very widespread and strongly encouraged practice, the use of educational reward, independent of guesses about efficient use of the educational experience, might become more common. Success in handling a drill press will not say much about an individual's chances for becoming a first-rate lawyer, but making public scholarships partially conditional on adequate job performance may be a relatively efficient way to assure conscientious effort at low-skilled work of limited duration.

---

11. The comprehensive survey of John Johnstone and Ramon Rivera, Volunteers for Learning (New York: Aldine, 1965), is a little out of date given recent federal efforts in job-training and basic literacy programs, but the positive strong relationship between socioeconomic class and participation is still found to hold in later more limited studies such as Jack London, "The Influence of Social Class Behavior Upon Adult Education Participation," Adult Education, 21, 3 (1970): 140-153.

Legitimate expectations

Sudden loss of occupational job status can occur, often for reasons which involve factors far outside the control of the individual and nearly impossible for him to predict. Demand for the sorts of services the individual is skilled in rendering may drop off due to changes in product demand or changes in the technology of production. The supply of individuals in his occupation may become overabundant and the new-comers may enjoy competitive advantages by way of the freshness of their skills. Individuals could be made to accept the brunt of these sorts of changes without assistance, but a host of governmental programs already stand ready to aid in such transition times, and a more thorough-going network of re-education programs would be highly consistent with what exists. A more comprehensive system emphasizing re-education might be thought of as a provider of somewhat more complete "social security" geared toward full maintenance of status rather than mere provision of some employment or income minimum.

Adding to the equity case for such activity, at the present time, is the fact that a fair amount of current occupational dislocation, especially among high-skilled individuals, is due to the vicissitudes of governmental spending decisions. Governmental program cutbacks have coincided unfortunately with the appearance of multitudes of new graduates from colleges and universities, many of whom were encouraged to get their degrees by large increases in governmental subsidies to higher education during the past decade.

Systemizing Equity Considerations

The earlier section on efficiency noted potential conflicts between equity and efficiency. This sub-section resumes that discussion and offers a systematic way of treating the problem.

First, note that any of the equity considerations posed so far may be consistent with efficiency in a given case, and that some of the policy guidelines suggested by these equity principles might even be given efficiency justifications more powerful than the equity argument. For instance, the vertical equity suggestion that individuals of relatively low economic status should be subsidized more generously might also be a reasonable efficiency rule of thumb in that lower status individuals may have difficulty in financing even a well-paying educational investment and may have a tendency to underestimate the rewards of education. It can be expected, however, that not only will some equity considerations be at general odds with efficiency, but even those that have some consistency with efficiency will be pushed beyond the point where that consistency continues to exist. If the equity considerations really do have social support, and if social policy reacts towards these considerations in a rational way, this loss of consistency is nearly guaranteed. A socially valued equity consideration is, almost by definition, one we are willing to pay some price for; the price likely paid is some departure from decision rules that maximize efficiency in the usual sense. Hence, sticking with the vertical equity example, we should expect that policy would be even more charitable (relatively) to the relatively poor in subsidization formulas than if efficiency were the only goal. The public should be willing to pay something in terms of less total consumption and investment benefits, from a given budget, to see still more vertical evening-up take place. We should expect a different result only if the equity principle in question has been so thoroughly served already that it has been "consumed to the point of satiety."

Reasoning in this way is also a start towards taking some of the mystique out of equity arguments. Progress toward an equity goal can be considered simply another social benefit to be dealt with as one would any other "public good." Its valuation, in relation to the amount provided, can be thought of in the same way as the valuation of any other externality whose benefits are not measurable in market terms. The appropriate basis for the valuation in a democratic society is the preferences of citizens, summed and reflected in a reasonable manner through a political process.

The pragmatic advantage of this approach is the weakening of the imperative connotations associated with equity principles and the consequent promotion of discussion about quantities and trade-offs rather than the bogging down in quandries and dilemmas of our own making. Operationally, it means decision makers should seek to find out how much equity of various sorts can be purchased with compromises on efficiency, and what a responsible valuation would be for varying degrees of attainment of each of the equity goals.

To be more specific, consider the following example, which focuses on a narrow range of considerations and requires knowledge that is attainable though not presently available in any detail.

Assume that our only equity concerns are (a) horizontal equity, (b) greater fiscal generosity to those with relatively less current income, and (c) bolstering the income status of individuals whose income positions are threatened by unanticipated market forces. Assume also that the only other goal of policy is to increase income net of investment costs, this being a proxy for economic efficiency. This suggests a "social welfare" function that looks something like this:

$$W = F(B-C,\ N_t,\ Y_c,\ Y_p-Y_f)$$

Where W is total social welfare resulting from public policy towards recurrent education; B-C is total economic benefits minus cost, which in turn is approximately equal to the gain in lifetime income experienced by those participating in (and attributable to) the recurrent education programs plus any economic externalities (both properly time-discounted) minus the direct resource costs and the foregone-earnings costs of the programs; N_t is the total number of individuals participating in the program; Y_c is the current average income of the participants; and Y_p-Y_f is the difference between the past average income of the participants and their expected average future income if they had not participated in the recurrent education programs.

Note that more than budgetary costs are included in the equation. Note also that the horizontal equity goal is explicitly represented only by N_t, the relevance of N_t being that it is more equitable that many, rather than a few, benefit from the system. Horizontal equity can be furthered additionally, however, by the Y_c term, as shown below. Finally, with Y_p-Y_f there are the problems of the time period over which to average and under what specific circumstances a potential fall in income really amounts to disappointment of a "legitimate expectation."

If such a social welfare function is acceptable, it would be useful to have available, for each potential participant in recurrent education programs, not only the benefit-cost ratio associated with his participation but also details on his current, past, and projected future income, as well as the budgetary costs of his participation. (Low budgetary costs of participation means that additional individuals can be participants in the system, and hence N_t will be greater.) As noted earlier, the relative importance of each of these factors must be established sooner or later. A convenient time to establish this is at the stage of ranking individuals for sequential selection into the system. That is, each of the factors associated with each individual can be given a numerical coefficient and a total "score" for each individual can be computed which would determine his place in the queue for subsidization in the same way that the benefit-cost ratio determined his relative efficiency.

Horizontal equity according to current economic circumstances would be served in a quite restricted sense: if two individuals have identical current income they will be ranked equally only if they are also equal in all the other respects noted above. Vertical equity is served by the numerical coefficient associated with the current income term. If many "points" are assigned to relatively low incomes, as compared to the points assigned to the other relevant characteristics, then relatively poor individuals will receive a relatively high proportion of the subsidization.

The technique for determining relative position should proceed on a trial and error basis. One reason for this is that experience with a more systematic recurrent education system will generate more accurate information on benefits and costs than we presently have. A more subtle reason is that the original assignment of the numerical coefficients might generate extreme results of one kind or another. For example, what seems like a reasonable coefficient for current income may lead to a system which subsidizes affluent individuals with greater frequency than it does low income people; conversely, the original formula may lead to a situation where only very low income individuals are subsidized, also an unacceptable outcome from both a political and equity point of view.

The above is a very brief sketch. Implementation not only requires information not now in hand but also bold guesses on the relative social importance of various considerations. Additional variables should undoubtedly be inserted in the social welfare function (e.g., race, sex, age) and coefficients assigned to them. Benefits and costs should be made to include psychic (consumption) components. The two-part problem of selection within a budget constraint and determining appropriate expansion or contraction of a budget remains, with the added difficulty that a benefit-cost ratio of unity is no longer the clear-cut point for budgetary limits.

The very last of these problems presents the trickiest conceptual difficulties. As shown above, there is little choice but to make some sort of politically responsible estimate of what the public at large is willing to pay for the furtherance of equity aims. Assuming the public is willing to pay at least something, it would seem to follow that budgets for encouraging continuing education should be extended past the point where benefit-cost ratios are less than unity.

How much past the point of unity is dependent not only on the social importance attached to equity but also on the scope and flexibility of the transfer payment system. If, for instance, the typical individual cares only about his disposable income and how it relates to that of others in society, then society itself should be inclined to define social equity in disposable income terms as well. If also there are no ethical or institutional constraints on transfer payments and work effort effects are negligible, then it would follow that the individual should not receive additional subsidized education to move him to the disposable income level thought equitable in his case unless the benefit-cost level associated with the educational change is greater than unity. If benefits are less than costs, then achievement of the designated disposable income level can be achieved through direct transfer payments with less social cost. The introduction of psychic returns into the decision clearly complicates things, but detailed analysis would, I believe, show that much the same prescription would follow. The key element would seem to be the existence or nonexistence of a transfer compensating mechanism. Without this alternative to rectifying "unjust" distributions of income and other personal or social advantages, education will continue to be an important vehicle for achieving equity, and the equity-efficiency trade-off in education--recurrent and otherwise--will remain a prominent problem.

recurrent education for women

GISELA SCHADE

Introduction

The increasing participation of women in education, though appearing as a consequence of general educational expansion, poses many interesting questions.

What do women do with their education?

Is their increased participation, especially at the higher level, worthwhile from an economic point of view?

Is it compatible with prevailing patterns concerning the division of labor between men and women? Would it be "worthwhile"--and from what points of view--to change those patterns?

Does the concept of equality of opportunity in education necessarily imply equality of opportunity in employment? And what does the concept "equality of opportunity" mean: equal rights, equal chances or equal achievement? How to judge achievement in different branches? Does equality imply identity of choice? If not, is equality possible in our present value system?

What are the objectives of education?

Those are complex and broad questions. Although difficult to answer in the framework of this paper, they show the perspective in which education for women is being considered here. Without being able to answer what "equal achievement" between men and women means and what is meant by "equal chances" for the two sexes, the order of magnitude of disparities in education (as in employment and incomes as well) is such that one can say categorically that granting "equal rights" in education has proved to be insufficient and that equality of opportunity has to be interpreted in a more ambitious way.

As Torsten Husen puts it, "The core of the problem is whether equality should be seen as a starting point or a goal." The traditional interpretation of equality of opportunity meant equality of exposure to a given curriculum. The modern, more radical concept implies that "in order to achieve greater equality in school attainments, society has to adopt special means to compensate for the deficiencies of the environment in which the child grows up or to supplement what may have been done at home."[1]

Recurrent education is one of the proposals aimed at reducing social inequalities. It may offer a second chance to workers. It also offers a second chance to women who did get a chance during their youth, but who could not exploit fully the opportunities offered since marriage was accepted as their main goal in life. Many women need a second opportunity in their thirties to plan their lives, or at least the part of it which they have to face with their new realities.

Recurrent education aims at providing everybody with access to knowledge throughout his whole life in line with his interests, aspirations and abilities. The single group which, as a whole, is cut off from this early in life is women. At present, most women are badly trained for long-term careers. Recurrent education may provide a framework for solving this problem. It will also help to overcome --or perhaps even avoid--the obsolescence women suffer after an interruption in their employment.

The Relevance Of Greater Participation Of Women In Education And Employment

The decrease in the rate of infant mortality in the last century, combined with the fall in the birth rate in Western societies, has resulted in a considerable shortening of the period of women's lives being reserved for motherhood:

> In the 18th century maternity filled practically the whole life of a married woman. A woman of 50 years old having married at the age of 23 would have 7 or 8 children on the average. Many of these died young (1 on 4 before 1 year, and 1 on 2 before 20 years), but the successive pregnancies and care of young children largely absorbed women's time and energy during married life....With the old mortality

1. Torsten Husen, Social Background and Educational Career (Paris: OECD, 1972), pp. 27-38.

rate about 7 children per "complete family" were indeed necessary to keep stable the population number: today an average slightly above 2 is sufficient.[2]

Moreover, there seems to be a recent tendency in the U.S. and Sweden for women to have children earlier. The fertility rate of very young women (under 25 years) has increased. Meanwhile, there is a decrease in the fertility rate of women over 30 years and especially over 35 years.[3] Life expectancy, on the other hand, has considerably increased over the last century. This means that women now have a higher proportion of their lives "available" for a career.

From an economic viewpoint, the limited participation of women in the labor force can be--especially in the case of "educated" women--a form of disguised unemployment or underemployment. This is true for all housewives, regardless of their education, once their children have reached school age (see tables 1 and 2).

In this connection it is interesting to mention the issue of flexibility in working life: new patterns for working time, while facilitating combinations of paid employment with domestic tasks and leisure activities, could allow married women to join the labor market more easily and, at the same time, offer greater opportunities to *all* individuals to play a more varied role in society.

Women's increased participation in employment might compensate for losses due to a general reduction in working hours, while at the same time enabling women to take a greater share in the financial responsibility of keeping a family. This could increase both men's and women's relative freedom and allow couples to support each other in periods of transition linked to retraining, further education and changes in career orientation.

Finally, greater female participation may help to improve the quality of candidates in the running for top jobs by widening the field of recruitment, and influence women's performance on the lower levels by offering better career prospects.[4]

---

2. Francoise Guelaud-Leridon, "Recherches sur la Condition Feminine dans la Societe d'aujourd'hui," *Travaux et Documents*, 48 (Paris: Presses Universitaires de France, INED, 1967): 22.

3. Evelyne Sullerot, *L'emploi des Femmes et ses Problemes dans les Etats Membres de la C.E.E.* (Brussels: European Economic Community, July 1970). See also, Centre d'Etudes d'Emploi, INED, *Bulletin d'Information*, 1 (Septembre 1971): 6.

4. Michael Fogarty, Rhona Rapoport, and Robert Rapoport, *Sex, Career and Family* (London: George Allen and Unwin, P.E.P., 1971).

Table 1. Labor Force Participation of Men and Women in O.E.C.D. Countries.

(in percentages)

Total labor force x 100 / Population 15-64 years		1960 Males	1960 Females		1970 Males	1970 Females
Austria	(1961:)	81*	45*	(1969:)	86	50
Belgium		89	36		87	40
Denmark		100	44		92	58
Finland		91	66		84	62
France		93	47	(1968:)	87*	46*
Germany		95	49		95	49
Greece		92	42	(1971:)	87*	32*
Iceland		97	38		94	38
Ireland	(1961:)	100	36	(1966:)	99	35
Italy		93	37		84	29
Netherlands		94*	26*			
Norway		92	36		89	39
Portugal		100	20		84	25
Spain		100	24		94*	30*
Sweden	(1962:)	93	53		89	59
Switzerland		99*	42*		96	51
Turkey		99	71	(1965:)	98	62
United Kingdom		99	49		93	52
Canada		92	32		87	41
United States		92	43		87	49
Australia	(1964:)	94	39		93	45
Japan		92	60		89	56

Note: Variations between countries are greatly affected by the relative importance of agriculture and the extent of urbanization.

Source: Labour Force Statistics, O.E.C.D., Paris.

* Figures marked with an asterisk have been calculated on the basis of data published in the Yearbook of Labour Statistics, ILO, Geneva.

Table 2. Proportion of Men and Women in Civilian Employment in Selected Countries, by Percent.

		1960				1970		
		Males	Females			Males	Females	
			Proportion of all women in civilian employment	Proportion of married women in civilian employment			Proportion of all women in civilian employment	Proportion of married women in civilian employment
Denmark		68%	32%	12%		61%	39%	24%
France	(1962:)		35*	18*	(1968:)		35*	19*
Germany		62	38	17		64	36	20
Sweden	(1962:)	64	36	20		61	39	25
Canada		73	27			67	33	19
United States		67	33	18		62	38	22
Japan		59	41			61	39	23
Australia	(1964:)	72	28	14		68	32	18

Source: Labor Force Statistics, O.E.C.D., Paris.

* Census data.

From a political viewpoint, the limited participation of women in political life cannot be considered a healthy practice of democratic government. As a group, they are isolated. This is not only the case for the housewife with small children who spends her days in a small closed circle. It is also true in a more general context. Women's participation in the labor market is limited and takes place generally at the lower levels. This means that only very few women happen to be in channels from which people are recruited for decision-making functions. The possibilities for participation in the decision-making process by women as a group are thereby very much limited.

Education may help to improve this situation by making them conscious of their possibilities and by enabling them to seize opportunities which exist, but which they have ignored so far or considered to be out of their reach.

From a cultural viewpoint, the education of the young is mainly in the hands of women. Not only is there a positive correlation between the level of education of the mother and the achievement in school of her children,[5] but the mother is an important factor in the more general transfer of culture, attitudes, and aspirations. Broadening women's horizons may, therefore, have an effect which is multiplied through the next generations, and especially through the girls, enabling them to take a more active part in imagining and constructing the future.

From the viewpoint of human relationships: The "nuclear family" of today is a relatively recent phenomenon. After having been an important factor of economic growth in Western society, it may have reached the limits of its unquestioned priority at the same time as economic growth itself is coming to be questioned. Getting mothers out of their household confinements through education, employment, or active community involvement is a first step toward enlarging the social awareness and culture of families.[6]

Considering these points, it seems that the organization of society has been by-passed by the technical evolution of our time. Women's recent claims for "liberation" can only be fully understood in the perspective of the profound changes that have taken place in their roles at home and in their level of education. Their emancipation appears

---

5. See, for instance, J. S. Coleman, Equality of Educational Opportunity (Washington, D.C.: Government Printing Office, 1966), and Central Advisory Council for Education, Children and Their Primary Schools (Plowden Report) (London: Her Majesty's Stationery Office, 1967).

6. For the effects of employment of the mother on her children (according to social background, age of the children, etc.), see for instance F. I. Nye and L. W. Hoffman, The Employed Mother in America (Chicago: Rand McNally, 1963).

now to be a necessary step towards a greater degree of freedom for the individual in general, both in relation to family structures and to flexibility in working life and division of labor. Beyond changes in sex roles, women's emancipation could bring about a fundamental change in values and a better functioning of society and democracy.

The Female Demand For Recurrent Education

When talking about the demand for recurrent education, we have to keep in mind a distinction between existing or observed demand and latent demand or underlying need. The usefulness of present inquiries is limited in that they tend to confirm existing trends. It is a well-known fact, for example, that at present adult education attracts mainly already educated, highly motivated students in their 20's rather than their 30's. Present statistics do not make much sense if the completely different cultural and sociological context of different groups (social class, age, sex) participating in education is not taken into account.

Demand for recurrent education by women has been measured in several European countries.

An investigation in the city of Malmo, Sweden[7] showed that in 1964 a quarter of all women were interested in further education at junior or senior secondary school level. As to participation in study circles or short courses, 37 percent of the gainfully employed women had taken part in such courses in their leisure time during recent years against 28 percent of housewives.

Another concrete indication of women's interest in recurrent education is given by the early experience of the "Open University" in the United Kingdom: housewives constituted 9.2 percent of the applicants in 1970, 11.0 percent in 1971 and 13.0 percent in 1972.[8] During the first year of its operation, drop-out rates were lower for women students than for men: 15 percent against 21 percent.[9]

In Germany, the number of female participants in vocational further education who received a grant under the Labor Promotion Act amounted to 16,901 against 82,231 men (end 1970), i.e., 17 percent.[10] That act

---

7. T. Husen, Talent, Opportunity and Career (Stockholm: Almqvist and Wiksell, 1969).

8. "Shorter Notes" in Education (March 31, 1972): 309.

9. Times Higher Education Supplement (June 9, 1972).

10. Die Forderung der beruflichen Bildung, Ergebnisse des Jahres 1970 (Bundesanstalt fur Arbeit, ANBA No. 7, 1971), pp. 2-14.

532-819 O - 74 - 11

was passed in 1969 in order to prevent or to cure bottlenecks in the employment market by improving the vocational mobility of the labor force. It provides organizational and financial facilities exclusively for the vocational side.[11] Professional promotion was the aim of two-thirds of the male participants, but only of one-third of the women. About 50 percent of the female participants took courses preparing for office work.

Table 3. Distribution by Age of Men and Women in Vocational Further Education.

	1970	
	Women	Men
Up to 25 years	44.5%	33.2%
25-35 years	32.2	51.2
35-55 years	22.7	15.3
55 and older	0.6	0.3
Total	100.0%	100.0%

Source: Die Forderung der beruflichen Bildung.

Men were concentrated in the age-group 25-35 years, whereas in the older age-groups, women's participation was relatively stronger. This may indicate that many married female workers cannot or do not want to combine further education or retraining with a job and family responsibilities, especially when they have children to look after. Seventy percent of the female participants had no children against 58 percent of the male participants; 36 percent were married against 61 percent of the men.

The influence of domestic tasks is also reflected in the fact that one-third of the women who wished to re-enter the labor market took retraining courses preparing them for a new job which was compatible (in claims and time-schedule) with the work they had at home.[12]

The number of applications during 1970 was 263,588, of which 58,008 were women, i.e., 22 percent.

---

11. CERI, Recurrent Education in the Federal Republic of Germany (Paris: CERI/OECD, October 20, 1972).

12. Die Forderung der beruflichen Bildung.

In the same year, women constituted 35.6 percent of the labor force. More than half of these (56 percent) were married.[13]

Most of the courses were full-time: 73 percent against 27 percent part-time.

Female participation was concentrated in the courses of shorter duration, as shown in the following table:

Table 4. Participants According to the Duration of Further Education.

	Women	Men
Up to 1 year	71.4%	34.4%
1-2 years	23.3	43.2
2-3 years	4.9	17.6
More than 3 years	0.4	4.8
Total	100.0%	100.0%

Source: Die Forderung der beruflichen Bildung.

For Denmark, the following table may give an indication of women's interest in further education.

Table 5. Number of Participants in Evening and Evening High Schools and Folk High Schools in Denmark, 1971-1972.

	Evening and Evening High Schools	Folk High Schools (full-time compensatory adult education)
Men	171,824	3,163
Women	357,713	5,386
Total	529,537	8,549

For the Netherlands, the only figure that can be given here for the time being is a total number of 310 authorizations for scholarship provisions given to women in the framework of existing adult education programs during the year 1970.[14] The figure is so low that

---

13. Labour Force Statistics 1959-1970 (Paris: OECD, 1972).

14. "Rapport Interderdepartementale werkgroep onvolledige gezinnen" (April 28, 1972), p. 24.

it may be worthwhile mentioning here in spite of the poorness of the information. It is also an obvious example of the ambiguity between existing demand and supply. The figure probably expresses, more than anything else, the limits on the supply of facilities, such as the fact that the Dutch centers for adult vocational training provide almost exclusively training for jobs which are not traditionally filled by women.

When turning to the latent or potential demand for recurrent education, it may be useful to make a distinction between different groups of women:

1. those who wish to return to the labor market and need training or retraining but are prevented from taking it by lack of training facilities;

2. those who would like to return to the labor market but who hesitate to make the leap; and

3. those to whom the idea of schooling or training is still entirely out of reach, materially and/or psychologically.

The kind of recurrent education that is needed is different for these three groups. Group 1 needs an increase and extension of training and retraining opportunities as exist under present adult education programs.

The second group needs a more general orientation and education to overcome the material and psychological problems posed by the transition from housewife to gainful employment. This would seem to indicate a need for informal, small meetings where women can talk freely about these problems, combined with general occupational orientation and vocational guidance. Only in a second phase would training or retraining for a specific occupation (as for group 1) be needed.

The third group consists of women, probably mainly working class, who are not aware of (re)training possibilities, who often need to take up paid employment, but who have no alternative other than unskilled labor. This group--the largest--must be made aware of educational and retraining opportunities. The latent demand for training from this group could become an effective demand through campaigns via mass-media and through active information services in cities and villages.

This leads to the conclusion that women's demand for recurrent education cannot be separated from their emancipation. The concept of emancipation has to be defined.

The report on the Swedish view of recurrent education mentions emancipation in the context of "emancipating the individual from the various social constraints laid upon him in a capitalistic society."[15] The same report stresses the fact that in Sweden it is generally assumed that both the adaptation of the educational system to the needs of the labor market and the above-mentioned emancipation of the individual could be better obtained through some form of recurrent education than within the present educational system.

Van Doorn[16] defines emancipation as the "theoretical and practical possibility to achieve equality of opportunity," which does not necessarily imply the "holding of equal functions and power positions."

Verwey-Jonker[17] does not entirely agree with this definition and thinks that the criterion has to be whether "the sub-cultures of different groups are sufficiently integrated in the total culture," which means that (1) "members of the sub-cultures have free access to the total culture" and (2) "the total culture must have adopted certain elements from the sub-cultures--or at any rate be prepared to do this."

This last definition makes incomprehensible the one which is implicit in the conclusion of a conference of sociologists held in Hrazany, Czechoslovakia, in 1964: "The position of women in contemporary socialist society is characterised by a contradiction between their emancipation and economic activity on the one hand, and their biological and social functions on the other."[18] Women's emancipation cannot be opposed to their biological and social functions. The latter underlie their sub-culture and should therefore be integrated into the basis of the total culture if the objective is emancipation as defined by Verwey-Jonker, which is the definition adhered to in this paper.

Women are not a homogeneous group, of course. All women are also members of other social groups so the problems posed by the specific condition of women in a given society are superimposed on the ones that are related to social class, age, and so forth. In the last analysis women's emancipation cannot be separated from the emancipation of all individuals, but steps which can now be taken to blur the rigidity of sex roles may contribute to this general emancipation process through

---

15. Jarl Bengtsson, "The Swedish View of Recurrent Education," CERI/RE/72.01 (Paris: OECD/CERI, August 7, 1972).

16. J.A.A. van Doorn, "De emancipatie der Nederlandse Rooms-katholieken in de sociologische literatuur, Sociologische Gids, 5 (September 5, 1958): 202.

17. H. Verwey-Jonker, "De emancipatie bewegingen" in Drift en Koers, Een halve eeuw sociale verandering in Nederland, edited by A.N.J., Den Hollander (1962), p. 122.

18. M. Kucera cited in J. Berent, "Some Demographic Aspects of Employment in Eastern Europe and the USSR," International Labour Review, 101 (February 1970): 192.

a change in values. Changes which have occurred in fundamental factors underlying women's past and present situation in society--as set out in the Introduction to this paper--seem to make possible some progress along these lines.

The full recognition of women's place in society as equals with men in the social, economic, political, psychological and cultural spheres ought therefore to be one of the general objectives of education in the coming years at the pre-primary, "basic" and adult or "recurrent" level, in the interest of all members of society.

The end of this emancipation process can be reached only in a society adapted to different life cycles of men and women as well as to different aspirations and different aptitudes of different individuals, i.e., in a hypothetical ideal future, where the various subcultures have been integrated in the so-called "total" culture and at the same time transformed the total culture.

As long as the need for a comprehensive policy in this field has not been recognized, existing educational opportunities (both formal schooling, informal education and adult education) may reinforce rather than weaken traditional choices and sex roles. The branches of study which girls tend to choose are an illustration of this point: the increase in female participation in higher education in O.E.C.D. countries since 1950, for example, is much greater in fields that lead to traditionally "feminine" professions, much higher in humanities than in sciences[19] (see table 6).

At the secondary level, the findings of the International Study on Achievement in Mathematics[20] point in the same direction: "it is possible that the studying of mathematics at school may be influenced not only by the educational opportunities available to males and females in a community but also by the role of women in society and their freedom to enter certain occupations. However, it is important to note that in most of the countries associated with this study the restrictions on women entering certain occupations arise from concepts of the role of women in a society rather than from a formal lack of freedom."

The specialization in humanities and social sciences when taken seriously may well prove to be better appreciated in the near future if the debate on "quality of life" is going to have practical consequences. For the time being, however, it reflects in many cases

---

19. Development of Higher Education 1950-1967, Analytical Report (Paris: OECD, 1971).

20. T. Husen, International Study of Achievement in Mathematics, Vol. II (Stockholm: Almqvist & Wiksell, 1967), p. 235.

Table 6. Rate of Female Participation by Field of University Study.

Country	Pure Science		Technology		Medical Sciences		Humanities		Law		Social Sciences	
	1955	1965	1955	1965	1955	1965	1955	1965	1955	1965	1955	1965
Germany	12.6	12.7	0.5	0.6	35.6	29.8	31.5	39.7	11.2	11.3	12.8	13.4
Austria	-	-	1.6	2.4	29.1	30.5	32.1	41.8	15.1	15.3	17.9	17.2
Belgium	26.3	27.6	0.6	0.9	16.8	22.7	39.5	45.5	13.6	18.8	14.4	17.2
Denmark	23.1	22.3	4.0	4.2	24.5	31.3	37.4	50.8	17.9	30.0	3.0	6.1
Spain	19.6	25.7	0.0	0.5	18.1	22.6	67.0	61.2	4.8	13.2	6.1	16.8
Finland	32.3	36.2*	2.8	3.7	36.0	37.8*	70.8*	75.5	14.4	26.1	32.0	43.3
France	27.6	31.0	-	-	29.6	34.9	56.9	65.0	26.2	28.0	-	-
Greece	15.0	20.6	2.1	5.5	21.7	29.9	50.2	69.3	18.4	36.2	12.1	24.9
Ireland	29.0	26.6	0.0	0.1	26.8	26.9	39.9	45.7	11.3	20.2	32.3	31.0
Italy	47.1	31.4	0.4	0.5	18.6	17.0	71.6	74.0	17.2	15.0	7.9	15.8
Norway	19.3	14.6	...	3.1	23.5	23.4	38.0	43.0	7.0	11.8	2.1	8.2
Netherlands	13.0	12.3	0.8	0.7	19.4	19.2	35.4	40.5	28.6	22.7	11.7	12.7
Portugal	55.7	65.8	5.3	9.1	23.2	27.2	71.7	76.9	10.7	14.8	15.6	21.9
United Kingdom	20.7	22.1	1.6	1.8	21.1	24.1	37.0	42.1	-	-	18.6	31.1
Sweden	23.8	25.0	2.1	5.9	23.0	26.4	47.9	63.0	14.1	20.3	5.0	38.3
Switzerland	11.0	15.2	0.2	0.8	12.4	21.4	36.5	41.6	7.8	11.7	10.3	11.7
Turkey	23.3	25.5	2.4	5.8	19.4	25.3	51.5	37.2	12.4	26.0	10.3	16.4
Yugoslavia	43.0	38.1	7.4	12.7	31.1	48.1	55.6	56.9	18.8	32.8	28.0	33.5
Canada	...	17.9	...	0.9	...	45.5	...	40.4	...	6.1	...	19.1
United States[1]	20.7	26.1	0.3	0.4	34.0	43.9	42.6	49.7	3.5	3.4	23.4	24.0
Japan	13.1	12.4	0.8	0.4	24.8	35.1	23.4	42.8	-	-	4.8	5.7

1. First degrees.

Source: Development of Higher Education 1950-1967, Analytical Report (Paris: OECD, 1971), p. 150.

a lack of long-term career commitment on the part of girls who use their studies more for developing personal interests than for achieving a specific professional career. Their attitude is perfectly in line with an education which has presented them from a very early age with the image of fulfillment through marriage. The fact that in most countries female students are socially selected to an even greater extent than their male colleagues may also have an influence in this respect. Though the emphasis on sex roles is probably even stronger in the lower classes, the idea of education for cultural purposes seems to be the prerogative of the middle and upper class woman in our society.

An example is given by Kilian[21] of an average girl from a middle class family, brought up according to the model of a girl of that milieu and thus not career-minded.

> If she does start working (as a secretary, for example) she will consider this as a transitory phase before marriage, or else as a possibility for finding a better husband. In her work as a secretary she will make use of all the skills and behaviour patterns she acquired during the early years of her life at home, which formed her character. She is more willing to prepare coffee and run various errands, work overtime and help her boss than a man would be under similar circumstances. However, there is no doubt that she will develop her initiative to a lesser extent and also tend to underestimate her intelligence. If she does not get married by the age of 30 or 35 she will most likely develop certain symptoms of a psychosomatic nature, symptoms which are characteristic of working women who have found satisfaction neither in their private lives nor at work.

This example, given in 1958, may no longer be valid in all its details for the new generation, but it applies to many adult women of today and illustrates their need for a second chance through recurrent education.

The emphasis on developing personal interests rather than concentrating exclusively on "career education" can be interpreted in a very positive way provided that it is placed in a different context. The

---

21. Hans Kilian, The Role of Women and the Education of Girls: A Sociopsychological Viewpoint, report on the meeting "Education and citizenship of girls today" convened by the UNESCO Youth Institute in Gauting (13-18 October, 1958) as cited by M. Sokolowska "Some Reflection on the Different Attitudes of Men and Women Toward Work," International Labour Review, 92 (July 1965): 18-19.

option is related to the issue of whether education ought to be considered as cultural consumption or as an economic investment. However, attitudes as well as specializations should be the result of a "free choice" and not of a conditioning process that starts at birth and affects both boys and girls. As long as this process exists, equality of opportunity is likely to remain a hollow slogan.

The Supply Of Facilities For Recurrent Education

The supply of facilities for recurrent education is obviously a function of the demand for this education and, therefore, of the interpretation given to demand. As far as women are concerned, demand should be stimulated by measures with an emphasis on changing sex roles.

The rise in women's--especially married women's--participation in the labor market over the past 20 years (see tables 1 and 2) may have been a factor contributing to an increase in the supply and demand of training and retraining opportunities. However, the importance and scope of such facilities have remained limited since married women tend to be considered as a reservoir from which additional workers can be drawn in times of economic boom and manpower shortage, while they are frequently the first ones to be dismissed again when the economic activity slows down.

As long as education for women is not seen as an end in itself, existing training opportunities for adult women are likely to result in a strengthening of present differences in types and levels of jobs between men and women.

Another important aspect which has to be taken into account in the elaboration of out-reach activities for adult women is child-care facilities. The participation of mothers of young children in adult education programs depends to a large extent on the possibilities for leaving their children in care.

Part-time courses adapted to the time schedules of women's work will be needed and patterns at home will be needed and training facilities should preferably be located near the home. This means an enormous decentralization and is obviously not possible for all kinds of training. Providing courses through television and correspondence widens the range of possibilities, but poses other problems. The experience of the Open University will certainly be instructive in this respect, but a key problem remains: how to reach a busy working-class woman through television; how to motivate her sufficiently to make the effort required by regular study.

An active policy will be needed here and, above all, coordination with appropriate social and economic policy measures. Effective employment opportunities after the finishing of a training or retraining course will certainly help as an incentive in making the first step. A lot of imagination is clearly needed to find a way through all the obstacles.

Although it will take time to elaborate good schemes, it is important to put women's education near the top of the list of governments' preoccupations at the moment and to involve women in the preparatory work. By not doing so, there is a risk of decisions being taken in other fields that do not take into account the interests of women. Present discussions on shortening working time provide an illustration of this: trade unions tend to ask for a shorter working week instead of shorter working hours per day, but it is the latter proposal that would facilitate women's participation in education and employment as well as men's contribution at home.[22] Shorter working days would also fit in better with children's school hours.

Organization Of Recurrent Education For Women

The organization of recurrent education for women is linked to its content and structure. As far as its content is concerned, recurrent education should not be limited to vocational training but should also cover general educational objectives. Though one of its purposes should be to facilitate women's integration into the labor market on an equal footing with men, this is not an end in itself but only one step on the long road towards emancipation.

Whereas the organization of general education rests mainly with governments, employers and the private sector generally have an important contribution to make to recurrent vocational training. Their initiatives should, however, be placed in the framework of a comprehensive policy if further accentuation of existing differences between social groups is to be avoided. Taking women again as an illustration of this point, attention will have to be given to the question of whether they have access to training facilities that go beyond an initial training for low-level work, especially in "mixed" occupations. A second question is whether further training receives as much attention in occupations mainly filled by women as in those filled by men.

As to vocational training set up by public authorities, a Dutch study mentions the fact that in the Netherlands training opportunities for predominantly "feminine" occupations seem to lag behind. Many "female" jobs are of recent origin (such as dentist's or pharmacist's assistant, laboratory assistant), but the lack of public training facilities might be due to <u>general</u> reticence of the government in these matters. The training for these jobs has been left to private

---

22. See for instance, <u>The Status of Women in Sweden</u>, for the United Nations (1968), p. 4. "It would be advisable to study how reductions in working hours could best be distributed over the working week with a view to making it easier for husbands to do their share of work in the home."

courses which recruit girls mainly from social classes that can afford to pay the higher tuition fees. As long as a sufficient number of women are being recruited to fill the sectors concerned, there is no immediate economic reason for the government to intervene, but the result is that women with lower social backgrounds have a very limited occupational choice.

Another drawback of private courses--in the absence of compensatory policy measures and government control--is the fact that they may take advantage of the possible ignorance of the student about manpower and skill demands. This danger seems to be greater for women than for men.

Costs And Benefits

The question of whether recurrent education will be more costly than conventional education is difficult to answer. Some general arguments on this aspect have been developed in Recurrent Education: A Clarifying Report.[23] Therefore, the discussion here is limited to those costs that are likely to be different for men and women, in particular, the costs which are related to the support of the individual and his family during his participation in the courses.

The following figures taken from the German report on recurrent education[24] give an indication of the increasing importance of the share of subsistence funds in total grant aid given to individuals under the Labor Promotion Act: from 28 percent in 1968 to 52 percent in 1969 and 65 percent in 1970. Total grant aid to individuals went up from 116 million DM in 1968, to 189 million DM in 1969 and 572 million DM in 1970.

Compensation for earnings foregone is a problem which at present seems easier to solve for most women than for men. Relatively few women have to support a family or dependents. The majority of single women work to maintain themselves only; married women's earnings are rarely the main income of their family. Costs involved in recurrent education for women will, therefore, be basically limited to the financing of courses (teachers, building, etc.) and of child-care facilities. For single women, a maintenance grant is necessary.

It should be added that the social costs of not providing recurrent education for women are high, as shown by the numerous tragic cases of middle-aged and older women, who are often obliged to support themselves and who have great difficulty in finding a job except on an unskilled level.

---

23. Centre for Educational Research and Innovation, Recurrent Education: A Clarifying Report (CERI/OECD, 1972).

24. Recurrent Education in the Federal Republic of Germany.

Since recurrent education for women aims at improving their educational level, it is useful to have a look at cost-benefit analysis of education for women in general, and more particularly higher education, before examining the specific returns to recurrent education.

The measured "rate of return" to higher studies for women appears to be not much lower than that for men, and in some cases even higher.[25] This is because:

1. far fewer women than men receive higher education (see tables 7 and 8);

2. higher education substantially increases a woman's chances of being in the labor force; and

3. the less educated woman is more likely to suffer from discrimination in the labor market than the highly educated one.

Women earn less, on average, than men.[26] These overall figures take no account, however, of differences in occupational structure, in qualification, in working time, in productivity, rates of turnover, and absenteeism. It is difficult to know, therefore, how much of the differential in earnings is due to pay discrimination and how much to other factors (including other forms of discrimination). Besides, married women who re-enter the labor force after a period of interruption are often willing to accept jobs which give new interests and scope but low financial return.[27]

An American study shows that in the U.S. the average income of workers in occupations at least 51 percent female and for which the median years of school completed is greater than 11.1 is lower than the median income for the total male labor force. This is despite the fact that the educational level of both men and women in these professions is higher than the educational attainment of the average male worker. "In other words, the more educated labor in several female occupations is not rewarded by a proportionately higher income."[28]

---

25. Maureen Woodhall, "Investment in Women: A Reappraisal of the Concept of Human Capital," <u>International Review of Education</u> (forthcoming, March 1973).

26. Sullerot, <u>L'Emploi des Femmes</u>.

27. B. N. Seear, <u>Re-entry of Women to the Labour Market after an Interruption in Employment</u> (Paris: OECD, 1971).

28. Valerie K. Oppenheimer, "The Female Labor Force in the United States," <u>Population Monograph Series No. 5</u> (Berkeley: University of California at Berkeley), p. 99.

Table 7. Proportion of Girls in Secondary Education in 1950 and 1965 in Selected Countries, by Percent.

	1950				1965			
	General	Technical and Vocational	Teacher Training	Total	General	Technical and Vocational	Teacher Training	Total
Germany	45%	42%	...%	43%	45%	47%	...%	46%
Austria	35	...	62	...	39	...	73	...
Belgium	43 b)	54 b)	67 b)	48 b)	46 g)	47 g)	67 g)	48 g)
France	52	44	62	49	52		68	52
Netherlands	45	40	...	42	48 g)	43 g)	...	45 g)
Denmark	50	...	35	...	52	...	43	...
Finland	57	...	...	...	57	...	...	...
Ireland	...	...	70	...	...	...	78 g)	...
Norway	...	34 b)	...	...	48	37	...	45
England and Wales	...	...	...	49	...	...	...	48 g)
Sweden	54 a)	...	...	...	54	...	...	...
Spain	35	73	73	...	41	...	62 g)	...
Greece	37 d)	...	...	...	43 f)	...	...	...
Italy	38	21	85	38	45	27	87	43
Portugal	47	27	47	38	50 g)	33 g)	91 g)	42
Turkey	25	27	9	24	27	29	43	28
Yugoslavia	45 c)	25 c)	64 c)	35 c)	53	38	61	43
Japan	...	...	...	46	...	...	...	48

a) 1951.
b) 1952.
c) 1953.
d) 1955.
e) 1956.
f) 1963.
g) 1964.

Source: Educational Expansion in O.E.C.D. countries since 1950 (background report No. 1), prepared for the Conference on Policies for Educational Growth (Paris: OECD, 1971), p. 35.

Table 8. Proportion of Girls in Higher Education Around 1950 and 1965 in Selected Countries, by Percent.

	Beginning of Period		End of Period	
	Year	Proportion	Year	Proportion
Germany	1950	20% a)	1965	23%
Austria	1951	21	1965	24
Belgium	1952	26	1964	32
France	1955	32	1965	39
Netherlands	1950	20	1965	25
Switzerland b)	1955	13	1965	18
Denmark	1950	24	1965	35
Finland	1952	39	1965	48
Ireland b)	1950	27	1964	31
Norway b)	///	...	1965	24
Sweden	1951	29	1962	38
Spain	///	...	1964	21
Greece	1955	23	1964	29
Italy	1950	25	1964	32
Portugal	1950	24	1964	35
Turkey b)	1950	20	1965	25
Yugoslavia	1951	33	1965	34
United States	1950	32	1965	39
Japan	1950	10	1965	24

a) excluding engineering schools.

b) university only.

Source: Educational Expansion in O.E.C.D. Countries.

The relation between women's level of education and their participation in employment has been shown by various studies:

--In Norway only 9.5 percent of all Norwegian married women worked outside their homes in 1960, but 55 percent of married women graduates did so.[29]

--A Polish study quoted by Fogarty et al. found that the proportion of married women who return to work after maternity leave ranges upward from 35-40 percent in low skilled work in the clothing industry, or as waitresses and barmaids, to 75-85 percent in most professional and managerial occupations and 95 percent in the case of doctors and teachers.[30]

--In France 70 percent of women graduates were working at age 50 in 1962 compared to about 45 percent of women with only primary education.[31]

--In England and Wales 40 percent of all married women aged 25-44 were working at the time of the census of 1961, but the figure was 57 percent for those women who completed their education at 20 years or over.[32]

--Of American women aged 45-54 in 1964 the proportion working was 43 percent for those with elementary education, but 85.5 percent for those with five or more years of college.[33]

Education is, of course, just one of the factors influencing women's labor force participation, but it is an important one. Expanded educational opportunities for women will influence society in a number of other ways as well.

An indirect effect of women's education is the reduction in the birth-rate which for developing countries with high birth-rates may be considered as an important benefit.

---

29. H. Holter, "Women's Occupational Situation in Scandinavia," International Labour Review, 93, 4 (April 1966): 383-400.

30. Fogarty et al., Sex, Career and Family.

31. "L'Emploi Feminin en 1962 et son Evolution Depuis 1954," Etudes et Conjoncture, 12 (Decembre 1964): 62.

32. Fogarty et al., Sex, Career and Family.

33. U. S. Department of Labor, Women's Bureau, Handbook on Women Workers (Washington, D.C.: Government Printing Office, 1965), p. 195.

It could also affect children's learning. Various studies have shown the correlation between the children's achievement in school and the educational level of the mother.[34]

Recurrent education for women would affect the distribution of work between the sexes and allocation of women's time. Is the existing distribution really the best and most rational we can think of? Tables on women's "time budgets"[35] are very revealing in this respect and show that on the whole married women work more hours per week than men. Only the ones who have neither children nor any professional activity seem to work less (and the ones who have daily domestic help, of course).

The issue is in the last analysis one of priorities which must be more clearly defined than they are at present. It is not sufficient to point out the positive aspects of certain activities, it is also necessary to know their opportunity cost in real terms (i.e., their possible substitution by other activities in the same length of time) for a conscious choice to be made.

The Returns To Recurrent Education For Women[36]

At present, it is generally very difficult for a woman in her 30's or 40's to get back to the labor market with the hope of starting a career leading to an interesting job. There is no reason--not even in economic terms--why this should be so. Allowing for normal discount rates, most of the "present value" to individuals--and hence probably to society--of a course of education is earned in the first 20 years after educational expenditure has been incurred. Training schemes for women in their 30's or early 40's followed by effective employment opportunities could, even on these narrow economic criteria, prove very profitable and should form an integral part of educational and

---

34. Coleman, Equality of Educational Opportunity and Children and Their Primary Schools.

35. See for instance, F. Guelaud-Leridon, "Le Travail des Femmes en France," Travaux et Documents, 42 (Paris: Presses Universitaires de France, INED, 1964), p. 43, and M. Guilbert et al., "Enquete Comparative de Budget-Temps," Revue Francaise de Sociologie, 6 (1965): 502-503.

36. A more detailed exposition of the material in this section is given in Gisela Schade, "Notes on Recurrent Education for Women," Higher Education, 1, 4 (November 1972): 477-481.

employment policies.[37]

Taking into account the economic gains of women's increased labor force participation, the social "rate of return" of recurrent education would be higher for women than for men in the younger age groups who are likely to have to work in any case. However, this is an area in which considerably more research is needed.[38]

Conclusion

Although this paper has dealt with education for women, it has placed women's interests in the framework of society as a whole. One of the most important aspects of women's emancipation today is the fact that for the first time in history, mankind has the

---

37. The income stream can be represented by:

$$y_t = A(1-e^{-kt}), \text{ where A is the upper limit.}$$

If the income rises by r% in the first year of a career, then $k = \ln 1/r$.

The present value (PV) of total expected lifetime income is (i = discount rate):

$$PV = \int_o^T y_t . e^{-it} dt$$

$$= A\left(\frac{k}{i(i+k)} + \frac{e^{-(i+k)T}}{i+k} - \frac{e^{-iT}}{i}\right).$$

Suppose $i = 0.1$, suppose $r = 0.15$ (a discount rate of 10 percent per year which is not unreasonable for this kind of investment), then: 87 percent of the present value of an expected lifetime income spread over 40 years occurs in the first 20 years of working life.

Therefore, other things being equal, a course of education finished at the age of 45 years should yield about 87% of a similar course finished at the age of 25 (for $i = 0.1$ and $r = 0.1$, one also finds a percentage of 87).

38. G. Psacharopoulos has collected about 50 rate of return studies from 32 countries. Only about half a dozen of these provide estimates of rates of return to women's education. See G. Psacharopoulos, The Returns to Education: An International Comparison (Amsterdam: Elsevier, 1972).

possibility of controlling its reproduction. This fact does not only concern women, it also affects men's lives and their responsibilities.

The effects of medical progress on the condition of women have not yet been fully appreciated by most people, including many women, but they probably will be within the next generation. It is not the small group of "educated" women today nor the often superficial lip-service given to feminism in recent years that is going to bring about a fundamental change in women's place in society. It is the increasing efficiency of contraceptives that will give freedom of choice to _all_ women. Motherhood will become a free and responsible option for all instead of being a destiny for the great majority. Governments will have to take their share of responsibility in this field too and recognize the social utility of child-raising much more than they do at present.

Women's emancipation appears then as an historical event influencing the organization of society at large in line with developments taking place in other fields.

The measures necessary in the educational field to accompany these changes have been briefly set out in this paper. It has been argued that women's education should be centered on the concept of emancipation and that this idea is not in contradiction with economic objectives. The necessity for a _comprehensive policy approach_ has been stressed on various occasions, comprehensive in the sense that:

1. it should cover all education, from pre-primary to adult, both formal and informal, general and vocational;

2. coordination with economic and social policies as well as employment practices is required; and

3. all social groups and not only women should be considered. (Recurrent education for women makes sense only in the framework of a _generalized_ recurrent education system, in which all individuals participate.)

However ambitious such a policy approach may appear, it has to be seen in a long-term perspective, the planning for which should be started now.

Specific policy measures which should be undertaken include:

1. curricula from pre-primary to adult education within the framework of general educational objectives that:

   --prepare for parenthood (in order to increase parents' capacity to assume fully their role);

   --stress changing sex roles;

2. special emphasis on emancipation and sex roles in the training of teachers and of people in charge of vocational guidance;

3. better informed public opinion through mass media: less exclusive representation of women as sex-objects and as gullible consumers;

4. counseling services for adult women;

5. increase in training and retraining opportunities for women, linked to an active employment policy;

6. extension of the fields covered by training (types and levels of jobs);

7. special attention to vocational training for women in the framework of an integrated nonbinary system; and

8. involving women in the preparatory work for new provisions, not only in the educational field, but also in town and country planning and community design, new patterns for working time, community care, etc.

educational planning for mature women

CARYL M. KLINE

In 1787 when the Constitutional Convention was meeting in Philadelphia, Abigail Adams wrote to her husband John, "If special care is not paid to the concerns of women, then we are determined to foment a rebellion and we shall not be bound by any law in which we have not had a voice or representation." The last decade has seen that rebellion, sometimes quietly and sometimes vociferously, move across the U.S. In its wake have come increased employment for women, higher wages--although still not equal to men's--real efforts to diversify areas of employment for women, the Equal Rights Amendment that 27 states have now ratified, and a nationwide effort to increase the educational opportunities for mature women.

Lewis Mumford once said that by their very success in inventing labor-saving devices, American men had created an abyss of boredom in this country which only the most affluent in earlier civilizations would have been able to bridge. The "abyss of boredom" has been most critical for the American woman. All the household labor-saving devices, the factory processing of food, the manufacture of wearing apparel took from the average American woman the tasks which had occupied her in her home. She had extra time on her hands, but what to do with it? Tradition says a woman's place is in the home and the woman who tried to abide by that admonition found herself making work for herself. She began to mother excessively, to make full-time jobs of busy-work housekeeping, to participate in social activities that were meaningless. Women began to express their frustrations and to seek a way out. In far greater numbers American women began to turn to the world of work but found they were not qualified for the jobs they wanted. Liberal arts graduates were completely demoralized and not just a little angered when they were asked finally, "Well, can you type?"

The problem became a concern to the nation's educators; conferences were held, articles and books were written. Obviously, a new current in American education was developing. For example, in October 1963, Edward Litchfield, Chancellor of the University of Pittsburgh, called to the attention of the university community America's failure to educate her able women to the full extent of their intellectual capabilities with the resulting loss to every phase of America's economic and intellectual life. The Chancellor announced his intention to appoint an assistant "to take an inventory of the professional and semi-professional needs of our region, determine to what extent they can, with or without persuasion, be filled by women, announce these needs to the women in our region, and invite their return to the University to prepare themselves to meet those needs."

It was expected that women who held M.D., Ph.D., M.A., and M.S. degrees would return to the university and refurbish their training and turn again to their professions. However, this did not happen. Women who had not completed their baccalaureate degrees, some with as much as three and one-half years of academic credit, came to complete their undergraduate work. Many others began college education.

In the intervening decade more than 200 colleges and universities in the U.S. have established programs for Continuing Education for Women. At the University of Pittsburgh, ages of the women in baccalaureat work range from 25 to 72. The average age is 39.

There are those, of course, who come because they feel there must be something more than children, house, and the same treadmill day after day. They look to college for direction and purpose. Then there are those who feel a very real need for individual development.

The majority come, however, with very definite goals in mind. They want an education to enter the labor force and contribute in a very tangible way to the upward socioeconomic mobility of themselves and their families. For many it is a vision of college for their children which would be impossible on a single income. For others it is a desire for career mobility. Then there are those who come out of a driving necessity. Many women are already widowed, divorced, or separated and have families to support. Sometimes they have sufficient money to support themselves for a short period of time but must find a way to begin earning a good salary within a period of three to five years.

The effects of the mature women returning to college are many. First, since she is there because she wants to be and she is anxious to get the most for her time and money, she expects excellent teaching and well-organized courses. At first some deans and professors were opposed to "frustrated housewives" returning to college, but the women soon won the respect of their professors by the excellent quality of their class participation and now professors ask that older students be in their classes.

Another beneficial effect is that in most cases the grades of children have gone up at least a letter grade. Although it is seldom intended, a sense of rivalry seems to emerge between mother and children. A side effect is the necessary division of tasks about the home. A greater sense of responsibility and cooperation is engendered in the children because it is necessary.

There are also serious problems. There is usually a struggle to find the money. While there seem to be grants, scholarships, and low-interest loans for the young student, there is little understanding of the needs of mature men and women for like financial assistance in continuing their education. Scholarships and loans are usually awarded only to the full-time student, but most mature people returning to the classroom must weave their attendance around family obligations or employment schedules. Many employers are now paying a percentage and sometimes all of the tuition of employees who take courses that are immediately applicable to the job they are doing. However, this meets only a very small fraction of the need, for before the student can take the professional courses, there are usually many required background and general education courses for which the employer will not pay. Another difficulty with such a system is that it is usually on a reimbursement basis where the employee is paid only after completing the course with a satisfactory grade. It is very difficult for older men and women in moderate economic circumstances to pay a lump sum for tuition. It would be most helpful if business and industry could make tuition grants when the money is due, with salary deductions provisions if the course is not successfully completed. Many service clubs, both men's and women's, Federated Women's Clubs, even organizations of professional educators frequently give scholarships but rarely are they designated for the mature student. It is unfortunate that education and educational aid seem to be designed primarily for the younger full-time student. If we are truly committed to the idea that education is a lifelong process necessary to the well-being of our society, then government, business, and private organizations must be persuaded to set aside monies for individuals interested in continuing education.

Among other problems is the fear of mature women that they are incapable of intellectual achievement comparable to that of the 18-22 year old student. Experience with mature students has shown that regardless of how good her college record was at 20, she will do even better when she returns after 30. If her college record were abominable at 20, she is sure to be pleasantly surprised by her achievements as a student of 30 plus.

A most important part of returning to the educational community is establishing some associations with other returning women and provision should be made for the formation of such groups. The women themselves will be most anxious to put together an organization and to spend time building seminars or programs to meet their own needs and to encourage other women who may be interested in continuing their education but lack confidence or understanding. Frequently, these mature women student organizations reach out into the community and present public seminars, lectures, and TV programs on women's education. The know-how gained from the necessary budgeting, fund-raising, sale of advertising, program planning, and public relations proves to be very valuable when the women seek to enter the business and professional world.

It is also important that there be an office within the university itself to assist mature women students. Here they will find counseling, academic advising, and a place to bring their serious problems, both academic and personal. Another service which this office might perform is the keeping of a file of old examinations. Students are much more confident if they have some slight idea of what their examination may be. If time permits, it is well to conduct some mock examinations followed by an analysis of the questions and answers.

For the woman returning to college after some years of working or of participating as a volunteer in community projects and activities, there is a great likelihood that through her varied experiences, from reading, from TV and public lectures, and from travel she has learned much that could be equated with the academic work of the classroom. Therefore, there has been much agitation for the granting of credits for "life experience." In the fields of social work, political science, public administration, business administration, and teaching, the work experience can be equated with the required practicum of the senior year.

The next question is, of course, how do you evaluate the experience of the mature woman student who has lived her life in the ghetto and participated in the block organization, who has raised a family within the constraints of public assistance, who has dealt with the problems of drugs, public housing, the geriatric citizen, the unwed mother, the latchkey child? Is there some credit for "life experience" for this student? Immediately after the assassination of Martin Luther King, when there was tremendous pressure for rapidly upgrading the employment of blacks, blocks of credit were given for "life experience," sometimes as many as 30 credits or the equivalent of one college year, without much thought of transferability of such credits to another institution or the applicability of these credits to the jobs that were being or would be done by the individuals to whom the credits were given. Soon the recipients of such credits began to point out that this practice was not very helpful to them and they did, indeed, need specific equating of their life experience with course work so that they could complement their life experience with formal training and be properly prepared for professional employment. Very real attempts have been made to equate life experience with academic courses particularly in the social sciences. Success has been achieved in the fields of sociology, social work, anthropology, cultural geography, and education. Many black mothers acting as teacher's aides, with no formal training in psychology or professional education, can handle the problems of motivation (so long neglected in our ghetto schools) and learning more effectively than the professionally trained individual with no practical understanding of the children with whom she must work. Therefore, to these women helping in the classroom, specific credits can be awarded and equated with required courses in schools of education or social work.

A further question raised on behalf of the returning mature student has been the granting of credit by examination. The Educational Testing Service developed the College Level Examination Program (CLEP) which affords to people who have gained their education outside the classroom the opportunity to assess their achievement (i.e., knowledge gained from work experience, correspondence study, television courses, independent study, on-the-job training, travel, wide-ranging reading habits, etc.). Almost without exception, the colleges and universities of the U.S. devote the first two years, or approximately 60 credits of the 120 required for the baccalaureate degree, to general education in the arts and sciences. These are usually called the "core courses" or "distribution courses" and include certain requirements in the natural sciences, the social sciences, and the humanities. It is, of course, requisite that college students be able to express themselves lucidly in writing. Therefore, the CLEP examinations cover five areas--English Composition, Mathematics, Natural Science, Social Science, and the Humanities. A student may seek examination in as many areas as she wishes. Each educational institution decides how the results of these examinations will be used. Varying numbers of credits are usually awarded on the basis of the score earned. In some colleges and universities, it is possible to satisfy a full two years of college credit by successfully passing all five areas included in the CLEP examinations. Credits are usually awarded on a sliding scale in a ratio to the scores received on the examination and equated with the number of credits required by that college in a given subject area. For example, if X University requires 12 credits each in the Humanities, Natural Sciences, Social Sciences, English Composition, and Mathematics, 12 credits will be awarded for an excellent score in any of these areas, nine credits for a good score, and six credits for an average score. Many women returning to college after an absence of several years have received from 42-60 credits. Usually credits already earned in a subject area are deducted from those gained from the examination. Thus, if you received 12 credits in English Composition as a result of an excellent score on the CLEP examination, but had already earned six credits by taking the courses, the net gain from the CLEP examination would be six credits.

Another very important value of the CLEP examination is to determine the value of credits earned by an individual in a nonaccredited institution. Many women attended small local or religiously oriented colleges which may not have been, at least at the time of attendance, accredited by the regional accrediting agencies. Therefore, the credits earned there are not transferable. By taking the CLEP examination, some salvaging of credits is possible.

The College Level Examination Program also offers examinations in specific subject areas which enable the student who has done independent upper-level work to take an examination in the subject and submit her score for consideration in the granting of advanced credits. Each college or university will determine how it will use these scores in the granting of advanced credit. Many colleges and universities have established an internal system of giving examinations for credit. Sometimes it is possible to petition and gain permission to take the final examination in a course without having attended lectures. Usually there is a fee for taking the examination and if successfully passed, there is a fee for the granting and recording of the credits although it is much less than the cost of taking the course. By examination, therefore, it may be possible for the continuing education student to eliminate several semesters of classroom courses.

Furthermore, more flexibility must be engendered in university administrations. Unfortunately, there are still some very conservative academicians who cannot countenance the granting of university credit for anything but classroom performance. An internal metamorphosis is needed in many educational institutions before there will be a real acceptance of continuing education for women.

Continuing education in the U.S. was given a great impetus some 15 years ago by the community college movement. It is possible to take at a community college two years of academic work similar to the first two years of any four-year college. The difference is that at the end of two years at a community college the student receives an associate degree which in many cases enables the individual to give proof of some college attendance and therefore gives an advantage in gaining employment over the individual who may have gone three and one-half years to a four-year college without a credential. In this credentially oriented society, there seems to be a need for a like piece of paper to be given to the drop-out or stop-out student in the four-year college.

A second option at the community college is a vocational school. In two years a student may get a certificate in inhalation therapy, pedology (child development and child care), accounting, nursing, computer science, etc. These certificate programs are very helpful to the mature woman who must qualify quickly for a well-paying job. There is some academic work included in each certificate curriculum which could be applied at a later date to the requirements for an academic degree.

At its inception, the community college was for the student who did not want to go to a four-year college or whose academic prognostication was insufficient to merit enrollment at a four-year college. As it has developed, the students who start at the community college frequently seek admission to a four-year college. Sometimes it is after some years in the job market or after raising a family to a point where the woman has time available for college attendance. A problem has sometimes arisen because of the refusal of four-year degree granting institutions to accept community college credits for transfer. A very important need for successful continuing education is the establishment of compatible curricula by the community colleges and the four-year colleges and universities. This may necessitate a greater diversification of course offerings on the part of the community colleges and a tightening of academic standards, but it also necessitates an elimination of derogative, supercilious attitudes of some four-year institutions.

An additional instrument for continuing education is beginning to flourish in the U.S., spurred on by the Open University in Great Britain. Many states are now considering the establishment of a system whereby a college degree may be earned entirely by independent study, or by a combination of independent study and brief periods of time on a university campus or at a center where the students meet with the professors who have been preparing the course material. This is not wholly new. The University of Oklahoma and Syracuse University have been pursuing a comparable program for many years and the land grant colleges have had extension programs for several decades. These were largely correspondence courses. Many universities are now starting modified external degree programs which means that a syllabus for a course and reading assignments are sent to the student and two or three times during the semester the students come to the campus to meet with their professor. For the woman with small children, the woman living in an area isolated from a higher educational institution, the woman who is employed full-time, the woman whose husband objects to her attending classes, the woman who is elderly, ill, or physically handicapped, the open university or the external degree program provides an excellent opportunity for her to continue her education. In this highly credentialled society, it is only fair to raise the question of the acceptability for graduate study or for job requirements of a degree from such an open university.

Another fortunate development which benefits the mature woman wishing to continue her education is the introduction by many educational institutions of evening programs which duplicate day programs. Not all courses are offered every semester but it is possible to complete a baccalaureate degree through evening study. In metropolitan areas, the professors frequently go to the suburbs to hold classes. Where such an opportunity has been offered, the women have frequently assumed the responsibility of getting the required number of registrants and of finding a place in the local schools or churches for classes to meet.

One of the weaknesses of the evening and suburban neighborhood programs is the unwillingness of regular faculty members to teach the classes. The result is that graduate students or men and women from high schools or business and industry are recruited to teach. The effect may be that the teacher is too engrossed in his own research to do a good job with the continuing education students, or the class is conducted on a secondary education level, or is too oriented to a specific experience. If continuing education is to meet its promise to returning students, then the same commitment must be made for quality education for the mature students attending in the evening and at satellite campuses as is made for the regularly matriculated day student. To implement this commitment, it is clearly understood in many university departments that each senior faculty member will teach in evening school or at an outlying location on a rotating basis.

Although much has been done to expedite continuing education for mature women, some colleges and universities still require mature women to meet regular admissions requirements. For the mature woman returning to continue her education after a long interruption, these requirements are ridiculous. For the woman who has been away from formal education for 10 to 30 years, college board scores are meaningless. The mature woman might do well in the verbal examination but she has little likelihood of being successful in the mathematical area and she is most unlikely to be successful in the achievement exams in specific academic areas. The mature woman seeking admission to college for continuing education should not be expected to take college board examinations or any other entrance examinations. Access to education should be possible at any point in life without exclusive barriers of any sort--academic, residential, or age.

Additionally, most admissions officers are oriented toward the recent high school graduate and must be made aware of the returning student. More effective for the continuing education program for women would be to have a mature woman in the admissions office who would handle all applications from women interested in continuing education.

Another meaningless requirement maintained by many admissions offices is the evaluation of a student by her high school counselor and letters of recommendation from three members of the high school faculty. In many cases, the schools are no longer in existence, and the principal and faculty who would have known the woman may well be deceased or long since moved from the area. Far more important to an evaluation of the ability of the woman to do college work would be the recommendation of her current employer, or the director of volunteers in the agency or organization in which she has served, the principal of the school where she is a member of the Parent Teachers Association, or a member of her political party who has watched her influence in the community.

In short, recommendations for the mature woman should be pertinent to her current activities, not to those of her adolescent years.

In the initial interview in returning to school, there should be a careful exploration of both the intellectual and economic needs of the prospective student. If the primary motivation for return to college is economic and the need is almost immediate, then the individual should be guided to other avenues of training. She should be encouraged to undertake an educational ladder which ultimately will enable her to satisfy her desires for a college degree but will give earning capacity more immediately; for instance, a paraprofessional degree program.

Intellectual readiness or capability is usually quite obvious in the initial interview with the mature woman. If a four-year college degree is not a possibility, then the woman must be persuaded in a gentle and kindly way to undertake another kind of program. Continuing or recurrent education for women does not necessarily mean a college diploma. If her abilities are more vocationally oriented, then every effort should be made to guide her to the proper individual or school to help her develop her skills.

Moreover, deans and administrators should alter some of their rules, regulations, and requirements. The woman with a family is unable to attend every day in the week or to take courses at just any hour in the day. Her program must be carefully scheduled around the school hours of her children taking into consideration whether they come home for lunch or are full or half-day students. Other women must fit their education around patterns of employment. Therefore, the university must be willing to accept a part-time attendance on the part of the mature woman.

Another requirement has been that each student must earn a physical education credit for each of four semesters. For the woman who, according to Chase National Bank, spends approximately 96 hours a week on household and family associated tasks which necessitate much physical activity, the physical education requirement is unnecessary.

Another sacred cow in American colleges and universities is known as the "statute of limitations." This means that unless a degree, graduate or undergraduate, is completed in a given number of years, all credits are forfeited. In many cases, departments or schools are willing to give extensions upon petition but in others the rule has been iron-bound, and women very near to completion of their dissertation have abandoned graduate work. This is a rule that must be permanently dropped if continuing or recurrent educational patterns are to have viability.

Another example of myopia on the part of deans, administrators, and their staffs is the unwillingness to accept a course for transfer unless its description is comparable to one at the new institution. Surely a general education course dealing with the Greek tragedies, the Iliad, the Odyssey, and the Bible is as suitable a course to meet a humanities general education requirement as a course in narrative fiction. If a broad cultural background is what we are trying to assure for each student, let there be some breadth of interpretation of what contributes to a broad cultural background!

Indeed this transferability should extend to universities of other countries so that when our mature women (and preferably any student) have the opportunity to study at a university in another nation, they can transfer the credit back to their degree-granting institution in the U.S.

Closely related to the problem of transferability is the possibility of cross-registration from one college to another. The need in the U.S. to get more mileage from every educational dollar means that every college and university in a city or a metropolitan area, or even a state, cannot have a full range of programs and courses. If Swahili is excellently taught at one university, there is really no need for another university two or three miles away to undertake a like program. Rather, the students should be permitted to take the course at the first university and have the credit accepted at the university where she matriculated. As simple and sensible as this proposal seems to some, it is remarkable how difficult of acceptance it is among some educational institutions.

Continuing education for women poses a problem for more than the educators and the institutions of higher learning. Employers, as well, must be convinced that a desire for additional education will develop in many of his women employees. If he is to retain these highly motivated individuals, he must find a way to encourage their return to education on a part-time basis or grant them periodic leaves without the loss of seniority or benefits. Many employers encourage their employees to continue their education by paying tuition. The union of one major industry has negotiated a remarkably generous vacation program which grants vacations up to 13 weeks in length. A few women have been able to return to college for a full-time semester by taking advantage of the long vacation and taking two more weeks without pay. Some employers have been persuaded to give released time during the day to enable women to take one or two courses. Such instances are still unusual in American business and industry. Indeed, only affirmative action programs have brought released time acceptance to many educational institutions.

The need for business, industry, and educational institutions to abide by U. S. Department of Health, Education, and Welfare's affirmative action requirements for the employment of women has brought the complaint that there are no qualified women to hire in many categories. The answer is, "Train them!" The result is that many employers are becoming aware of the value of upgrading by education the women already on their staffs. Another method of finding time for and enabling women to finance their continuing education is for an employer to permit two women to share a single job. It has been done successfully in many areas of employment. There are partnership teaching assignments, medical and nursing assignments, clerical assignments, and many others.

Frequently, women, whose careers have not been interrupted by marriage and family, are interested in changing careers just as men are, and there should be an opportunity for them to re-educate themselves for those new careers. Aware of the desire of mid-career women to find new and challenging job opportunities, a group of women at the University of Pittsburgh made a proposal to a foundation for a grant to establish a program for mid-career women in urban planning, development, and administration. The money is being used to finance women between the ages of 30 and 50 who wish to take graduate work in the urban field. There is need for many more such programs geared to the professional training of the mature woman. It is still very difficult for the mature woman to be admitted to law or medical schools. There seems to be a belief that the woman of 40 or over will not have time to make a meaningful professional contribution if she is a doctor or a lawyer. This is a myth that has been disproven many times but which continues to be used to eliminate the mature woman from most classes in schools of medicine or law.

The U.S. has a large surplus of elementary and secondary teachers, a great backlog of unemployed Ph.D.'s, and a surplus of nurses. If mature women are to be educated for financially remunerative employment, they must be encouraged to go into nontraditional fields, such as engineering, electronics, landscape architecture, and the health-related professions that are expanding in today's economy. Those fields are still looking for women employees.

In addition to increasing the opportunity for economic equality, the greatest value continuing education can give women is to allow them to participate actively in the maintenance of our nation's democratic institutions. It can help them serve less fortunate men and women and it can help them build an intellectual storehouse so rich that no woman, who has enjoyed the fruits of recurrent education, can complain of being empty, frustrated, and alone.

education and the world of work

532-819 O - 74 - 13

towards flexibility in working life

GOSTA REHN

Flexibility in working life, through new patterns for working time and allied reforms in education, training, vacation, and pension systems, are now on the agenda for policy debate in OECD countries. Some reforms have already been implemented or experimented with: flexible retirement, wide-ranging adult education schemes, "flexi-time" (i.e., variable working hours per day and per week), long-service leave and other intermittent "sabbaticals."

This development was to be expected since shorter hours and improved retirement conditions have created broader margins for both diversification and variation of work patterns, even though laws and collective agreements continue to prescribe the traditional uniformity of rules and to set rather narrow limits for deviations.

More specific factors, however, are also working toward a breakthrough for greater flexibility in timing our working day and working life:

--The rising level of education engenders a demand for individual self-determination and a rejection of standardized prescriptions and regulations.

--Adult ("recurrent," "permanent," or "lifelong") training and education, which is both an economic necessity and a method of promoting social equity is therefore expanding. These programs are by their very nature widely diversified.

--The growth of special programs to keep older workers in employment, together with rising pension levels, make it possible for a person to contemplate exchanging some of his expected old age pension for advanced, temporary, or partial retirement earlier than the ordinary age, and also to arrange for a less abrupt change from full work to full retirement.

--The growth of the number of women who combine family responsibilities with gainful employment leads to a demand for intermittent or part-time work with variable hours.

--The expanding service sector offers greater possibilities for non-standardized work-time arrangements than manufacturing industries and at the same time creates more demand for schedules permitting the customers to be served during their free hours or days.

--Continuing urbanization requires rearrangement of working time over the course of the day and the year to avoid traffic jams in big cities and overcrowding in tourist resorts.

--The growing importance of shift-work designed to utilize the capacity of increasingly capital-intensive industries leads to the use of special time patterns to make such work tolerable.

--The rising level of real income and the relative job security created by full employment permits employees to react against rigid work-time rules and other unsatisfactory conditions through absenteeism and high labor turnover; this in turn leads employers to offer more acceptable schedules (the time aspect of industrial democracy).

--The fading of remembrance of the labor movement's long and hard struggle to establish hours-of-work regulations and old age insurance systems make the workers lose their reluctance to accept arrangements which deviate from the rules set in these fields, particularly when the arguments about "not taking work opportunities from the unemployed" no longer apply, thanks to full employment.

--Finally, the difficulty of solving the inflation-unemployment dilemma through income or traditional manpower policies has led to a search for new methods of matching supply and demand in the labor market. The solution must be found in part in income maintenance and transfer arrangements which promote voluntary variations in the supply of labor without similar variations in the individual's flow of income, and replace involuntary and destructive unemployment with agreeable leisure and useful studies.

Policy Recommendations

Since a greater degree of freedom and flexibility thus seems both probable and desirable, some suggestions should be formulated as to how this development could be constructively channeled. The recommendations presented first are goals which are capable of improving the quality of life. They are followed by suggestions for specific institutional reforms and innovations to implement these and allied goals, and finally by some concrete examples on specific details.

Governments and industrial organizations should make it a policy goal to provide the individual with the greatest possible freedom to determine the allocation of his own time among different uses. An endeavor should be made to achieve this freedom through well-planned and prepared policy programs rather than by reluctantly and belatedly yielding to the social pressures for greater flexibility.

The individual should be free to switch between periods of income-earning work, education or training, and leisure (including retirement) according to his own interests. There should also be many different and variable patterns of working time over the course of a year, a week or a day so that the individual can always find something that suits his preferences.

Of course, this freedom cannot be unlimited; the task is always to find the best compromise between individual wishes and the technical and economic exigencies which have led to existing rules and regulations whose role in promoting both economic efficiency and social protection should not be overlooked. But the time has come to move the point of compromise toward freedom by offering more flexibility whenever possible.

Systematization Of Social Choices

The reduction in total hours worked over the course of a normal lifetime, which can be expected to continue, ought to be based on a systematic and simultaneous consideration of all the options. Decisions concerning retirement, vacations, weekly hours, years of schooling, and access to adult training and education should be an interrelated set of economic and social choices which are taken into account in improving the quality of life.

This recommendation is equally valid whether the intended result is achieved in the traditional way--i.e., by applying standardized rules--or by adopting more flexible arrangements which encourage deviations from the most common patterns of working time and from the average number of hours and years devoted to various purposes of work, study, and leisure.

Introduction Of Generalized Drawing Rights

An integrated insurance system for transferring income between different periods of life (under appropriate risk-sharing) should be created to make the desired flexibility and freedom of choice a practical reality. The many separate schemes for maintenance of income during periods of voluntary and involuntary nonwork which already exist are becoming chaotic, bureaucratic, costly, inequitable, as well as insufficient. Often they tend to reduce rather than increase the individual's freedom by acting as "golden handcuffs" which keep a man at a job he does not like because moving would mean loss of the advantages given by seniority.

Freedom of choice and flexibility in shaping one's own life presupposes an increased degree of self-determination in the use of the income transfer and maintenance systems. This freedom should apply both to timing and to interchangeability--a right, within limits, to sacrifice benefits of one kind during one period in order to get more of the same or another kind during another period.

This could best be achieved by combining into one single, unified system of individualized accounting all those fees, taxes, study loan payments, and other compulsory savings already used to provide the individual with liquid income during periods of nonwork. Part of those future increases of hourly earnings which could be regarded as compensation for shortened working time (as is customary with reductions in weekly hours) would also have to be directed into this unified system. Each person would be given the right to draw on his account for his own reasons just as he has the right to borrow on that part of his private life insurance which is not needed to cover the risk-sharing involved.

Limitations on such drawing rights would obviously be necessary. An individual account could not be drawn upon to a point where it endangered a certain minimum level of old age pension; similarly, advance drawings to finance studies could not be permitted to become so large that the account could never in future reach this minimum pension level. (Longer studies for advanced degrees will therefore always have to be financed by individual arrangements, whether through scholarships, private capital, or reimbursable loans.)

Theoretically, the individual was always able, by borrowing and saving, to arrange to switch liquidity between various periods in his life to suit any possible variations in his needs, including a profitable investment in his own human capital. In reality, the unavoidable element of risk creates obstacles to such rational behavior, particularly in low income groups. Belonging to a compulsory general income insurance system would make it more possible for everyone to mobilize a certain amount of liquidity and thus to overcome discrepancies between current expenditure and current income. This would create greater scope for following one's own preferences for amount and timing of work, study, retirement, and other periods of leisure.

Such an arrangement would remove part of the burden of decision-making in these matters from the political authorities and large organizations, whose standardized regulations cannot be optimal for all persons whose preferences diverge from the norm. It would also provide a democratic and elastic correction to situations in which the power of different pressure groups may have led the political authorities to a series of separate decisions which, taken as a whole, result in an unacceptable level of forced savings through taxation. Those who did not accept the situation could react by using part of their accumulated assets at the earliest permissible occasion, but still combining this with continued income-earning activities.

To some extent, everyone wants to belong to a compulsory savings scheme in order to do what he cannot do on his own--e.g., save adequately for his old age. The burden of this deduction from current income is more easily borne if everyone is under the same obligation to participate. But as this burden of taxes and fees to finance collective consumption and income transfers becomes very large, there is a growing need for both equity and elasticity in this "voluntary compulsion."

All citizens, including those with relatively low incomes, are already paying for generously encouraged secondary and higher schooling, as well as for recurrent training and other adult education activities. These mainly benefit a minority who can fully utilize such facilities. During the period of educational expansion through which most countries are currently passing, such studies must be financed by taxes covering not only the direct expenditure for buildings, teachers, and study grants, but also the mobilization of capital for study loans. Even if most of these costs come back to society later in various forms, equity demands a better bookkeeping system to register year-by-year every individual's contribution, e.g., by rechristening part of the value-added tax "contribution to the general income insurance" and crediting the individual's account for a sum related to his net earned income. Thus, <u>everyone</u> would eventually be permitted to regain some part of what he has paid to help others enter the above-average income bracket. This could take the form of access to late studies, early pensions or some other option left to individual choice. In some countries, this rather natural demand is already on the way to becoming a political reality.

Coordination Of Flexibility And Labor Market Policy

To promote the closest possible conformity between individual choice and the varying needs for manpower in different areas and sectors, supplementary benefits should be offered to anyone willing to use some of his assets to finance a period of training or leisure where this is desirable because of a decline in the demand for labor. Some countries already offer allowances to companies willing to use their accumulated profits to invest during slack periods; it appears both rational and equitable to give analogous incentives to individuals to counterbalance variations in employment.

Labor market policies and programs geared to this need (labor market training, redundancy payments, early pensions) exist on a limited scale, but their expansion is hampered because they constitute pure gifts of public money to selected individuals. Such grants require what is often an authoritarian and humiliating control: first, the applicant must show bona fide eligibility; and second, the financial burden must be limited and focus on those cases where the benefit is demonstrably higher than the costs, or expenditure is unavoidable for social reasons. If eligibility were determined simply by a person's willingness to debit a major part of the cost to his personal account in the income transfer insurance system (or in any separate system for study credits or social security), these restraints could largely be eliminated.

It might appear as if the switch from pure grants to a system of debits on the individual's account (in which grants were only used as a supplement) would be anti-egalitarian. In reality, as indicated above, the existing selective grants are utilized to a particularly great extent by those who are relatively well off, while the suggested general income insurance system would be neutral with respect to income distribution. It could even be used for reduction of income differences, e.g., by constructing at least part of the drawing rights (most naturally the advances for studies, given to everyone on passing compulsory school age) as flat-rate, although financed through income-proportional contributions.

The suggested incentives to desirable timing of individual switches between periods of work and nonwork could attract people in all income brackets, who believe they will find better jobs as a result of job search or retraining, or would like to have a period of extra leisure but want to return to the same kind of job when the demand for labor increases. It would be desirable in this way to undertake measures of adaptation voluntarily. At present, a disproportionate part of the total burden of adaptation to most adaptable changes in the labor market falls on the least adaptable--the old or handicapped workers most vulnerable to unemployment in cases of general or sectoral decline in employment. Also creation of employment, readjustment measures and income maintenance for these groups is particularly costly. In any case, it is desirable to encourage aging persons to use their drawing rights (or any other form of flexible retirement provisos) to begin to adjust their occupational lives to their declining capacities before they are too old to continue in their main occupation or to go over to something else.

A general and uniform reduction of weekly working hours is often suggested as a measure to fight unemployment. But both theory and experience have shown this to be an ineffective method, and may even stimulate inflation by narrowing existing bottlenecks. But if some part of the reduction in the total number of work hours over a lifetime could instead be applied selectively--if some people voluntarily abstained from work when the demand for labor in their sector declined, and used such time to reorient themselves towards expanding job opportunities--this would be a real weapon against unemployment. It would also alleviate the negative side-effects on employment, which can stem from general demand-decreasing anti-inflationary measures, and thus increase the chances of success of economic stabilization policies.

Some Illustrative Details

The following more concrete and detailed suggestions concern flexibility over the course of a lifetime as well as over shorter periods. The figures used are only illustrative, as different countries would require different programs. The suggestions could be applied whether or not a "general income insurance system" and drawing rights were introduced, but such a system would greatly facilitate most of them.

--It should be made possible for the individual to maneuver freely with the upper third of his future pension rights. He would then be able to choose between early but small pensions and later but larger ones; he could also return to work and build up new assets after a period of temporary retirement. Starting earlier in life to readjust to easier work for the later years should be encouraged, e.g., by access to "part-time pensions."[1]

--When vacations are extended to more than three weeks per year, the individual should be permitted to accumulate the right to a longer leave after a number of years. This is just one possible method for arranging intermittent periods of nonwork if there is no system of general drawing rights which combines all the various methods.

--Everyone who has passed the age of compulsory schooling should be given a basic study credit to cover living expenses and tuition costs for a certain number of years. The individual should be free to use this credit at any period of his life. Instead of putting pressure on him to stay in school (college, university or vocational school) as long as possible without interruption, this system should be designed to encourage him to take relatively low-skill jobs in his youth. This maturing experience would be an advantage (rather than as at present a drawback) in advanced studies or high skill vocational training or retraining. The difference between high-status and low-status jobs could thus, to an increased extent, become a matter of different stages in each individual's life rather than of early and definitive class distinctions. The hot-house subculture of large student populations having no experience of productive work life might also be modified with more mature groups.

Those who do not use the study credit for its original purpose should be allowed to use it at a later stage for leisure or to supplement pension incomes. This scheme could be modified in various ways to provide the right balance between long-term equity and the provision of educational incentives to persons who have little spontaneous motivation to study. It could, for example, be argued that drawing rights should be more generous if used to finance studies rather than leisure.

---

1. In 1971 OECD's Council approved conclusions of OECD's Manpower and Social Affairs Committee on Age and Employment, which suggest such arrangements. A 1970 amendment to existing rules about voluntary early retirement introduced a right to return to work and to new build-up of pension rights in Sweden.

--Any further reduction of weekly hours of work should be based on the "dispositive" principle whereby employees are given an unconditional right--but not a duty--to reduce weekly working time to a specified number of hours (lower than the intended average for the economy as a whole). Those who have particularly strenuous jobs and therefore prefer shorter than average hours would thus get the support of the law. On the other hand, local collective agreements could still provide for somewhat longer than average hours where workers would prefer more income to more leisure. This suggestion is designed to counteract the "undisciplined" use of permanent overtime, which is now widespread in several countries. Where this habit has become engrained, it hampers a reduction in hours (which may be desirable for health reasons) because the workers are reluctant to lose their overtime pay. It also narrows the margin for varying production, which is needed to meet temporary changes in demand. It probably implies a collective self-delusion on the part of the workers, who may gain less through overtime pay than they lose through decreased purchasing power during the ordinary hours as prices are influenced upwards by the high marginal wage costs, i.e., those for the last hours of every week.

--Legal obstacles to the use of nonstandard working hours should be eliminated. In some countries, existing social insurance legislation makes part-time work unnecessarily expensive. In others, hours-of-work rules limit variations in working hours to a very narrow range, and laws protecting working women are sometimes detrimental to those they should protect. All such obstacles ought to be reconsidered to facilitate the introduction of "work a la carte," "flexi-time" and other variable and unorthodox patterns for the allocation of working time. There is now a growing body of experience which shows that permitting individuals to choose their daily hours of work can benefit both employers and employees.

Reforms Of Social Policy Concepts

The suggestions made here have even broader implications than those indicated by the terms "flexibility in working life" or "new patterns of working time." Implied is the introduction of to some extent new concepts in social policy: the offer of economic incentives to the most adaptable to use their own funds to undertake adjustments in the labor market (similar to countercyclical investment incentives to enterprises) instead of waiting for the most vulnerable and least adaptable to become "social cases." It also implies recognition that much of what we pay into the social insurance system is in reality a transfer of income among different periods in our own lives. Utilization of these funds (created by "voluntary forced saving" as a more convenient method than unstable and uninsured private savings) should therefore be freed from unnecessary bureaucratic supervision and determined to an increased extent by the individual according to his own preferences, under influence of more business-like incentives, only with limitations necessary to safeguard the basic need of social protection.

We may also hope that the suggested reform programs will counteract the current trend towards limitation of individual freedom which is growing in some countries, particularly in the guise of guarantees of employment security and other devices to keep workers from displaying high rates of turnover. The more one can feel certain of one's own mobility (i.e., one's capacity to move away from an unsatisfactory or painful work situation, without prohibitive loss of security or economic advantages, in order to find something better) the less will be the need or demand for protective rules and fringe benefits which appear immediately advantageous but which also tie the individual to a given place of work. If the trend continues without being counterbalanced by measures to supply the individual with more means to cross the barriers to his mobility, in the long run both individual freedom and labor market adaptability will diminish. The result can also be a polarization of the labor force between those who enjoy security and economic privilege on condition that they abstain from individual freedom of movement, and those who are formally free and untied to any employer but who have to live in insecurity and poverty with only intermittent and marginal employment. This should be prevented.

local and regional centers for recurrent education: yugoslav experience and orientation

B. SEFER

In no country, including Yugoslavia, has recurrent education been integrated into the educational system. However, in every country faced with the present crisis in education, thought is evidently being given to recurrent education as a new educational strategy. The great interest in recurrent education and the exchange of experience in this field between various countries attest to the fact that solutions are being sought, as present-day educational strategy obviously does not meet the needs of modern society. In every country, Yugoslavia included, there exists in the present educational system and in the strategy deriving from it certain "seeds" that suggest a future reliance upon recurrent education. These seeds have been produced within the framework of the present educational system. They will gradually disrupt this system as they grow, destroying its hierarchy and particularly its division into youth and adult education, as well as changing the form of the educational process and its contents. To a certain extent, these seeds are alien bodies in the present system. But there is good reason to believe that we are dealing with factors upon which will be based future educational strategy, including the reorganization of education and different educational methods and content.

In the Yugoslav Report on Recurrent Education, it has been stated that recurrent education refers to postcompulsory education, namely, secondary and higher education, that it encompasses under the same conditions all age groups (i.e., youth and adults), and that it offers the possibility to all employed to return to education, either for acquiring higher qualifications, specialization, or any other reason. This right can be exercised many times during a person's lifetime, with the employee retaining all his basic rights: personal income, participation in self-government decision-making, accumulation of work years for the right of retirement, and health and social insurance for himself and his family.[1]

Yugoslavia is a multinational community. For 20 years it has been building a system--socioeconomic and political--based on self-government, as well as on public ownership of the means of production, which has provided increasing opportunities for decision-making by the workers.

These characteristics of self-government and multinationality call for a high degree of decentralization, while modern society and economy call for a high degree of integration, coordination, and an ability to make numerous overall decisions. The role of the state is being supplanted by correspondingly constituted communities, on the basis of self-government, state decision and reinforcement by social agreement, and thus acceptable to the interests of the whole community. This, of course, is a process, but an open one. In education, for example, self-governmentally constituted educational communities have appeared, consisting of educational institutions, representatives of social community, and labor spheres interested in education. Instead of state-financed education, the financing of educational institutions is affected on the basis of separate social contributions from self-governing associations, with the emphasis on allocating more and more funds to education in the future.

Annually, some 400,000 Yugoslav adults engage in general and vocational training without interrupting their employment.[2] This represents an imposing 10 percent of the country's employed population. Some 75,000 employees (or two percent of those employed) are receiving junior college and university-level education.

These figures show the need for on-the-job training during active life, the interest of adult employees in education during the course of work, and that in the present system of education appropriate institutions exist that have adjusted their work to the requirements of adult education.

The majority of adults are being educated at secondary-level educational institutions, namely, at postcompulsory schooling institutions of the following forms:

---

1. Recurrent Education in Yugoslavia (Paris: OECD/CERI, 1972), p. 17.

2. Stevan Bezdanov, On-the-job training in working organisations in our socio-economic and technical and technological development (Belgrade: Yugoslav Research Institute for School and Educational Problems, 1972).

1. Training Centers Within Enterprises.

Training centers are formed as a rule in larger working organizations, and sometimes also as a result of collaboration between several working organizations and educational institutions in a particular region. The center conducts an analysis and programming of personnel, and its educational activity covers three fields: (a) general education, (b) socioeconomic education, and (c) vocational training, with the emphasis naturally on the last. Principally they conduct the training of skilled and highly-skilled workers, but in some centers training is also provided for technicians and other professional personnel with medium-level education. Training centers often initiate cooperation with other educational institutions. Frequently youngsters and adults are educated side by side, and it is here, in fact, that differences and divisions between youth and adult education are the least significant.

2. School Centers.

School centers are formed as a community of educational institutions that include schools for industrial workers, skilled and highly skilled; secondary schools as well as vocational; and junior college institutions, technical and vocational. In these centers, training is conducted on the principle of gradual instruction, which facilitates acquisition of knowledge starting from the skilled worker level, via technician, up to junior college engineer. This, of course, varies from one center to another, depending on specific conditions and on their training targets. However, within these centers, integration of second-level education and the first degree of higher education is already taking place. Here, too, both youth and working adults are being educated together, with the adults' work experience being taken into account. The school centers are as a rule located in major industrial areas, and are of regional character. The centers maintain close cooperation with enterprises or with other institutions interested in the qualifications of the personnel whom they train. Joint planning is done of work, educational content, school programs, etc.

3. People's And Workers' Universities.

Workers' and people's universities are specialized educational institutions for general and vocational training of adults in a larger area than the two types of facilities mentioned above. The prevailing orientation of these universities is the education of personnel that the economy needs. They conduct training on behalf of enterprises or factories in their special centers and also through other forms.

4. Schools For Adults.

Schools for adults are a component of the present Yugoslav educational system. They involve either special schools or special departments of regular schools. About one-half of these schools provide education for adults who have not acquired elementary, eight-year compulsory education, while the other half provide occupational education after the completed compulsory schooling.

Hence, a great variety of adult education exists in medium-level education, the more so when the training centers within enterprises are taken into consideration, and school centers in particular, providing a link between second-degree and first-degree education, and in fact between all levels of the educational system. At each level a real possibility is given the student to either acquire a qualification for a particular job or to continue his education at a higher level. The barriers between youth and adult education are already being torn down in the centers. We, therefore, consider that from these two standpoints (division of education into autonomous but "open" cycles that provide both job qualifications and the possibility of further education, and integration of youth and adult education), the centers manifest characteristics of recurrent education.

While the seeds of recurrent education at the higher level are somewhat less distinct than at the medium level of education, they undoubtedly exist there as well.

Junior colleges have become a massive form of education after the completion of secondary school education. As a rule, they last two years, offer higher job qualifications (plant engineer, economist, teacher, etc.) and also provide a possibility of transfer to third-year university studies. Junior college or advanced schools are not a component part of universities, and as such are not well received by the majority of universities and faculty-level schools. Therefore, there are considerable barriers to university entrance after the completion of a junior college program. But the economy as a whole and public services have welcomed these schools, as have youth and employed adults. Adults as a rule attend as extramural students. In the system itself, these schools have been conceived as a "closed" cycle (first degree) study at a high educational level, providing an opportunity either to enter employment or to continue studies. Thus, although limited in time, this represents characteristics of recurrent education, inasmuch as it is already divided into definite degree-granting educational cycles that offer the choice of either entering employment or continuing studies. Moreover, some of these schools, as a rule two-year, have divided the educational process into two further cycles of one year each (e.g., the Junior College School for Work Organization). At the end of the first year, students can take up a job or return to the production process as a supervisor, while the second-year cycle produces work organization engineers.

A certain number of university institutions in the country have introduced multi-stage interconnected training. The first closed cycle comprises the first two years of studies, which qualify the student both for work and further studies. The other two years (three in a few faculties) result in final qualification and a university diploma. Continuation of studies for a further two years makes it possible to attain a master's degree. This, however, is a characteristic of only a small number of faculties within the universities. The majority of university-level educational institutions continue to provide four- or five-year consecutive training.

The most significant involvement of university institutions in adult education is in extramural studies. In the past 10 years, this has led to a considerable decentralization of universities and university institutions. Some universities have opened external campuses, or training centers for both full-time young students and adults. Decentralization of university institutions has considerably increased the accessibility to the highest-level education. In this context, many new university centers or individual university institutions have been formed, as a result of direct action, interest, and cooperation between the universities and other partners, such as the representatives of the economy of a particular region, social services, etc.

Yet the least satisfactory progress has been achieved in terms of changes in the character of work, in contents and forms of training, and in the relations among the participants of the educational process at the university education level. The most important characteristic of recurrent education is the alternation of periods of work and education throughout the lifetime of an individual, with guaranteed economic and social rights.

The position of adults during their schooling can correspond to any of the following cases:[3]

1. regular education without interrupting employment, but with time off from work for a certain period;

2. regular education with partial job interruption and reduction of personal income;

3. extramural (part-time) education without a job interruption;

4. extramural education with paid leave while taking exams;

5. educational leave of absence without interrupted employment, but without personal income allowance;

6. shorter working hours with personal income reimbursement;

---

3. The Yugoslav Research Institute for School and Educational Problems conducted a poll on the "seeds" of recurrent education in a certain number of working organizations and educational institutions. All data to be listed originate from this poll and the monograph published by the same Institute in 1972.

532-819 O - 74 - 14

7. payment of traveling costs to the place where the educational institution is located;

8. payment in full or in part of the costs of education;

9. adjustments in shift work to facilitate education; or

10. credits and grants.

The study reveals that the working organizations did not follow any fixed model in granting privileges to the trainees. But in the majority of the polled working organizations, these rights have been regulated by their rules and regulations.[4] It has also been shown that the number of facilities offered to the workers undergoing education has in the past 10 years substantially increased, and that in this respect, the enterprises organized on a self-governing basis give the workers during their active life increasing opportunity for education. It is worthwhile pointing out still another feature: Yugoslavia is not only a multinational country, but is characterized by a great economic difference between individual republics and provinces. Research has shown that in more developed republics and regions a relatively greater number of employed adults is engaged in the various forms of adult education than in the lesser developed ones. This suggests that higher development results in a greater need for education and that the corresponding conditions will be created, i.e., that the necessary provisions and arrangements as to both the educational offer and the necessary adjustments in workers' socioeconomic situations will be provided. In a way, this present situation gives a taste of what the future will be.

This indicates that the economic and social position of adults is still not on the whole harmonized with the principles of recurrent education. But the results of polling show that various provisions and allowances during the period of adult education exist in at least 75 percent of working organizations, which can be looked upon as a relatively positive situation, although far from the economic and social possibilities that recurrent education could offer. In something more than 50 percent of cases, the interests of the working organization and of the individual being trained coincide. In the case of temporary interruption of work (without interrupting employment), the time involved ranges from three months to two years, and only exceptionally is it of longer duration. But the prevailing interruption lasts from six months to two years. Some 75 percent of the polled working organizations have standardized their rules and regulations on education, rights, and facilities provided for employees during the period of education. About 20 percent of those previously without qualifications return to the same job after they

---

4. Some 75 percent of working organizations have Regulations on Personnel Training which regulate the rights of the workers.

acquire the qualification, while 80 percent change their work posts. New jobs are taken on after the completion of training by 50 percent of those who enrolled for education in order to obtain higher qualifications. This indicates that the change of the qualification structure brought about by the acquisition of qualifications during active life has important effects on the position of the workers in the working organizations.

A Recurrent Education Strategy

The strategy of recurrent education in Yugoslavia, in my opinion, must nurture those seeds that exist at present, and incorporate them systematically in an integral strategy of education, which will have as its fundamental characteristic the alternation through the whole life-span of periods of education with periods of work.

The present-day school centers are of great importance for the future of recurrent education as they already educate both youth and adults, and as they are often not only established as second-degree education institutions of the gradual, ladder-like type, but are connected directly with first-degree level university training. Of service to labor markets interested in the personnel which they train, these centers provide for an alternation of periods of work and education, great flexibility of training programs, and flexibility regarding the exigencies resulting from economic and social factors. Of particular importance is also their curriculum, as it opens the possibility both for entrance upon or return to work and for further education. Previous work experience has already become not only one of the criteria for admission to these centers, but has also influence on an educational content and form. Factory workshops are utilized for training purposes by the centers.

In the same sense, the training centers within the working organizations can also serve the strategy of recurrent education although the fact that these centers are related to particular working organizations limits their range. For this reason, they should be regarded on the whole as local, while the school centers can be regarded as regional in character.

By a system of school centers, it is also possible to organize training of personnel required by social and auxiliary services. In this way, conditions would, to a considerable extent, allow the secondary school to continue as a general second-degree education institution, providing no work qualification, but directed towards studies at university level. Thus, in fact, the conditions would be created for the formation of a comprehensive middle school that would provide general, as well as vocational, education and thus greatly reduce the present differences between the general education provided by secondary schools and other schools at this level.[5]

Already at the local and regional level within the framework of the centers, many issues essential to the functioning of recurrent education can successfully be resolved, such as programming, financing, etc. Within the framework of the centers, equalized financing of both youth and adult education can be insured. However, still greater opportunities are offered by the association of all centers into wider educational communities, by means of which the planning of education development and its financing is affected. The present educational financing system can successfully develop into the mechanism of social financing of the school centers and of their educational activities. It remains, then, to resolve the problems involving economic, working, and other social rights of workers. This also requires appropriate financial means. Some working organizations will be able to bear these costs by themselves, but others will be unable to do so. It should be possible, through a corresponding contribution to be paid by all organizations, to establish funds to cover all social benefits for workers during their job interruption and education.

Junior colleges and advanced vocational schools, as mentioned earlier, already provide a certain link between postcompulsory schools and university education. Although these schools are not university members, they often offer a type of first-degree university education. Their development indicates great viability, and suggests that the reorganization of university and university-level education toward recurrent education should rely considerably upon them.

It is, in this respect, important to effect several fundamental changes.

There must be a closer link between these schools and the interested spheres of labor. While this could be achieved through the formation of regional centers of advanced schools in which would be involved, in an appropriate way, the representatives of these other spheres of labor, it could also be achieved by linking the present school centers, which presently unite secondary-level schools, with junior college and advanced vocational schools. As these school centers already have established contact with the interested spheres of labor, the problem of creating further links with other interested spheres of labor does not pose great difficulties. It is important that a corresponding reorganization be affected in this respect to enable a greater degree of joint decision-making and coordination.

Advanced schools must be linked with postcompulsory schools and the university. This can be achieved either by integration of

---

5. Conference on Recurrent Education and the Organisation of the System and Process of Education and Training (Belgrade: Yugoslav Research Institute for School and Educational Problems, 1972).

advanced schools into school centers, or by close cooperation in the programming of curricula. This coordination need not be very formal. Already the advanced schools provide the corresponding qualification to enter employment, as well as the possibility of further studies at the final two years of university.

And, lastly, the character of advanced schools should tend towards a further breaking-up of strictly connected years (semesters) of education into cycles, which would facilitate further education or the return to work.

It seems likely that the greatest objections to the changes toward recurrent education will come from the universities, particularly those with a long-standing tradition. The newly-formed universities and university institutions have shown themselves to be much more flexible and adjustable in this respect.

For the university to start adapting itself to the needs of recurrent education, it is first necessary to break down the present unwieldy size of universities into smaller institutions. Further, the position of full-time and part-time students should be made equal, which could be achieved by a system of social financing for the universities and their institutions. The university should represent "unity in variety," united or closely connected with advanced schools, faculties, faculty-level schools and academies. The present experience derived from the decentralization of university institutions has already yielded positive results in the links with other spheres of labor. Thus, the decentralization of university institutions, opening of training centers, departments, consulting centers, etc., would bring university institutions closer to the direct beneficiary and would facilitate the strategy of recurrence, the aim of which, among other things, is equality of accessibility to education at all levels, including the highest.

While a ladder-structured curriculum has, as previously stated, been introduced at a certain number of university institutions, the majority have not accepted it. If medium-level education and advanced schools could orient themselves towards firm links with other spheres of labor, and could organize on the principle of self-contained cycles instead of years and semesters, this would undoubtedly influence the reorganization and essential reform of the universities.

It is evident that recurrent education calls for very profound changes, not only in the sphere of education, but in labor, social insurance, etc. Presently legal regulations often limit such changes; they should be altered not only to facilitate but to stimulate such a development. Present state regulations on education present an obstacle to positive educational change. The state, by providing exclusively, or almost exclusively by law, the funds for education (although these funds are now distributed on the self-government basis, and not through the state budget), and by exerting its influence on the teaching programs, supports conservatism in education and separation of education from other spheres of labor. By gradually relinquishing this position, the state could open possibilities for links between direct interaction of education and labor. Thus, the role of the state should be to establish the conditions for the development of recurrent education.

Recurrent education is an educational strategy suitable to the self-governing society which Yugoslavia is trying to build. It enables, or at least creates conditions for, a substantial increase of accessibility to education (and this is where at present the principal causes of social difference lie). It also qualifies the individual for increased participation in the process of decision-making, and raises his productive capacity, resulting in expansion of the material base for better satisfaction of personal and common needs. On the whole, recurrent education provides an opportunity for man to better adapt himself to changes in life, a chance to unite the process of education and work, and hence to form an all-round and emancipated personality. And this is the very aim of the socialist society.

Conclusion

In Yugoslavia, people have for some time been considering the fundamental reform of education, as the country's rapid development and the system of self-government in particular have brought the country face-to-face with the necessity for educational reform earlier than it would have under other circumstances. Life itself, as this paper shows, has "sown" some seeds of recurrent education. The present situation shows that there are certain points on which the new strategy of education can rely for its future. But, recurrent education calls for a change of attitude towards education both of the individual and society. Recurrent education is a long-term strategy, which, under Yugoslav conditions, should be made an essential element of change and progress toward a self-governing socialism.

labor-management policies on educational opportunity

HERBERT A. LEVINE

Educational opportunity programs for workers and their families, as they appear in collective bargaining agreements and in unilateral offerings of industry and labor unions, have a latent potential that could significantly alter the educational systems of industrialized and developing countries.

While these programs take many forms, including inplant training, scholarships, individual and institutional grants, this paper will highlight two methods now subject to collective bargaining in a growing number of industries: tuition refund and industry-union education funds. A third method now under international discussion, generally referred to as paid educational leave, will also be examined.[1]

In these times of cutbacks of financial aid to social welfare and education activities, it is bewildering to know that--while millions of public and private dollars are currently being spent on these forms--there are hundreds of millions of dollars which are available but which are not used by workers!

---

1. This is the fourth in a series of articles since 1966 on the subject of collective bargaining and education. See H. A. Levine, "Educational Opportunity: A New Fringe Benefit for Collective Bargaining," Changing Education (AFT AFL-CIO) 2 (Fall 1967): 5-12. Readers who might also be interested in a later discussion of this subject should see H. A. Levine, "Education: An Emerging Fringe Benefit," Federationist (AFL-CIO) 77 (March 1970): 11-16.

The fact is that hundreds of thousands of Americans work for companies which offer tuition refund and other educational fringe benefits, but most workers do not take advantage of these opportunities although their need and interest is great. This is true despite the fact that in recent years tuition refund programs have caught the attention of some American trade unions which have begun to discuss seriously this potent fringe benefit at the collective bargaining table.

Two startling examples are the United Auto Workers (UAW) and the International Union of Electrical, Radio and Machine Workers (IUE).

The UAW and the automobile-related industries have signed agreements which provide tuition refund entitlements which could amount to over $200 million per year.[2] Recent articles in Solidarity report an expenditure of $1 million for 1971.[3] The General Motors stockholders report, which includes management personnel, reveals a maximum expenditure of only $2.9 million.[4]

The IUE and the General Electric Company arrived at a similar agreement in 1970 which provides $400 per person annually or approximately $57 million per year potential.[5] General Electric reports that in the first six months of the newly negotiated plan, only an estimated $154,560 was expended.[6]

One might say that a $1 million expenditure on educational upgrading of worker skills and education is an achievement over yesterday and is a credit to the union, the worker and the company. It is the potential, however, that grips the imagination and calls urgently for unions, management and the educational establishment to develop a delivery system capable of relating the educational needs of workers to the available resources. Why are not these funds linked into some integrated adult education effort in cooperation with the enormous sums spent by governments and foundations? Who is to blame? The union, the company, the school system or the worker himself?

---

2. See UAW-General Motors Agreement 1970 as a sample provision.

3. Howard Lipton, "A Door to Old Dreams," and "A Million Dollar Fringe," Solidarity (UAW) 14 (October 1971): 5.

4. Progress in Areas of Public Concern, GM Proving Ground, Milford, Michigan, February 1971.

5. See Individual Development Program negotiated by IUE and GE available from GE Headquarters Office, Lexington Avenue, New York City.

6. Activity Data Report - Individual Development Program, General Electric Corporation, December 1, 1971, unpublished.

Can The Promise Become A Reality?

It would seem at first that all parties are in favor of making the promise a reality. Actually, educational opportunity for workers and their families through the tuition refund process will remain merely a promise for some time. Its consummation will require far more serious attention by unions, management, the educational system, and government.

It might be useful to pause here for a moment to consider the nature of an educational delivery system which might attempt to meet the needs of workers in advanced and developing countries. There are, of course, differences in the specifics of education and training needs and in the availability of technology and finances, but it seems all countries might approach educational opportunity with a similar perspective. Education from the primary grades through the Ph.D. should be integrated with work, leisure, and the physical stages of life and not separated from it. Perhaps the saddest words ever written by a university career guidance officer was his expressed regret that a current graduate of his distinguished institution had decided to be a carpenter--when he might have become, at least, a builder's technician! All too often some of us think of education as existing merely for a career. Yet we have a strong tendency to separate work from education. We even overlook the fact that education _is_ work, while at the same time many have suggested various forms of payment for those who engage themselves in educational effort. These include scholarships, stipends, paid educational leave, sabbaticals, and other financial incentives. The argument has been made, with some justification, that individuals as early as in primary and secondary schools should receive a wage for their participation in the educational enterprise. This is based on the concept of the social values the society derives from an educated work force which can fulfill its role as an educated citizenry.

I am not quarreling with the concept of recurrent education in its sense of providing continuing education over a lifetime, but if one stresses educational effort as something which occurs "in alternation with other activities," there seems to be an implication of blocked out periods of work and study. For example, the idea that students completing secondary school should automatically break with the school pattern and engage in one or two years of work experience is anathema to me. It assumes that youth will not engage themselves in an income-producing work experience throughout the primary and secondary grades. What kind of a job will uninitiated youngsters perform in this postsecondary period? How will they select the job? Will the opportunities be as class, caste or racially related as in current opportunities? If the student has already been working, where is the advantage?

Perhaps a significant aspect of this problem is a latent invidious comparison of full-time and part-time study. Part-time study, innovatively provided and integrated with work, should be the core of any educational system attempting to reach the mass of citizens.

Workers and their children, if not all citizens, require continuing opportunities for part-time study and part-time work. When educational facilities are not close at hand or if research-oriented study requires one to move or travel, or if a teacher or curriculum calls for special residential periods of concentrated study, then the strenuous adjustment to job, family and daily patterns of living should be specially financed.

Work-study programs came late to our society which for too long has held back our youth from a potentially rewarding learning experience. Perhaps it might be well to consider ways to design an integrated program of workers, vocational and adult education based upon the worker's relationship to his job, career and lifetime aspirations. It should enlist the cooperation of unions, management, government, the school system and the individual worker and his family.

Unions have begun to turn their attention to the nature, quality and accessibility of education for workers as it is currently being provided by management and the school system. As indicated above, a growing number of unions are negotiating educational opportunities. Let us consider for a moment the concept of education as a collective bargaining fringe benefit.

American unions have maintained an aggressive interest in education from the early days of the struggle for free, universal public education. To workers, education has been the "glory road" upon which they hope their children will march out of the mines and mills into the offices and professions. Large numbers of their sons and daughters have moved out, but more have been left behind.

On the national political scene, unions are strong supporters of legislation providing for educational opportunity, including federal aid to schools in all forms, from primary grades through colleges and universities, vocational education, labor education, apprentice training and manpower development programs. Yet these programs, vast as some of them are, have not been able to do much about the inequality of educational opportunity in America.

Perhaps the largest single group deprived of college education are not, as one might initially think, the minority groups, the aged, or the unable, but rather Americans organized into unions who have achieved a modicum of success, including a regular, decent income, a home, a car, and a pension. What's more, these groups contribute a good share of the taxes that undergird the educational system.

Once upon a time, corporations required a high school education from all employees hoping for reasonable advancement on the job. With great reluctance under government and community pressure, some modifications were made which appear to alter temporarily the educational requirements. In fact, however, many corporations have raised their educational sights to the two-year community college, the four-year college and beyond.

Some workers appear resigned to live with their educational deficiencies; yet many yearn for a second chance to acquire an education. Almost all workers hope their children will be educated. But large numbers recognize that their children too may be stopped at the college gate for educational and financial reasons.

For this reason, although unions continue to believe that education for all to their fullest capacity should be a social charge on the public treasury, they have turned to their area of special expertise to obtain for their members through collective bargaining that which is not yet fully available in the larger society.

Paul Jennings, President of the International Union of Electrical, Radio and Machine Workers, expressed the labor movement's new look at educational opportunities when he described the basic purpose of the demands placed before General Electric by the coordinated bargaining groups. "Much of the undercurrents of unease in our nation today," he said, "stems from frustrations of opportunity. What we are going to do is at least start to remove that frustration among our own members by creating the opportunity for a member to get what education he wants, to expand his understanding of his job and the world around him and to send his children on to college."

Not all managements have a clear notion of how to provide education opportunities for their employees. Roger O'Meara, in a brief overview of his interesting National Industrial Conference Board Study of Employee Tuition Aid Plans, suggests there is an emerging tendency on the part of company managements to think of tuition aid plans more as a training tool than as an employee benefit.[7] Of the 200 companies, 35 have discarded the employee benefit concept; others are contemplating doing so. A study made in a food processing organization, for example, suggests that the company's educational reimbursement plan "might be better positioned under a training program, rather than considered a 'fringe benefit,' so that it could be turned into a development resource which could be more effectively controlled by management." It seems safe to assume, however, that

---

7. J. R. O'Meara, Combatting Knowledge Obsolescence. II Employee Tuition-Aid Plans (New York: National Industrial Conference Board, 1970).

unions will press even harder for substantial participation in the "control" of educational programs and training.

Collective Bargaining Agreements On Education And Training

In 1969 the U. S. Bureau of Labor Statistics made an attempt to study the training and retraining provisions in major collective bargaining agreements in the United States. The study indicates that fewer than 20 percent or 344 of the 1,823 major collective bargaining agreements studied contained training or retraining provisions.[8] These applied to 2.4 million of the 7.3 million workers in the study. Most of these agreements contained scanty and inadequate clauses which provided training under rather narrowly defined limits. Only a very few contract clauses in the study provided education and training in the larger sense discussed in this paper. There are some current interesting efforts being made by Local 3 of the International Brotherhood of Electrical Workers in New York, the Amalgamated Clothing Workers Union, sections of the International Ladies Garment Workers Union and some building trade unions.

The International Union of Electrical, Radio and Machine Workers, the UAW and the American Federation of State, County and Municipal Employees, District Council 37 have concentrated on tuition refunds and education and training funds.

Tuition Refund Programs

The significance of the funds involved in tuition refund agreements in the UAW and IUE were discussed above. It is interesting to note how in a relatively short time advancements have been made even before anyone has seriously examined the workings of the educational provisions. The initial UAW auto agreements called for a $250 annual per worker entitlement. The IUE-GE negotiations resulted in a $400 entitlement. The second round of UAW negotiations raised the current maximum in the auto industry to $500. Individual agreements reached by the IUE and smaller companies have so far reached a maximum of $750.

A particular feature of the IUE demands on GE was that the tuition refund plan be made available to the children of workers. This demand was deferred by GE without serious consideration at the time although an International Monetary Fund (IMF) study of comparative wages and working conditions in Latin America indicates that the General Electric

---

8. <u>Major Collective Bargaining Agreements: Training and Retraining Provisions</u> (Washington, D.C.: U. S. Bureau of Labor Statistics, Bulletin No. 14257-7, 1969).

Company in several countries already provides tuition and other educational costs for the children of GE employees.[9] Incidentally, since that time the International Association of Machinists, a party in the coordinated bargaining effort at GE, has negotiated an agreement with a smaller company which provides up to $1,000 per year per child of an employee covered under the contract.[10] In this interesting contract, a worker with three years of seniority is entitled to $300 per child. The entitlement is augmented in the amount of $100 each year thereafter until ten years when the $1,000 becomes fully available for each child in college. What better way for a company to encourage young men to invest their future in the company? Pensions and some other deferred benefits have lost some of their appeal. Young parents would certainly tend to stick it out with a company if they knew their children were more or less guaranteed a college education. This could help the company retain desirable employees. It surely helps the worker and his family meet one of the potentially heaviest financial burdens in family life. It could, if universally applied and adjusted upwards over the years, make an astounding change in the number of workers, their spouses and their children attending college. It is not unreasonable to expect that the next decade will see tuition refund programs made applicable to the children of workers.

Although tuition refund programs are new to the collective bargaining table, employee tuition aid plans have been offered by management since 1904.

Management's View Of Tuition Refund Programs

Roger O'Meara's study mentioned above provides considerable insight and information into the nature of the employee tuition aid plans in the United States and Canada.

"Tuition aid allowances paid participants in 162 companies in 1967 totalled nearly $17 million. Tuition aid plan costs equaled .04 percent of payroll costs out of current income." At first look, $17 million is a large subsidy offered by American and Canadian corporations to the educational upgrading of the workforce. The report, however, goes on quickly to point out that in 155 companies, the median rate of employee tuition aid plan participation is 4.4 percent. About seven-eighths of the participants, who are usually salaried male employees, completed approved courses successfully. Why are 95.6 percent of all eligible employees not participating in the plans? It seems strange that $3.5 billion of education entitlement should lie fallow in the face

---

9. Comparative Wages and Working Conditions (Geneva: General Electric Company, International Metal Workers Federation, 1969).

10. IAM Contract District 508 and Xerox Corporation, Sunnyvale, California.

of the great needs of American workers.

The companies, for their part, generally consider their current expenditures in tuition aid plans a "good investment."

"Employees who take tuition aid courses are more highly motivated to begin with. What their participating in the plan does is to identify a competent employee," said a printing firm executive.

"I know there is little evidence of causative effect, but every time we need a man to fill an important opening, the one we select has a record of tuition aid plans participation," declared an engineering firm personnel director.

An electrical equipment manufacturer asserted, "The percentage or turnover among tuition refund graduates is far less than the percentage among college graduates." This view is reinforced by a survey of bank employee turnover which showed "employees using the tuition refund plan were twice as stable as those who did not." A vice-president of a food company states, "We know that our plan is well accepted and that it has a positive effect on employee morale."

GE asserts that "the individual development program is an important step forward in helping both the company and employees meet challenging job demands of the future."

The NICB report concludes that "So many jobs are being changed by technological innovations that more and more companies are either starting or enlarging tuition aid plans to encourage their employees to return to school for the new knowledge they need to perform at peak efficiency."

It does not appear, however, that management knows how to motivate workers to participate in their plans, nor have they received any imaginative assistance from the school system. The NICB report tells us that "all but 13 companies" want more employees participating in their plans. The publicity outlets used to encourage greater participation include special booklets, recruitment brochures, letters, bulletin board notices, employee publications, meetings and recognition awards. Efforts are made to win the support of supervisors in promoting the plans. All this to produce a 4.4 percent utilization of the plans.

Using The Union Organization As A Delivery System

The one missing ingredient has, up to now, been the lack of union participation in the development and promotion of these plans. The union can be a powerful motivating force, its shop organization an effective vehicle, and its organizing expertise a necessary ingredient for cooperation among companies, local, state and federal education agencies and schools. In cooperation with management the social and political weight of unions can be applied to legislation and finances.

In the past, corporations have instituted tuition aid plans unilaterally, with unnecessarily restrictive clauses, and in many cases to enhance their public relations image. Few have built their plan into a consistent system of education for career development.

Workers have not responded to the educational opportunities available to them for many reasons. For the most part, they are unaware of the existence of these opportunities, despite the public relations activities of many corporations. Secondly, these plans have only recently been extended to the blue collar worker whose needs have become so clearly urgent in our time.

Adult workers are diffident in applying for educational opportunity. Supervisors are not concerned about educating men out of a specific job assignment. Without effective counseling, workers do not know where to start in terms of their long-range educational needs or aspirations. The school system has made little or no adjustment to their special needs in terms of physical location of courses, schedule of hours--what is available for second shift workers, for example?--rigidity of curriculum, prerequisites, examinations and other class-based mores which are at times contrary to the needs of workers.

One union, the IUE, has tried to inform its members about the educational benefits in their collective bargaining agreements and to assist them to participate in available programs. Already there are indications that there will be greater educational activity among IUE members.

Union-Industry Education And Training Funds

The second category of educational demands is the proposal for the establishment of a union-company or industry education and training fund. Both the UAW and the IUE asked GM to allocate one-fourth of a cent per hour to be placed in an education and training fund. A similar proposal was considered but not actively presented by the powerful USWA to the steel industry. The UAW states: "Neither the worker nor his child should have to regard factory work as a dead end; and working in a General Motors plant should not foreclose an employee's future or that of his children." It suggested that a part of these funds be used to finance the UAW family education center at Black Lake.[11] The IUE at GM and at the GE negotiating table wanted the fund for innovative experiments in labor, vocational and general education which would benefit the worker and his family. The IUE proposed that one use of the fund might be to serve as a stimulant to experimentation with ways to help workers reach out for the larger millions lying fallow in the tuition refund provisions. It was

---

11. Education and Training Proposal UAW-GM 1969, unpublished.

proposed to combine the fund with other resources, both public and private, to even further enhance workers' opportunities in the field of education.

While these proposals were not considered acceptable by such occasionally forward-looking companies as GE and GM, they were found acceptable by a number of private and public employers when presented by the unions in their respective jurisdictions. Local 3 of the International Brotherhood of Electrical Workers, Local 1199 of the Drug and Hospital Workers, Local 122 Hodcarriers, are among those who in addition to District 37 of the State, County and Municipal Employees (AFSCME) have negotiated an education and training fund.

"The City Wide Training Fund" which was established in accordance with New York City contracts with several locals of District Council 37 AFSCME is intended to provide training opportunities that will help employees to improve their performance in their current job as well as prepare them for career advancement. Twenty-five dollars per employee were allocated to this fund over the life of the three-year contract. As a result of the educational efforts made by District Council 37 stimulated by this fund, some 1,400 members of the Council are enrolled in GED courses alone. Technical and vocational courses enroll thousands more and a new college refund program is being offered for 1973. The union appears to be gearing up to participate actively in open university and external degree programs and has declared its intention of bringing to its members the fruits of new educational technology, including TV, cassettes, programmed instructions and other self-teaching devices.

An Exciting Prospect

It is startling that our formal school system, the adult educators, colleges and universities, too often preoccupied with seeking out foundations, government and private funds, have made no serious effort to tap these readily available resources. Corporations have failed to make their offer of educational opportunity a substantial reality, principally because of a lack of organization and a misguided emphasis upon "self-interest" limitations. The worker himself is largely unaware of the opportunities, reticent to apply, distrustful, and fearful of rejection. The formal school system is lacking in innovative approaches and appears to him to have little concern for his work scheduling and family situations.

American unions pressed by new technology, the changing character of the work force, the introduction of minority groups and the hard-core unemployed, recognize the direct relationship of education to income. They have brought the issue to collective bargaining tables.

Paid Educational Leave

Similar pressures have brought another educational demand to the collective bargaining table and, in some countries, to the legislative halls as well. The demand for paid educational leave, while it has tentatively and occasionally been raised in the U.S., has achieved a more prominent status in European labor negotiations and legislative effort by unions. The ILO meeting of experts on paid educational leave, organized by the Workers Education Branch in January 1972, helped develop an interesting and useful report on this subject for the 1973 sessions of the International Labour Conference.[12] Substantial attention has been directed to the issue of paid educational leave by the ILO since 1965 and it has become a high priority item of the Workers Education Branch. Essentially the ILO conference advocated "the access of workers to various types of paid educational leave, as distinct from holidays with pay for recreational purposes, in order to give them the opportunity and incentive to acquire the further education and training which they need to carry out their duties at the workplace and to assume their responsibilities as members of the community."

The ILO report informs us that under collective agreements in Belgium between workers' organizations and management representatives, paid leave is provided for workers under 21 for vocational training. In France, in July 1970, a national inter-occupational agreement was negotiated between the National Council of French Employers, the General Confederation of Small and Medium Sized Undertakings and all the major workers' organizations. Some 10 million workers are thereby afforded opportunities for training at the skilled and unskilled level. In Italy, several of the more important collective agreements in the chemical, pharmaceutical, metal, rubber, petroleum, graphics, paper, plastic and glass industries provide arrangements for both vocational and general education.

In England, some four million workers, under formal and informal arrangements, are entitled to some type of paid leave. These are sometimes narrowly job oriented and limited with respect to age. Some grants include full fees, salary, travelling expenses and subsistence; others have fixed weekly or monthly amounts. Some grants vary according to whether they are made for "sandwich" courses, block release or day release. But for over 1.5 million workers, the leave provisions are fairly comprehensive. In Sweden, collective agreements in the private sector normally provide that the employer must pay a trainee his full salary while on study leave. But this provision is limited to educational activities desired by the employer and the decision is the prerogative of management.

---

12. Paid Educational Leave, Report No. 6 (Geneva: International Labour Office, 1972).

532-819 O - 74 - 15

In Latin America, several different types of conditions govern collective agreements with regard to paid educational leave, primarily but not exclusively for vocational and technical training.

The ILO report contains many additional examples of collective agreements and details a considerable variety of provisions. I would like to call attention here to the fact that in France, Belgium, the Federal Republic of Germany, Algeria, Austria, Poland, the USSR and other countries, national legislation exists providing some variety of paid educational leave. Perhaps the Act adopted in Berlin in 1970 is illustrative of the more liberal interpretation of the purposes for which workers can request paid educational leave. The Act provides for release during working hours of workers under 21 years of age to follow recognized courses to further social or political education. Leave with pay can be claimed for up to a maximum of ten days per year. The leave is granted if the courses are organized by recognized bodies concerned with youth and adult education, including public education facilities, democratic political parties or workers' and employers' organizations.

Trade Union Studies

A significant area of educational opportunity of immediate concern to labor and to enlightened management and government has been mainly neglected by the formal school system and by most public and private educational plans for meeting the workers' needs. This increasingly important area is trade union studies.

Very few of the millions of new workers who entered the labor movement since the last significant wave of union organization, in the 1930's and 1940's, know anything about the social, economic, and political developments leading to the situation in which they find themselves today. Unionists need to learn the practice of unionism, the meaning of industrial democracy, and the ability to perform in a participating democracy. They need to know parliamentary procedure, union administration, and grievance procedure. Union leaders need to learn how to communicate imaginatively with the rank and file. They must learn how to compete with television, so that members will be motivated to attend meetings, serve on committees, and understand the union's position on inflation, civil rights, and legislative programs.

Some 24 universities have labor education services which are struggling with small staffs and smaller budgets to provide education to union members and staff. Yet there is little research in the field of labor studies.

Surely management, perhaps even more than other segments of American society, should recognize the necessity for labor education. Yet it has shown little acceptance of the need to educate union members to perform their union tasks.

In Europe, according to the ILO report, the introduction of educational courses in labor for trade unionists is itself of recent origin. Thus there is little legislation providing opportunities for such study although trade unions in a growing number of countries have been encouraging the introduction of such legislation.

European unions have fared better at the collective bargaining table in a variety of countries through formal and informal arrangements. In the Federal Republic of Germany, 118 collective agreements covering some 2.6 million workers provide some form of paid or unpaid leave for educational purposes, including vocational training and workers education. Under one-third of these agreements, leave for trade union training is available to all categories of workers. In England, it appears that some three million persons are eligible for some form of trade union studies.

It is not possible at this time, unfortunately, to discuss the nature and extent of participation by workers in these European legislative or collective bargaining opportunities. This would certainly seem to be a priority area for research for those concerned with recurrent education.

Financing Union Education Programs

Organized labor's efforts to provide educational opportunities for workers have generally been overwhelmed by the financial drain on its resources. Some unions are spending considerable sums on their educational programs.

The International Typographical Union has tried desperately to upgrade the skills of its members.[13] The ITU "new processes" program is a great effort, costly to the union, but it has had some impact in maintaining the skills of its members.

The Plumbers and Pipe Fitters' Union began an extensive training program in 1955 designed to improve the skills of its membership.[14] Other unions in one way or another attempt to meet the vast need for training and retraining opportunities for their constituency; yet, the total sum involved is woefully inadequate to the task.

The UAW alone spends at least $700,000 annually on a per capita allocation on its education programs, and its local unions spend

---

13. Rennard Davis, "Retraining the Unemployed: Skill Improvement Training for Electricians and Plumbers," Monthly Labor Review 84 (October 1961): 1074-80.

14. David E. Christian, "An Assessment of Apprenticeship," Monthly Labor Review 87 (June 1964): 628-29.

an even greater sum.[15] Another international union, the Communications Workers of America, estimates its budget for education at $240,000.

Unions provide $1.4 million annually for college scholarship programs, but few scholarships are for adult workers.[16]

Educational Opportunity At The Bargaining Table

The accumulated total of all U.S. trade union expenditures on education for the 20 years since World War II would not equal the sum that could be raised in one year by two cents an hour negotiated at the bargaining table. For instance, in the 57 years from 1908 to 1965, the International Typographical Union spent $1,937,465 on educational work for apprentices.[17] In one year, the ITU on two cents an hour could raise almost five times that sum.

Could industries adopt an across-the-board two cents an hour? There are many which could well afford it. The USWA in one year could develop a fund of approximately $40 million; the UAW, $50 million; the IUE, $11 million; the IBEW, $33 million; the Machinists, $33 million; and the Carpenters, $31 million.

Unions Could Support Educational Experimentation

Union-negotiated educational funds might be used to provide educational opportunities at all levels, from basic literacy to the Ph.D., for workers and their families. Education itself is moving into new areas and unions should be in the forefront of those pressing for new methods and programs. Unions could support experimental programs which the formal school system is reluctant to accept or slow in adopting. They could help attract thousands, if not millions, back into the educational arena and develop imaginative financial incentives, including released-time, work-study, vacation-study, and travel-study programs which are currently so difficult to incorporate into the U.S. educational pattern. One has but to think of the influence of the Ford Foundation and other private foundations in urban and international studies, to get some idea as to what these funds derived from collective bargaining could accomplish.[18]

---

15. U. S. Senate 87:2, Daniel S. Bedell, Prepared Statement.

16. "Union Education Aid Totals $1.4 Million," AFL-CIO News (October 22, 1966).

17. Annual Reports of Officers and Proceedings of 107th Convention, ITU, Washington, D.C., August 14-20, 1965, p. 325.

18. Martin Mayer, "Washington's Grant to the Ford Foundation," New York Times Magazine (November 13, 1966): 58, 150.

It is true that union leadership itself is only gingerly entering the arena of collective bargaining and education. What are now relatively unknown provisions tucked away in the recesses of negotiating packages or matters discussed at international conferences by a small group of forward-looking labor representatives may have a latent potential that could cause a revolution in the educational system of industrialized and developing countries.

impact of trade union education efforts on recurrent education

RUSSELL ALLEN

American unions have traditionally supported public education at all levels--beginning with advocacy of free public schools in the early 19th Century--as a means of achieving full citizenship for their members; later came the realization that an increasingly credential-oriented society, opportunities were rationed in large part by access to education. In more recent years, the impulse has been one of survival in a period of rapid technological change accompanied by skill and even occupational obsolescence.

It was consistent and understandable, therefore, that in the 1960's the unions advocated an "active manpower training policy" as a supplement to fiscal and monetary policies to achieve full employment. Thus, beginning with the depressed areas legislation and continuing through the vocational and manpower acts, the unions have stood for a large public role, especially a large federal role, since the state boundaries are artificial in economic, if not political, terms.

The unions have not yet, however, advocated anything as sweeping as the "educational bank" through which all individuals would have a right to so many units of postsecondary education. The exception has been the various "GI Bills" providing educational benefits to returning servicemen. The emphasis instead has been on federal aid to higher education institutions and to scholarship and loan programs, though with little emphasis on the latter.

Thus, American unions have supported piece-meal legislative programs that fall within the purview of recurrent education but have not yet addressed the general question of a total system of recurrent education.

This paper discusses the relationship of recurrent education to trade union education efforts, very much in terms of the American scene. Since the education structures and relationships between universities and unions--not to mention the economic systems and ideological bent--are obviously quite different among countries, what may loom as major problems here may be readily soluble in other national environments. However, from the labor education perspective in the United States, the close ties between union and university education are of major importance to better educational opportunities.

Labor Education

Workers' (or labor) education in this country is defined as those educational activities undertaken by unions and universities having the aim of improving the skills and understanding of trade union activists in subjects related directly to their union functions and goals. Since the union social, economic, and political program is broad in scope, however, these labor education programs frequently range into social and economic policy issues, as well as collective bargaining concerns.[1]

This definition of workers education does not include vocational education, even where the union is a partner in the educational program, nor does it include the general education of the membership, though here again unions have acted as facilitators in helping members achieve fundamental education and in some cases high school equivalency. The American unions have not seen it as their function in their education programs to provide their leaders or members with means to remedy deficiencies in general education.

A system of recurrent education, however defined, is tangential to labor education. Labor education is a form of recurrent education --limited to the training and education of a cadre of secondary labor leaders. It reaches only a very small number of union rank-and-file who presumably would be the candidates for any widespread recurrent education system.

The greatest impact on recurrent education might come if a financing mechanism is created that provides a universality of educational benefits and defines labor education as compensable under the financial provision. While labor education facilities would be hard pressed to meet any large new demand under such financing, the pattern has already been set and provision could be made by great expansion of both union and university programs along the lines already laid down.

---

1. For the most current, comprehensive treatment of this subject, see Lawrence Rogin and Marjorie Rachlin, Survey of Adult Education Opportunity for Labor; Labor Education in the United States (Washington, D.C.: U.S. Office of Education, Education Resources Information System, 1968).

The already-close liaison between union and university labor education is a positive factor in the American situation. Some 30 universities--mostly publicly-supported state universities--have at present time year-round extension programs for labor education. These programs are generally well-staffed and much of the union education work in the U.S.--I would judge most of it--is done in conjunction with these university labor education centers. University staff and materials as well as physical facilities are used. In fact, most unions would find it difficult to conduct their education programs at all without at least supportive services from universities.

A mechanism already exists for a system of recurrent education that permits trade unionists to return to school for varying periods of time to pursue a program of "labor studies" rather than taking the traditional academic curriculum. This opportunity is enhanced when the university also has a program of labor studies in either its undergraduate or graduate offerings, although the number of universities having such programs is much smaller than the number having labor extension programs.

One feature of such labor studies program should be some orientation away from the "tool subjects" which form the core of most university labor education courses. On the other hand, the program would end up being less academic than the normal student programs. It would almost certainly have a more vocational cast to it, although it would be vocational not in the sense of specific job or skill training but in terms of preparation for a career as a union official or as a labor functionary in a community or governmental agency.

The advantages of a broader based recurrent education of this sort for trade unionists are obvious. But particularly in the field of labor studies, some work and organizational experience of both work and organizations is essential to understanding. The self-selection of students into these programs meets the problems of low-motivation and of muddled career objectives and expectations.

Vocational-Technical Education

As mentioned above, unions have supported vocational-technical education in varied legislation and have an immediate interest in its extension for reasons of both job security and upward mobility. Unions have sponsored their own training programs in some instances under the manpower acts. This aspect of recurrent education, therefore, is not new and its mechanisms are well established. Provided it can be offered on a part-time basis, without breaking the employment nexus, it poses no apparent difficulties.

What does raise problems, however, is employer financing or released-time if the purpose of the training is to make the individual more employable generally. A laudable social purpose may be less than gratifying to a particular employer under these circumstances. The test of "job-relatedness" that is usually applied in such schemes may be the reverse of what is needed in a thorough-going system of recurrent education. When a worker is seeking a new career, job unrelatedness may be the correct prescription.

New Directions

Any consideration of recurrent education must take account of recent changes in the educational level of workers as well as stirrings within the academic community itself. Some changes seem to be creating a favorable environment for a break-through in further education.

To begin with, there has been a dramatic increase in the educational attainment of the civilian labor force since World War II,[2] as the following table shows:

Table 1. Educational Attainment of the Civilian Labor Force, 1940-1972.

	Percent completing 4 years of high school or more	Percent completing 4 years of college or more	Percent with some college (1 to 3 yrs.)
April 1940	32.0%	5.7%	
October 1952	44.5%	8.1%	
March 1962	54.9%	11.1%	
March 1972	69.2%	14.1%	14.0%

(18 to 64 years of age in each case)

Almost 70 percent of those in the labor force in 1972 had completed high school and 28 percent had some college. These figures, coupled with the changing age and occupational structure of union membership, suggest that a growing proportion of unionists have already had 12 years or more of formal education.

There are some public policy declarations in the 1972 Amendments to the Higher Education Act of 1965 that show uneasiness with present forms and indicate a desire for at least some modest experimentation. Among the stated purposes of the Amendments were these:

> encouraging the reform, innovation, and improvement of postsecondary education, and providing equal educational opportunity for all;
>
> the creation of institutions and programs involving new paths to career and professional training, and new

---

2. William V. Deutermann, "Educational Attainment of Workers, March 1972," Monthly Labor Review 95 (November 1972): 38.

> combinations of academic and experimental learning...;
>
> the introduction of institutional reforms designed to expand individual opportunities for entering and reentering institutions and pursuing programs of study tailored to individual needs...; and
>
> the creation of new institutions and programs for examining and awarding credentials to individuals, and the introduction of reforms in current educational practices related thereto.[3]

Even applying a generous discount to the customary Congressional pieties, these declarations of purpose show concern with the efficacy of the present educational system. In the future Congress may well be more receptive to more dramatic proposals.

Within the universities themselves, there are rumblings of discontent--and not all from students. One manifestation is the growth of the "external degree"[4] through the State University of New York, the University Without Walls sponsored by the Union of Experimenting Colleges and Universities, and many others. This is not new; it has been done by the University of London for over 100 years. The Open University in Britain is a prime example of adaptation to the needs of adults alongside the traditional higher education system.

Although its dimensions are undetermined, there is a latent demand for release from "The space/time/place/course sequence/credit framework usually characteristic of an educational institution."[5]

Union members, officers, and staff are caught up to some extent in the demand for credit for labor studies. In part, this stems from the credit pressure of the society; it is also a response to the accreditation of similar programs for businessmen and white-collar types. More and more union members are taking part-time college-credit courses in other subjects and see no reason why they should not also receive credit for their labor studies course.

---

3. Public Law 92-318 (June 23, 1972): 93.

4. John A. Valentine, "Higher Education: Has It Found a Better Idea?" <u>The Conference Board Record</u> 10 (February 1973): 61.

5. Report of the Commission on Non-Traditional Study, <u>Diversity by Design</u> (Washington, D.C.: Jossey Bass, January 1973): 11, Section I.

All of this runs counter to the historical currents of labor education, which was based on the cooperative rather than the competitive ethic. Overemphasis on credit programs can warp labor education programs and lead to an elitist psychology.

The Auto Workers have worked out Associate Degree programs with community colleges; the Operating Engineers have a dual enrollment system under which apprentices receive college credit (and an Associate Degree) for their classroom training. Empire State College of the State University of New York and Cornell University's School of Industrial and Labor Relations have started Associate Degree programs for unionists. Rutgers has had a labor studies credit program for some years, partly but not exclusively for unionists.

For the most part, these programs have been fairly traditional since most work is structured through the classroom. I know of no systematic effort to provide for external degrees. The AFL-CIO Labor Studies Center is seeking a national mechanism to provide college-credit programs leading to the baccalaureate degree for full-time union staff and officers. Work taken at the Center itself would form the focus of an individual's study but most work would be done in the home community through an advising team, using available educational resources. Formal classroom work is not necessary unless required by the study plan.

What the demand will be for this type of program is uncertain, but preliminary soundings indicate that there is a good deal of interest. The program represents a second chance for unionists who plunged into work without ever having college as a realistic, full-time alternative. Many of them have functioned in responsible jobs and have moved up to leadership in the union hierarchy. Since they do not have financial credits "in the bank," they will have to carry a large share of the cost themselves. But the financial cost is small compared to the cost in time, energy, and sheer endurance that they will have to pay to complete such a program. Serious experimentation should be done on this external degree program to help find workable solutions to the problems it poses.

Financing: A Critical Problem

If every individual is to have an opportunity, say, for two years of postsecondary education in an educational bank, the problem of financing must be resolved. Labor-management agreements on educational leave and tuition refunds deal inadequately with the problem of recurrent education. They are completely dependent on the accident of the locus of employment--the larger firms and the stronger unions. In addition, they do not provide for subsistence payments: educational leave--for blue-collar workers at least--merely provides for re-employment rights.

Realistically, workers cannot contemplate a year or more without income--or even with limited income from part-time employment. Not, at least, if one is talking about full-time study. The only precedent in this country on any scale for payment of both tuition and subsistence is the "GI Bill" for educational benefits for ex-servicemen. Similar approaches have to be considered if recurrent education is to be made available to workers on a substantial basis.

The GI bills have been financed from general tax revenues. That may not be politically feasible for a system which would include not only servicemen but anyone who wants the opportunity since such a commitment would be essentially open-ended with no way of calculating its cost for any given year.

A social security approach has been suggested with a trade-off between educational benefits and pension and unemployment payments. Such a scheme has much to recommend it. However, safeguards on pension reductions are needed. There is a precedent in manpower training programs for setting subsistence payments equal to unemployment benefits.[6] Heads of families with three years of labor experience could qualify for up to a year of training allowances equal to the average unemployment benefits in their states.

Use of the unemployment compensation mechanism seems to offer the most promising funding vehicle for recurrent education. Some changes would have to be made so that individual employers were not penalized under the prevalent "merit rating" provisions that tie any employer's tax to his own employment experience. The duration of benefits--typically 26 weeks--would have to be increased, and limited supplementary earnings should be permitted. Special arrangements would have to be made for that relatively small group not under unemployment compensation. Through this device, the individual would "pay" for educational benefits through his years of labor. It would remain to be seen what level of payroll taxation would be necessary to finance the scheme.

Without a clear-cut financing device, it is doubtful that tax funds will be voted out of general revenues on a continuing basis. The experience with manpower training should be instructive. When full federal financing expired, state programs lagged although matching federal funds were available. This was true even though, using only the narrow calculus of cost-benefit analysis, the programs were generally efficient.[7]

---

6. Mangum Garth, MDTA: Foundation of Federal Manpower Policy (Baltimore: Johns Hopkins Press, 1968), p. 19.

7. Ibid., p. 125 passim.

This is not to say that federal, or even state, expenditure for postsecondary education is pressing the upper limits in this country. In 1971, the federal government spent $4 billion on higher education; in fiscal year 1973, the authorization of Congress was for $7.4 billion, or 3 percent of the total budget. For the states, the national average per capita appropriation of state funds for higher education was $37.85 or 0.8 percent of per capita income.[8]

Nevertheless, there is strong resistance to tax increases at all levels; therefore, it would be better to rely on a certain and specific mechanism such as unemployment compensation than on general revenues.

Conclusion

Recurrent education, while not new, offers new opportunities if utilized through a system that makes it realistically available to many individuals. If labor studies can become a part of that system, both unions and universities can greatly expand their present labor education offerings. The way labor education develops within recurrent education will be very much a function of the public policies adopted. This development will not happen, however, unless a dependable financial mechanism is worked out.

---

8. John Sessions and Alan Ostar, "College Costs Squeeze the Worker Out," The American Federationist (AFL-CIO) 79 (November 1972): 23. The authors used U.S. Office of Education figures.

industrial experiences in middle management training

ANDREW DALY

The growth of training outside of educational institutions as an established function of industry has not followed consistent patterns throughout the world or even in a particular country. Large variations have evolved in the organization, the staffing, the philosophy, and the scope of the training functions.

Training takes place in all types of manufacturing, mercantile, and governmental organizations. It occurs in big and small companies, in one location and in multilocation organizations. There are one-man training departments, or even situations in which training is but part of one man's job with most of the significant training being done within the line organization. On the other extreme, there are training departments having several hundred or more professional staff people, and of course there are many organizations with no incompany training.

Some training staffs act primarily as consultants or coaches to the line organization. In other organizations the emphasis is on highly formal classroom activities within the organization.

Training content ranges from basic company orientation to the equivalent of university graduate level courses. The employees being trained range from unskilled workers to top scientists and company presidents. The nature of the training includes apprentice programs, sales training programs, customer training, engineering education, management and executive development. Just as important, the people who work in the training functions vary tremendously in their educational and experience backgrounds. Some instruct, other coordinate or administer the training function. These extremes make it difficult to generalize about industrial or corporate training activities.

Training outside of formal educational institutions to date has been implemented in the following major ways: (1) customer training, (2) basic skill training of employees, and (3) middle management development.

Customer Training has been undertaken to market, install, and utilize manufacturers' products or services and in the case of a government or public agency, to help implement a policy or procedures. Many changes in this category are not forseen except perhaps in the emergence of specialist schools such as we have seen in the area of computer programming.

Basic Skill Training has been provided by varied industries including engineering, manufacturing, sales, administration, finance, etc. The training has been done by industry and government in order to get the job done well. Some basic training is and will continue to be carried out in technical schools, but the training of staff in the basic skills required for performance on the job will continue to be done by the industries. One area in which significant changes may be anticipated is in the retraining of employees for second and third careers.

Over the last 20 years we have seen the need for management training develop and grow as business and systems of government have become more complex and competitive. The problems of today's world will result in the next two decades in an even greater growth in management training demanding a considerable amount of innovation skill and imagination. Toffler in his book has coined the term "future shock" to describe the shattering stress and disorientation that we induce in people by subjecting them to too much change in too short a time.

The pace of change--social and technological change, the knowledge explosion, and the population explosion--is so great that we must inevitably be influenced by it. We must have a pervasive sense of change. Change will be too fast moving and too varied to provoke a generalized and consistent response throughout the world or even in one country; it will require the utmost flexibility on the part of all levels of management, both a difficult and demanding challenge.

How will businesses and organizations throughout the world respond to these new challenges? There are a great many questions but no "right answers."

On the basis of discussions with many training directors throughout the world, the following summary has been extracted.

The first question asked was: "What changes that might have an impact on the future teaching and learning process are you considering in planning your industrial training programs for 1973 and 1978?"

The replies fell into three general categories. The first may be termed the environment response. The changes that the training directors indicated include: (a) greater international interdependence, (b) a more affluent society throughout the world, (c) expansion of multinational organizations, (d) the increasing use of automation, computers, and management sciences, (e) the increase in knowledge and rapid development in technology, (f) a shift from a production to a service economy, and (g) improved communications, particularly press and television. Also as part of environmental change, the respondents were in favor of a shorter work week (four-day, forty hours, or the flexible work week) and a shorter working life-span with persons entering the work force later and leaving earlier in their lives.

The second group of responses called attention to the changing population. Changing population was defined as changes in the work population such as: (a) a changing mix in the work force, (b) the "new generation," (c) minority groups, (d) increased number of women employees, and (e) senior employees.

The third area of response concerned other challenges and changes. Gordon Lippitt,[1] one of the best-known among the training men of industry, enumerated new directions in organizational arrangements, in the humanization of industrial processes, and in interrelations of formal education and industry. More specifically, he emphasized the following:

--Organizations will require new structures and processes to cope with change.

--Many jobs and skills will become rapidly obsolete, pointing to second and possibly third careers to keep pace with this rapid change.

--Employees will insist on greater responsibility.

--Conflict and confrontation will grow.

--Interaction between government, education, and industry will become more urgent.

Let us now look in more detail at some of the changes and responses.

The "new generation" clearly has different attitudes and values than those to which we have been accustomed. They claim to be less materialistic, and seem to have less respect for authority, or as they often refer to it, the "Establishment." They demand more influence on organizations, and request greater intellectual challenge. They express

---

1. Dr. Lippett is with the Department of Management Science, George Washington University, Washington, D. C.

532-819 O - 74 - 16

moral concern for social improvements. Their education seems to have given them high expectations, but they lack old time loyalty.

I do not think this should be considered a passing phase. Schools and universities are producing more high school and college graduates, and the population trends for the decade 1970-1980 show that persons aged 34 to 44 will decrease in relative numbers while persons aged 25 to 34 and those aged 15 to 24 will increase.

One statement from Australia forecasts that individuals and students there will expect to have a greater say in the learning process. The U.S. has experienced a display of student concern about the governance of universities, as seen by students asking and sometimes demanding more say in university practices.

Many countries expect a great increase and emphasis on employee and management training with, however, more attention to scheduled training programs by industry in place of casual on-the-job training.

It seems paradoxical that with the increase of better educated employees, some respondents forecast a shortage of competent, experienced managers. Today, with very few exceptions, most senior managers are in their late 40's and early 50's. Given the population trends, in the near future we will have managers and executives in their 30's and 40's. To assure the competence required for these high level positions, new training programs and not just business courses are needed.

Changes in the value systems of individuals and groups, particularly job values, were reported from several countries. Fear as prime motivator is lessening. In the past, the possibility of losing a job was a strong motivation for the job to be done well. Today with the introduction of laws protecting the employee and with substantial unemployment benefits, new motivations have to be recognized, developed, and implemented Education programs within industry play a key role in this activity.

The second question posed to the training directors reads: What can be done to make individuals recognize that lifelong learning is imperative?'

The second question reads: "What can be done to make individuals recognize that life-long learning is imperative?"

The society ahead is a continually learning one in which the knowledge industry is among the fastest growth industries in its production and distribution branches. To assure the motivation for learning, we must make sure that learning will be immediately productive and rewarding. The learning that will be successful is that which capitalizes on the experiences of the individual and provides immediate feedback in new jobs and job advances. Educational methods will have to be overhauled. Building adult interests and competence must be the cornerstone, with outmoded academic rituals debunked and textbook theories deemphasized. An environment conducive to adult learning must assume that the limits of understanding can be declared within a group without loss of dignity. Experience suggests that most people are willing and anxious to continue learning when there are meaningful, practical, effective opportunities for them to do so. They are receptive to change. The willingness of personnel to retrain when given the opportunity has certainly been proven. The mining and textile industries have experienced technical development with ever increasing speed. Thus, two and three careers in a person's lifetime will be common, putting heavy demands on incompany training departments.

Training to overcome problems of technological advance is matched in its demands on industry by training for employee career paths. Organization career ladders are important management tools that require identification of skills and knowledge minimums for each part of the industrial organization, and they require adequate recognition and rewards for the accomplishment of the above minimum achievements unless rewards are restricted to those who meet minimum requirements.

"What changes in the level of knowledge and skill will be required between now and 1978?" This question in the survey was intended to identify those areas that today are not adequately covered and to look further into the future to see where improvement is required. Among the industrial training needs to be filled by subsequent action, these types of training were noted: training for conference leadership and in group dynamics skills, training for planning and goal setting, imparting better understanding of computers and their applications, training in principles of organization, education in social, political and economic issues confronting industrial organizations and management, training in use and control of own leadership style, imparting knowledge about motivation theories and their applications, developing teaching and coaching ability, aiding in career planning and individual growth, and developing ability to work in task force groups.

Within industrial training programs, subordinate managers are surveyed to determine the needs of their superiors and to formulate training programs to meet those needs. The lack of ability to teach and coach subordinates and to assist in career planning are critical areas often identified. Inquiries suggest that more emphasis in training is needed on theories of motivation and leadership which would insure that the reward system is consistent with those items on which a manager is being held accountable.

"What can companies do to improve the training system so as to contribute to the continued growth, competitiveness, and survival of the organization?" Preventive rather than corrective training was emphasized in the responses. To assure such prevention, each manager must understand the learning process.

Training must be viewed as a management tool; it is the way management gets its job done, not solely the function of the training department in the classroom. Furthermore, evaluation of training is essential. The fact that a training program or school is popular is not a valid measurement of its need or its effectiveness. More quantitative research about evaluation should be used. Has it improved performance and accomplished the objectives now? Six months later? A year afterwards? This is important, particularly in terms of job performance.

To achieve better training programs, industry must move away from training fads and gimmicks, including packaged programs that are unrelated to the real needs of the organization. Many packaged programs, although good in design, are not related to the needs of specific organizations or persons. Where possible, industry has little option other than to build its own "inhouse" capabilities. Outside experts and resources cannot be depended upon to do the firm's job well.

Training rests on a research and development base. Much more research and development must be done by training organizations to secure creative and innovative approaches to the solution of business and administration problems. These solutions should be presented in nontraditional ways. Excessive use of role playing, case studies, group dynamics, etc. that do not assist in achieving the program objectives should be avoided.

Motivation is an essential ingredient of training. Motivation depends on reinforcement and followup experience for trainees that permits persons trained to apply what they have learned to the job. Individuals, in order to learn, must be self-motivated. Systems should be developed whereby employees are able to elect or select those opportunities for training that will correct or improve areas in which the employee is dissatisfied or deficient. This process, of course, leads into career planning, which itself encourages the employee to continue learning. No one should be forced into a pre-planned program for which he feels no need.

"What type of cooperation between companies, between higher education and companies, and between professional organizations and companies is possible and recommended to assist in meeting these training and educational requirements?" Some business organizations will and should be able to conduct all essential education activities, but many others for reasons of size, cost, and staff, must rely on outside assistance. The survey results of this question indicate major weaknesses in the ability of higher education to assist business. Responses from many nations including the United Kingdom, Brazil, Australia, as well as the U.S., confirm these weaknesses. There is a great communications gap between business and formal education. Education does not understand the needs of business and, therefore, does not provide programs to assist in meeting those needs. Some new relationships and new types of institutions are essential to meet the different and rapidly changing kinds of learning requirements, and to develop the capacity to fully utilize new educational technologies.

Educational institutions may exist--some already do--without faculty or campus and are accredited for degree purposes, equivalent work experiences, and company-taught courses. Professional associations or even companies may be able to award credit for courses in the future, with the rapid expansion of informal education. This suggests that a company or a combination of companies may establish their own educational centers, and will be able to grant degrees, particularly at the graduate level. Degree granting by informal means points to a need for new attention

"How will the role of the professional training person change in the next five to ten years?" In the years ahead, training departments of industrial firms should comprise a mix of both professional educators and experienced businessmen. These departments should be capable of scanning training programs and determining their use in terms of an adequate return on the investment for the organization. By such determination they will earn the right to be part of the senior organizational planning group.

Professionalism in the training field is needed. Staff members should be well educated and above all they must have creditability and acceptability. The impact and influence trainers can have on the organization is large. The training officer or manager, by the information he has and acquires, can contribute to decision-making regarding changes in organization or other changes that influence or impact manpower management. As such uses are made, the training professional's image will gradually change from that of a teacher operating only in the classroom to that of a consultant and advisor to managers. A trainer must be a learning and information specialist and be able to plan programs or educational experiences, determine needs, establish objectives, be current on the most advanced educational technology in learning systems, and above all, be able to continually evaluate and quickly change educational efforts. To achieve this type of training program, organizations must be willing to invest money, resources, manpower, student time--which is employee time--in the educational effort, whether this effort is within, or outside the company. In the future, organizations must have comprehensive training programs and not just merely provide lip-service to this very important company and management responsibility. The recognition system for employees and managers must support this concept. Line managers, however, cannot abdicate the total responsibility to the training department, but must continue the learning process during the day-to-day operations.

Each organization has the responsibility for the growth and development of their human assets just as much as the capital assets and profits. The nature of the present and future industrial society is changing to organizations of workers who put knowledge to work, and who work with their minds rather than their hands.

to be given to university training on general concepts of curriculum areas rather than for specific knowledge and applications in a particular company. Concentration of training inhouse comes about for reasons of a proprietary and confidential nature. The concern of new centers for industry-sponsored training must be for quality of education and the training evaluation that shows that the company can save money in training and also get better performance results using the services of centers of training in place of inhouse training.

A move to multicompany training in higher education requires much greater attention to the selection of instructors, the training of instructors, and the selection of participants. A better exchange of talent needs to be developed between the training centers and business. Capable business representatives should teach in schools, and school and college instructors should have greater work experience in the area of their specialty. Some action has already started in this area, but more exchanges have to take place. The problem of rewards and remuneration needs particular attention.

A sufficient supply of trained and capable instructors to serve the needs requires new and immediate action. New and different learning and education concepts and training technology will be needed. Already we are beginning to hear of technology and methods such as programmed instructions; instruction by video tapes and video cassettes; instrumented training methods; simulations and related training exercises; laboratory training; computer assisted instruction (CAI) in the office and perhaps even in the home; and closed circuit TV. By and large, the technology to improve the methods of teaching exist, but the application needs attention and improvement. The reception by educational institutions and students to these methods is often limited by preconceived attitudes.

The trend seems to be towards learner-controlled instruction. A variety of resources are provided for the students' use after he has determined his specific objectives through self-analysis instruments or other types of pretesting. An increase is indicated in training based upon the findings in the behavioral sciences ranging from sensitivity training in its many aspects to organization development and team building. It is possible that organization development or team learning experiences whereby two, three, or four levels of management in an organization participate in a learning experience simultaneously, will assist in the creation of a bridge, between staff and managers.

Many of the technologies are already in use in industrial training. As a result, newer teachers or educators will become more planners of the learning process, consultants, as it were, to the students, and creators of learning materials, than they have been in the past. Education is likely to become a part of each person's way of life. It will be essential, therefore, that management be ready to assist subordinate staff members in working through their career plans and developing those skills that would be most helpful to both the employee and to the organization.

labor market improvement and economic trade-offs

CHARLES C. HOLT

The prospect of "recurrent education" raises many new questions on how work experience complements formal education. Unfortunately the work side of the relationship cannot be taken for granted. What aggregate economic policies should be pursued to influence general economic conditions, and how these conditions influence labor markets and interact with governmental manpower and educational programs are vital questions that need to be analyzed jointly. This paper concerns the compliment to the educational side of recurring education, recurrent work.

Inflation And Unemployment

Lord Keynes developed an analysis for understanding the unemployment problem of the 1930's and prescribed a solution in terms of regulating aggregate demand with monetary and fiscal policy. As a result, the gross business cycle has become a problem of the past. Unfortunately the two major economic aggregates, inflation and unemployment, are perversely linked so that efforts to reduce unemployment tend, with a lag, to stimulate wage and price inflation. Either problem alone could easily be resolved but in some countries no aggregate demand policy exists that would successfully resolve both. A compromise is the best policy, but it may be far from satisfactory, depending on the inflation-unemployment

---

* This paper draws on research supported by the Manpower Administration of the Department of Labor, the National Science Foundation and the Ford Foundation. The views expressed are those of the author and do not necessarily reflect those of The Urban Institute or its sponsors.

trade-off prevailing in the country at the time. For example, figure 1 gives Erich Spitaller's[1] estimates of the trade-off for 17 countries. This and other work indicates that the U.S. and Canada must cope with much more adverse Phillips curves[2] than most European countries. However, increasingly severe European inflation problems in recent years may indicate worsening trade-offs there. The long lag in the inflation response can make the regulation of aggregate demand a complex dynamic control problem. The effect of such lags can be seen in figure 2[3] which shows the recent inflation-unemployment history of the U.S. and an estimate of its long run trade-off relation based on data through 1969. For the U.S., the best that aggregate demand policies can achieve with tolerable inflation still leaves an unacceptably high level of unemployment, and with it a high degree of dispersion of unemployment rates between different groups of workers,[4] a similarly high dispersion of earnings, and low rates of worker upgrading.

Improving the inflation-unemployment trade-off requires structural changes in the economy through one or more of the following policies: dynamically directing the composition of demand toward relatively slack industries and regions, reducing the market power of unions and employers through union and antitrust policies, reducing the inflationary exercise of those powers through incomes policies, restraining inflation through direct taxation of wage and

---

1. See Erich Spitaller, "Prices and Unemployment in Selected Industrial Countries," International Monetary Fund Staff Papers 18 (November 1971): 528-569. Estimates of Phillips curves for Japan, U.S., and U.K., using the same labor market specification, are presented in C. Duncan MacRae, Stuart O. Schweitzer, and Charles C. Holt, "Job Search, Labor Turnover, and the Phillips Curve: An International Comparison," in American Statistical Association, 1970 Proceedings, Business and Economic Statistics Section (Washington, D.C.: American Statistical Association, 1971), pp. 560-564.

2. Named for British economist A. W. Phillips, who first quantified the relationship between inflation and unemployment overtime.

3. The inflation rate is measured as the percentage increase in the GNP deflator over the agerage of the previous year and the unemployment rate is the annual average percent of the civilian labor force not employed. A full discussion of this figure and broad policy implications is given in Charles C. Holt, C. Duncan MacRae, Stuart O. Schweitzer, and Ralph E. Smith, The Unemployment-Inflation Dilemma: A Manpower Solution (Washington, D.C.: The Urban Institute, 1971).

4. For example, a 4.5 percent national unemployment rate for the U.S. carries with it a 31 percent unemployment rate for black teenage girls.

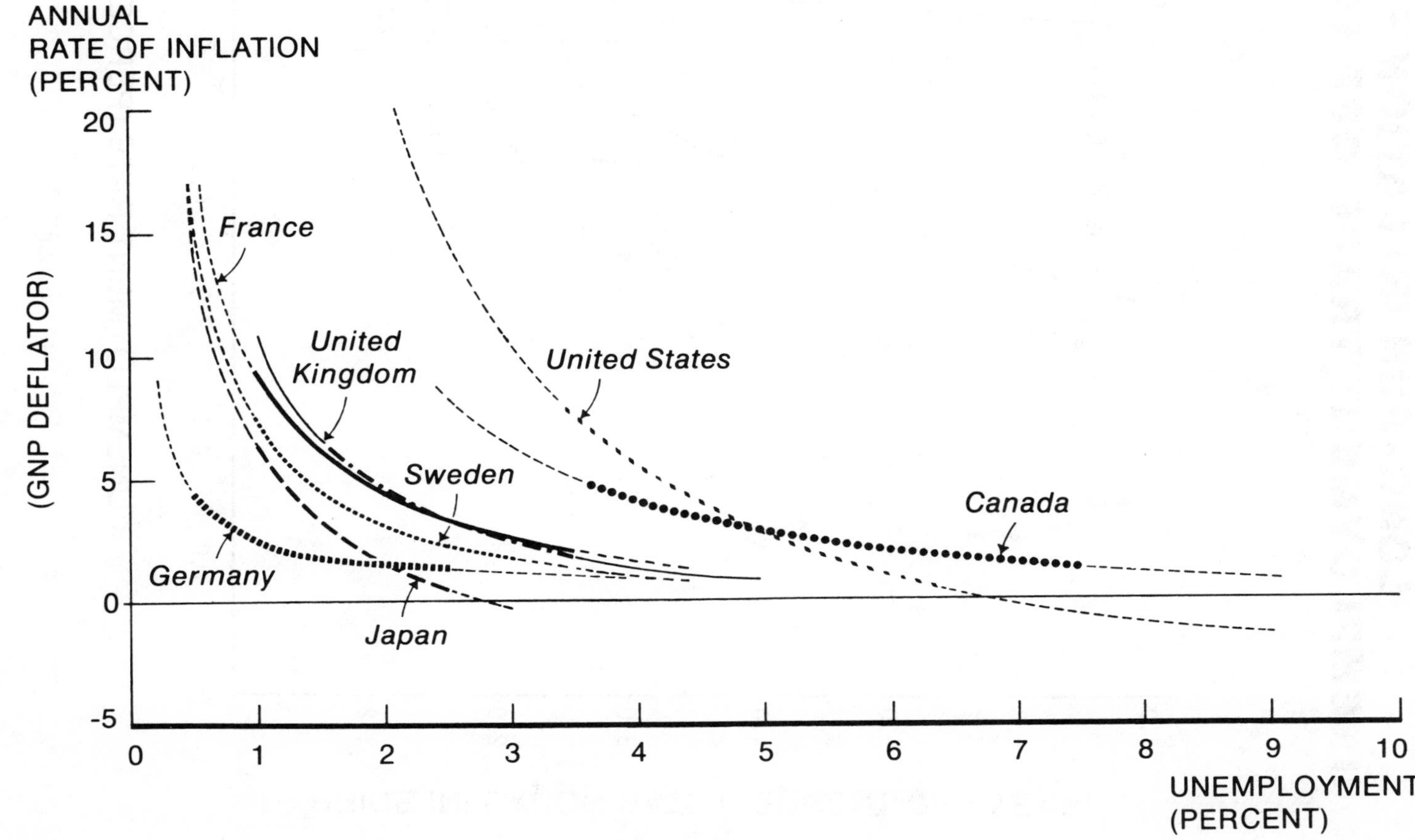
STEADY STATE RELATION BETWEEN
INFLATION AND UNEMPLOYMENT
ANNUAL
RATE OF INFLATION
(PERCENT)
(GNP DEFLATOR)
20
15
10
5
0
-5
0
1
2
3
4
5
6
7
8
9
10
UNEMPLOYMENT
(PERCENT)
France
United
Kingdom
United States
Sweden
Canada
Germany
Japan

FIGURE 1

LONG-RUN INFLATION—UNEMPLOYMENT TRADE-OFF 1954-1969*

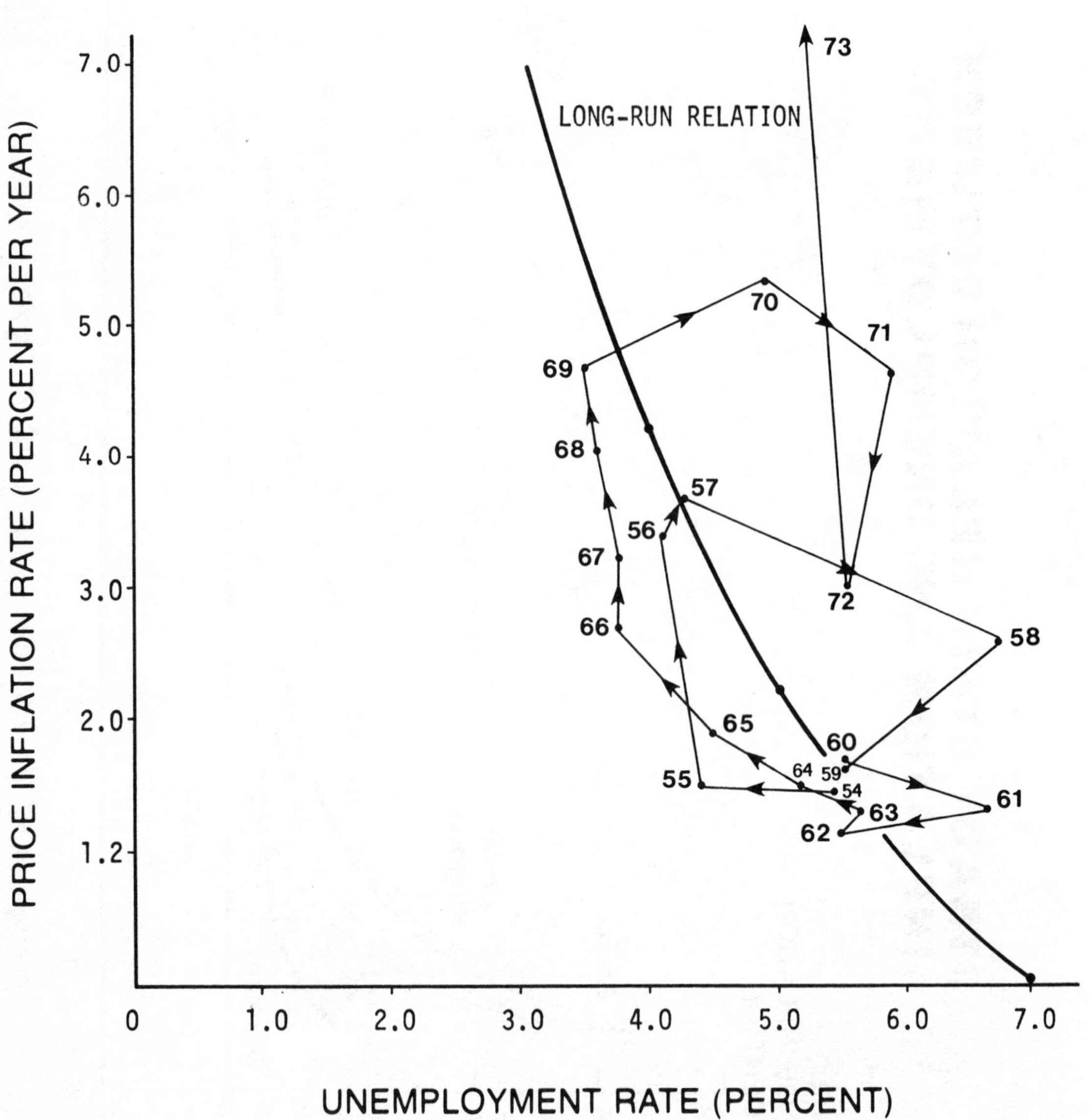

FIGURE 2

*The 1973 figures for the unemployment rate and price inflation are based on the first two quarters of 1973.

price increases, and/or improving the operation of the labor market so both unemployment and inflation are reduced. Unfortunately, the relative efficacy of such policies is not well understood, and may involve one or more of the following: severe political problems, long-term efforts, high costs, and economic inefficiency.

Whether or not this problem is solved will have an important influence on the economic environment in which recurrent education operates. Improving the operation of the labor market is one of the more promising solutions. Recurrent education could contribute toward that solution as well as benefiting from it. Before considering this issue of interdependency, we need to look at the labor markets themselves.

The Operation Of The Labor Market

A great deal of progress has been made in recent years in developing and testing the job search turnover theory of the labor market and its relation to the inflation process. Although there is still substantial disagreement on the quantitative magnitudes involved, an important consensus is developing among economists on the essential processes that are involved.

It is necessary to discard the simple static conception of the labor market in which the demand for goods and services directly determines the labor that will be employed, leaving the balance of the labor force unemployed. This implies that two kinds of people are in the labor market, the employed and the unemployed. Of course, an increase in aggregate demand is indicated when unemployment is below the best trade-off point on the Phillips curve. But a more refined analysis is needed that takes into account changes in labor participation, productivity, and population. When we find that increases in demand lead to excessive inflation, the above static picture of the labor market offers no useful insights as to what other policies might help to reduce unemployment without causing inflation.

A much more accurate and useful picture of the labor market stresses its dynamic character. There are large flows of people making transitions continually between family pursuits, unemployment, and work. "Unemployment" does not describe a type of person, but rather designates a state lasting weeks or months through which large numbers of people pass. Then the direct determinants of the stock of temporarily unemployed people are seen as the quit and layoff rates which determine employment turnover, the search time required to land new jobs, the withdrawal rate of discouraged workers who abandon further job search, and finally the rate at which people leave family pursuits for job search. The duration of search to find a job is, of course, influenced by the number of available job vacancies which in turn is influenced by aggregate demand, but many of the other flows into and out of unemployment also are influenced by the level of vacancies.

Increased economic demand has an impact on reducing unemployment. However, institutional and motivational factors also lead workers to change their probabilities of making various labor market transitions. These in turn can change the unemployment rate even though demand remains constant.

The operation of labor markets is further complicated by their inherent segmentation by geography, occupation, race, sex, age, union seniority, and licensing. Of course, workers can make transitions between segments by moving, training, job restructuring, and the lowering of barriers.

The various flow rates and search times between jobs differ between different segments of the labor market. Welders may find jobs quickly in some regions and slowly in others. Within a single area, bookkeepers may have abundant opportunities, but there may be a glut of school teachers. Six months later all of these situations may be reversed.

In general, the numbers of workers and jobs in the various segments and the number of workers in various states of fulfillment or frustration motivate workers to enter the labor force, leave it, accept jobs, or quit them. These, in turn, affect the motivations of employers to create vacancies, make job offers and lay off workers. Interactions between employers, workers and unions determine changes in earnings and labor costs.

From this complex labor market process, an equilibrium pattern of employment, unemployment, labor participation, and wage rates tends to establish and maintain itself. Some groups of workers end up with high unemployment rates and others with low. In the U.S., the former groups are made up generally of workers who are young, black, female, and low-paid. The differences in unemployment rates are largely accounted for by differences in turnover rates rather than differences in job search times.

On the other side, changes in aggregate demand change the levels of vacancies in the various segments and, in turn, change job search times and unemployment rates. As aggregate demand increases, the vacancy-unemployment ratios rise in the various market segments. Pressures to increase wages and reduce hiring standards are thereby generated. Simultaneously, prices increase. The resulting price and wage advances interact to mutually support each other so that the levels of wages and prices are inflated and produce arbitrary transfers of income and wealth in the economy. The collective market power of unions and employers, of course, influence these atomistic adjustment processes.

If the resultant inflationary rate is too high for governmental authorities, actions are likely to be taken to reduce aggregate demand. This occurs even though many workers are still in overcrowded labor market segments with low wages and high unemployment. At the same time, segments of the labor and product markets that are very tight generate inflation throughout the economy through diffuse wage and price interactions. Thus, the reduction in aggregate demand which is undertaken to restrain inflation tends to occur long before prosperity has reached the most handicapped segments.

Barriers between segments often limit the search for a new job. Friends and relatives can tell of local job opportunities, but use of such channels by employers and workers helps to maintain highly segmented markets and long search times.

The inequities and production losses which result from an inefficient and segmented labor market can impose intolerable burdens on a society. The flux and uncertainty that characterizes labor markets put an undue premium on the worker's knowledge of market opportunities, and his ability and willingness to search, change occupations, and move. Employers may think the rigidities of a highly segmented labor market serve usefully to block the "escape" of their workers. On the other hand, workers seeking to increase job security and advancement support the erection of barriers in the form of union seniority, credential requirements, discrimination, etc. Unfortunately such segmented barriers contribute to unemployment, and the inefficiency of the market as a whole. The recognition of these problems has led to recommendations for governmental intervention.[5]

Manpower Programs And Policies

If the classical justification for a laissez-faire system--that social optimality of the decisions made by workers, consumers, and businessmen in their individual self-interests--were true for workers, there would be no case for such intervention.

However, it is well known that worker decisions do not necessarily achieve the social optimum of freedom and self-interest. A strong case can be made for social intervention when: (1) all the costs or benefits of the action in question do not fall exclusively on the decision maker, (2) social welfare would be increased by redistributing income, (3) markets for credit discriminate against investments in human capital because it cannot be used as collateral, or (4) the combination of high risk and risk aversion at the individual level lead

---

5. For earlier work urging extensive manpower programs, see G. Rehn, "Trends and Perspectives in Manpower Policy," in M. S. Gordon, ed., _Poverty in America_ (San Francisco: Chandler, 1965); and Manpower and Social Affairs Committee, _Adult Training as an Instrument of Active Manpower Policy_ (Paris: Organisation for Economic Cooperation and Development, June 15, 1971).

to less than the social optimum investment in human capital.[6]

The external benefits from education have long been widely understood and used to justify the social support of education. The other points have been considered mostly by economists, but the applicability of all of these to the manpower area has been increasingly understood and used to justify governmental intervention. Because of the similarities and interrelations between manpower programs and recurrent education, the above points also can serve to justify governmental responsibilities in the latter area as well.

The historic pursuit of human fulfillment and democratic values supplies at least part of the motivation for social intervention, but it has been and will continue to be difficult to supply fully adequate hard-nosed justifications for such programs and policies. Subtle conflicts are bound to occur as bureaucratic agencies try to contribute to the liberation and development of individual workers. Some _mix_ of public and private decision-making is needed.

Making a case for governmental intervention to increase workers' job options is relatively easy. Manpower and educational programs are widely deemed socially valuable. The hard question is determining the appropriate extent of the programs. C. Duncan MacRae, Stuart O. Schweitzer, Ralph E. Smith and I have made a preliminary analysis[7] of this issue for American manpower and have reached the conclusion that a very substantial expansion of manpower programs is needed to improve the trade-off between inflation and unemployment in the United States. As indicated previously, the unemployment rate depends importantly on the behavior of most workers and employers involved in large turnovers rather than the behavior of a small group of chronically unemployed. Thus, a very _extensive_ program is required to shorten the placement process and extend employment duration. The costs of that program would be high but the benefits great. Several European countries, most notably Sweden, have more fully developed manpower programs,

---

6. Burton A. Weisbrod, "Benefits of Manpower Programs: Theoretical and Methodological Issues," in Gerald C. Somers and W. D. Wood, eds., _Cost-Benefit Analysis of Manpower Policies: Proceedings of a Non-American Conference_ (Kingston, Ontario: Queen's University Press, 1969).

7. C. C. Holt, C. D. MacRae, S. O. Schweitzer, and R. E. Smith, _Manpower Programs to Reduce Inflation and Unemployment: Manpower Lyrics for Macro Music_, Paper 350-28 (Washington, D.C.: The Urban Institute, December 1971). Robert Hall has made judgmental estimates of program impacts which are less optimistic than our largely econometrically-based estimates. See Robert Hall, "Prospects for Shifting the Phillips Curve through Manpower Policy," _Brookings Papers on Economic Activity_ 3 (1971): 659-701.

and that may partially explain their superior inflation-unemployment trade-off relations compared to the U.S.

Unfortunately, our knowledge of the complex labor market described above is still inadequate to make valid estimates of costs and benefits. But we estimated that an increased expenditure of $14 billion on manpower programs in the U.S. would enable an increase in GNP of $30 billion.

I would like to summarize the particular manpower program and policy recommendations my colleagues and I believe are needed by the U.S. These recommendations cover four broad program areas: job matching services to speed placements and reduce turnover; vocational counseling and employment opportunities for youth to reduce their high turnover and increase subsequent productivity; and training and job restructuring to reduce inflationary labor shortages and pockets of high unemployment. Research is needed, however, to determine how to effectively implement these proposals and reduce institutional barriers in the labor market that contribute to unemployment and inflation.

Matching Workers, Jobs, And Manpower Services

There is a great potential for improvement in bringing together workers, employers, and employment-related services. We recommend that the federal-state Employment Service be restructured so that each office will assign staff counselors and interviewers to serve the specific needs of workers and employers (IV-a).[8] To help motivate and guide the staff to make matches to best reduce inflation and unemployment while giving special consideration to workers and employers, we recommend the use of incentive formulas suggested by labor market theory (IV-b). In particular, quality of placement, measured in terms of job tenure, should be stressed to reduce turnover.

To improve private agencies, we recommend that fee splitting, standards, and so forth, be established so public and private agencies can cooperate in a flexible nationwide placement system (IV-c).

We recommend the urgent development and installation of a nationwide computerized man-machine system for matching workers, jobs, and services (IV-d). The system should incorporate behavioral relationships to help predict which of the astronomic number of possible matches hold the greatest promise of both worker satisfaction and productivity.

We recommend upgrading and expanding the staff of the Employment Service and establishing salaries to attract and retain well-qualified professionals (IV-e).

---

8. The numbers and letters associated with each recommendation correspond to the recommendation numbers in C. C. Holt et al., Manpower Lyrics for Macro Music, where the detailed proposals and their analyses are presented.

We recommend that the federal government take the lead in organizing, funding, and coordinating the nation's public-private employment service system to triple its present capacity (IV-f).

Reducing The High Unemployment Of Young People

Certain groups, including youth, blacks, women, and the disadvantaged, suffer relatively high unemployment rates. Reducing the unemployment problems of youth contributes to solving the labor market problems of other groups, and getting youth off to a good vocational start can produce lifetime benefits. For both teenagers and blacks, more emphasis needs to be placed on preparation for lasting and valuable jobs and less on short-term placements. Their high unemployment is due largely to high turnover, not prolonged job search.

We recommend that existing vocational education and manpower programs serving youth, such as the Neighborhood Youth Corps and those under the Manpower Development and Training Act (MDTA), be redirected toward preparation for more stable employment as measured by reduced turnover (V-a).

High school programs, even in vocational schools, are weak in vocational counseling. There is less than one counselor per school. Many lack suitable training. We recommend more cooperation between schools and the Employment Service to double the number of vocational counselors and improve their training (V-b).

To improve the transition from school to work, we recommend school work-study programs for younger students. Employers could be subsidized to offer students valid experience. About one million new work-study and subsidized after-school and vacation job opportunities are recommended (V-c).

Reducing Critical Skill Vacancies

When the composition of the local work force does not match the distribution of skill requirements, wages go up in the shortage occupations. Those increases spread through the economy to produce inflation. Therefore, we urge recruitment of labor from less tight occupations and more job training to fill shortages. To accomplish this, we recommend a data and analysis effort to anticipate or, at least, quickly identify the occupations in short supply (VI-a).

To respond to scarcities, we recommend a major expansion of training closely tied to anticipated needs for skilled workers (VI-b).

Less than 70,000 unemployed workers who are not disadvantaged now receive training annually in government-sponsored programs.[9] We recommend that the number be increased by 1.1 million trainees--both advantaged and disadvantaged, in both on-the-job and institutional slots--with training oriented toward skilled-labor shortages. Even though labor demand is always in flux, the occupational composition of job vacancies remains quite stable.

Many shortages could be avoided by restructuring jobs so that they could be filled by available workers. We recommend that the Employment Service add 4,000 industrial engineers and psychologists (an average of two per office) to the current staff of 35,000 to assist employers with shortages of skilled workers (VI-c).

Many skilled women, or women capable of readily learning skills, are unable to work because of the lack of adequate child-care facilities. We recommend subsidizing day care centers to enable these mothers to become skilled workers (VI-d).

Reducing Geographical Imbalances

The long distances between job markets mean that able workers and good jobs go begging simultaneously. Self-adjustments of the market are inhibited by travel and relocation costs only part of which are financial. This hurdle is especially high for the poor and disadvantaged. We recommend a new mobility assistance program for regional labor shortages and the disadvantaged (VII-a). About 200,000 workers and their households (about 10 percent of the migration flow) might be aided annually. We recommend an employment service that will function nationally to help workers move (VII-b) and supply financial assistance (VII-c).

Reducing Institutional Barriers

Institutional labor barriers, based on discrimination, licensing, union membership, and so forth, inhibit the response of labor to production needs. These barriers increase unemployment, skill shortages, and inflation. We recommend that a Presidential commission develop policies for dissolving artificial barriers to employment (VIII-a).

Research: Design, Experimentation, Evaluation, And Demonstration

Knowledge to implement fully effective programs is still inadequate. Hence, we recommend a carefully designed, integrated, and expanded program of basic and applied research, including large-scale field experimentation and evaluation (IX-a and IX-b). Behavioral research for computer matching, counseling, training, and motivation is especially important, as is the prediction of the broader impacts of programs.

---

9. These recommendations were made in late 1971.

532-819 O - 74 - 17

Additional programs of government service employment, wage subsidies, and compensating changes in the composition of government expenditures may be useful in complementing the proposed programs.

The important role of vocational education and skill training in the above scheme is very closely related to recurrent education. Joint planning and possibly joint operation are in order.

Interactions Of Recurrent Education With The Labor Market

Unfortunately, we in the U.S. cannot be sanguine about either the support of such extensive recommendations, or their early effective implementation. The way in which the labor market operates, including its training, placement, and other institutions, will have a great deal to do with the effectiveness of recurrent education--and vice versa. Issues of interaction between the two programs need to be examined deeply. For instance:

Will workers be reluctant to leave jobs for education, for fear of losing their jobs?

Will educational programs be merely a better alternative to unemployment--without other motivation?

Will workers leave educational programs prematurely when jobs become available?

Will educational credentials be more significant in placement than the increase in job productivity?

Will further education appear futile because available jobs will not utilize it?

Is the income distribution so rigidly set by the organizational hierarchies of employers that educational programs can have no effect on the distribution, but only on who occupies the slots?

Are job tenures so short as the result of sporadic product demand and inadequate smoothing in scheduling employment that careers are so often disrupted that educational development is seen as going nowhere?

In the proposed reorganization of the U.S. federal government, there is a plan to set up a Department of Human Resources which would merge responsibilities for both education and manpower programs. While one can question the size of such an agency, we need to achieve functional integration in these two areas.

The concept of recurrent education opens an exciting prospect which in addition to other benefits can contribute importantly to making labor markets work better. But unless equal imagination is applied to solving labor market problems, recurrent education will not reach its full potential.

If by improving the operation of labor markets we are able to lower unemployment without inflation, both work and education will be more meaningful. As was indicated earlier, other policy measures such as income policies have potential for dealing with aggregate economic problems, but as far as recurrent education is concerned, there is <u>no</u> alternative to improving labor markets.

financing and politics of recurrent education

educational leave and sources of funding

F. EDDING

In 1961 the OECD held an education conference which concentrated on the importance of school expansion for economic growth, "school" meaning institutionalized education for the age group 5 to 24, and "growth" referring to increases in material output. The growth rates of indicators for school activities as well as the rates of economic growth have been high since 1961; there still appears to be a causal relation between these two phenomena. But there is no longer a consensus on the thesis that every year young persons spend in school serves the general goal of better education, or as to whether continued high growth rates of material output are desirable and compatible with educational goals.

In contrast to the ideas prevalent in 1961, two new points of view have remolded the education issue: quality of life as the supreme goal and the de-schooling movement with its challenge to the present school system. The new basic concept for educational planning emerging from this remolding process is recurrent education. This new concept involves breaking the quasi-monopoly of education held by the school, and extending the chances for recurrent change among learning situations beyond the traditional phase of institutionalized education to the whole period of adult life.

One of the fundamental tools of recurrent education is educational leave.[1]

Educational leave for some young people may mean leave of absence from school for periods of practical work, participation in youth camps, or a stay abroad. For others it will mean periodic release

---

1. In 1970 France introduced paid educational leave as a legal right for the gainfully employed, and in 1969 the Federal Republic of Germany moved substantially in that direction. Some form of legal provision for educational leave exists today in many advanced countries.

from gainful occupation or apprenticeship. For adults it can mean leave of absence from paid employment, independent work, or duties as a housewife. Generally, the concept remains in flux and is highly debated. But in any case, there are costs involved, and alternative ways to meet these costs must be considered.

The complex problems associated with the financing of educational leave can be structured around the following three interdependent questions:

--who pays the bill?

--who ultimately bears the burden?

--who decides on the allocation of the financial resources?

To evaluate alternative ways of financing educational leave, an appropriate set of criteria is proposed:

--integration of vocational and nonvocational education;

--optimal motivation to participate;

--"justice" of financial burdens;

--exclusion of domination by partial interests;

--democratic participation;

--promotion of innovation; and

--efficiency.

These criteria are derived mainly from the general goals of recurrent education.

Individual Financing

When discussing financial contributions to the costs of educational leave by individual participants it must be borne in mind that the individual will contribute anyway. If the costs are financed mainly from public funds, he will contribute by paying taxes; if they are financed by private enterprises, he will be affected by increased prices.

First, the question of whether individuals have the material ability to pay for educational leave has to be considered. If participation in educational leave implies a loss of subsistence funds, the existence of either property income or savings is a necessary prerequisite. It is often argued that financial contributions by the participants are justified, as it is mainly the individual who benefits from educational leave. There is, however, no positive proof for this argument.

Society and its economy benefit as well from an educated and better skilled work force.

But will people choose vocational education that will meet their long-range needs and assure them of retaining jobs in an ever-changing economy? The evidence suggests not: people select educational investments with immediate payoffs.[2] Furthermore, it is often supposed that financial contributions from participants promote motivation for learning. In this context it is helpful to answer the following two questions:

--are financial contributions likely to create motivation?

--will existing motivation be sustained by paying fees and sacrificing income?

The answer to the first question is probably no. The groups hitherto underrepresented in adult educational activities are almost identical to those having had little education in their youth. They found it an unpleasant experience then and are likely to find it so again. It is also unlikely that those persons could be motivated by prospects of financial sacrifices. On the contrary, learning may seem a greater burden than working. To get them to return to school might require an educational leave higher than wages.

The second question might well turn out to have a positive answer since it is in line with the theory of consumer behavior. People normally value goods they have paid for and as a rule consumers associate high prices with high quality. Thus, if my reasoning is valid, charging participants in an educational leave program would presumably motivate only those already motivated, and would not create new learning motivation.

Whether valid or not, the idea that participants should pay their own way has been defended with the argument that an informed consumer can best decide what is better for his needs, and the institutions will respond accordingly as in any market situation.

It has been argued that the dominance of particular interests is best prevented if the individuals decide upon the programs to be realized and make the allocation of funds. However, since the individuals as consumers do not represent an adequate counteracting power, it is illusory to hope for decisive influence from their side.[3] Besides,

---

2. Whether the dichotomy between vocational and nonvocational programs would be eliminated if the participants were more problem-oriented will be discussed in the context of the innovation criterion.

3. The position of the participants in educational leave is further weakened by the fact that the relevant educational activities are of short duration.

the organizational and curricular structures of the educational system are an obstacle to responsive and frequent change and within a short time frame.

Individual financing of educational leave is said to optimize didactical innovation by stimulating competition among the educational organizations. However, since innovation is risky, educational organizations may well form a cartel restricting their programs to a medium level of quality. Insofar as competition works, it may center on marginal points similar to product variations in the consumer goods market. The chances of such tactics being successful are quite good since it is extremely difficult for potential participants to evaluate different programs. A public information system might change this situation, but consumer sovereignty seems rather far away.

As for efficiency, it must be recalled that the market mechanisms do not care about social needs, benefits and costs. Consequently, it is highly probable that a system of educational leave regulated by supply and demand only will result in social under-investment.

Furthermore, individual financing would not provide justice or equal opportunity; it would rather result in selection of participants according to their financial means. Empirical data from the Federal Republic of Germany and France indicate that under the existing financial arrangements for educational leave, which make at least some monetary contribution by the participants obligatory, some social groups --especially low-income groups, older people and women--are largely excluded from participation. These defects could hardly be remedied by credit or grant systems.

Financing By Private Enterprises

When private enterprises pay for educational leave, the burden normally does not fall on them, since, as a rule, they have a good chance of shifting it either forward (onto the consumers) or backward (onto their suppliers). Whether and to what extent this burdens the consumers depends mainly on market conditions, the amount of monopolistic concentration, the power of trade unions to shift the burden back to the enterprises by way of tariff negotiations, and the basis on which the payments are calculated.

Besides these uncontrolled shifting effects, financing of educational leave by private firms probably has another negative effect: the willingness of private entrepreneurs to invest in educational leave depends to a large degree on the aims and content of the programs envisaged. According to their market situation, investments are made if an adequate pay-off can be expected. Consequently, they normally favor programs with immediate or short-term benefits. Even if an entrepreneur is sufficiently farsighted to see the weaknesses in such a strategy, in a competitive system he cannot help but conform to the general practice, especially if he is not in an exceptionally good market position.

The short-term perspective of planning in private enterprises cannot do justice to the goal of the unity of vocational and non-vocational education. That professional roles do not consist of "vocational" components only and that qualifications are the less affected by technological change the broader the basis, are facts that are all too often ignored because of the acute demand for skills rather than learning.

Financing of educational leave by private enterprises, together with their possibilities of influencing aims, content, and participation, may have consequences for the motivation of possible participants. On the one hand, it could lead to positive reactions inasfar as it is interpreted as a special program in favor of the employees; on the other hand, it may stress the consciousness of the dependence on the employer and thereby reduce learning motivation.

Compared with alternative ways of funding, some arguments seem to support financing of educational leave by private enterprises:

--they are materially in a position to pay;

--they benefit not only from the productive contributions of the working population but also from their educational activities; and

--they normally can pass on at least part of the financial burden and thus should not be too opposed to the introduction of new levies.

The first argument neglects the differences in solvency between firms and in changing market situations. A warning must be given also as regards the shifting processes. It can hardly be anticipated who will ultimately be burdened and whether social and/or economic distortions will ensue.

The financing of educational leave by private enterprises must be looked at critically from the criterion of the exclusion of the predominance of partial interests. As mentioned above, the entrepreneurs are likely to concentrate on their short-term interests, with the consequence that those learning targets whose benefits are likely soon to be "internationalized" will be given preference. The prospects for democratic participation in a concept of educational leave depending on financing by private enterprises are rather weak. The organizational structures of educational activities of private enterprises tend to reflect the industrial hierarchy. Entrepreneurs will not as a rule favor other structures, because democratic decision-making processes in the educational sector could lead to a critical reappraisal of traditional practices in general.

Financing by private enterprises does not hold great promise for the promotion of innovation. Even entrepreneurs who enjoy taking risks on capital investments might be reluctant to invest in unconventional educational measures that are not really their task. For this reason, this method of funding didactical innovation in educational leave programs is likely to be restricted to a minimum. Motivation for innovation must be accompanied by the material possibility.

On the other hand, private enterprises as financiers of educational leave are well-prepared to judge efficiency. They may in many cases have a good estimate of their medium-term manpower needs. But present practice shows that firms' educational programs intended to meet this demand all too often conflict with the interests of the participants, one of which is to promote their professional security by broadening their vocational flexibility. Educational leave based exclusively on financing and allocation decisions of private enterprises is likely to result in under-investment of capital, both financial and human.

Financing By The State

Considering the social and political aims associated with educational leave, it seems quite obvious that financing by the state would be the most effective way. The arguments in favor of state financing concentrate on two main points:

1. as the state is assumed to be in a position to attain generally accepted aims for the benefit of society and to enforce public control, it can best secure educational leave for all employees, and

2. consequently, financing by the state seems to be the most promising way of guaranteeing the correspondence between educational activities (e.g., educational leave) and general political and social aims.

In reality, however, state decisions are largely influenced by economically powerful groups which might be afraid that their interests will be challenged by such integrated education. This thesis is confirmed, for example, by the development in the Federal Republic of Germany where the dichotomy between vocational and nonvocational education has recently become more noticeable.

Furthermore, it could be difficult for a state to obtain public approval for integrated programs for educational leave if, apart from the institutional costs, wage payments or payments foregone are to be financed from state budgets. Whether state financing of education is more just than other alternatives depends on the tax structure. There are strong indications that state financing burdens primarily the dependent labor force.

Prevention of dominance by partial interests is not automatically met by state financing of educational leave. There are good "informal" opportunities for vested interests to influence public authorities, while the majority of the people generally have no possibility of articulating and expressing their needs.

In a system of state-financed educational leave, a shortage of funds can easily be used as an excuse for delaying controversial innovations. But innovation could be promoted, since state financing rests less on the willingness of third parties to implement new ideas. On the other hand, state administration is likely to restrain innovations that might challenge their traditional way of thinking.

But despite these drawbacks, state financing has two very important contributions: motivation and efficiency. Quite simply, more people will be motivated to gain further education if the state pays for their leave from work. As for efficiency, state funding can compete adequately with financing by private enterprises. The difference between them lies in the likelihood that the aims will be achieved.

Financing By Collective Funding

In examining the implications of different ways of funding, specific deficiencies become apparent. As already indicated, the inadequacies center on the following criteria:

--individual financing is problematic, especially in view of the requirements of integrating vocational and non-vocational education (and in this context of innovation), of justice in financial burden and, most of all, motivation;

--financing by private enterprises is not compatible with the criterion of integration; and

--financing from state budgets does not guarantee the curbing of the dominance of partial interest and seems unlikely to sufficiently further innovation.

Each of the methods of financing so far discussed has, if applied in isolation, distinct shortcomings. But certain advantages can also be presumed to be potentially available. Therefore, the aim is to find a way to exclude most disadvantages and retain the greatest assets. This is called here "collective funding under public responsibility." A rough sketch of such a scheme would include the following provisions:

...We propose to charge all private enterprises by law a levy according to their economic capability. The revenue from this levy would not form part of the state budget but be transferred to a national foundation for the promotion of educational leave.

...The state as a rule would pay into the national foundation fund only a small contribution, as a sign of interest. But in times of recession the state would be bound to compensate the revenue from the levy by amounts large enough to allow a stepping up of educational leave in times of unemployment. In addition, the foundation may in times of depression raise funds on the capital market.

...Minimum qualitative standards should be set for educational leave. To the extent that firms and other organizations come up to this qualitative level set by the government, they get standardized costs refinanced out of the national foundation's collective fund.

...Special incentives for innovation would be provided; additional subsidies can be given for educational leave with integrated programs so as to reduce the additional burden and risk normally associated with innovative educational activities.

...Continuation of wage payments would be guaranteed by the national foundation during educational leave. This does not necessarily mean that the total former wage must be paid. Alternatively, the wage payments could be graded, ranging for example from a minimum wage for unskilled workers up to a maximum, following regulations in most social insurance systems. The lower limit should be high enough to give special encouragement for participation to the lower income groups.

...The foundation would be governed by a board in which representatives of the state, private enterprise, and trade unions, plus independent experts, have equal voting rights. The foundation would have to decide within legal limits, the amount of the levy, curricular targets, and other quality standards.

The guidelines set forth for the national foundation would insure a high degree of continuing independence from partial economic and political interests. It would promote motivation and innovation, particularly in integrating vocational and nonvocational education. By introducing democratic participation at all institutional levels, this funding organization may counteract bureaucratic sterility and stimulate local initiative. There is, of course, some danger that this may impede efficiency. On the other hand, it has often been proven that adequate organizational forms of participation can enlarge the problem-solving capacities of social subsystems.

Nobody can predict how the volume of finance needed for educational leave will develop. The figures we have for recent years are no adequate basis for projections. They show the strong increase of educational leave under present circumstances. Under the conditions here envisaged an even faster development could be expected. Our proposals for funding would insure the flexibility needed to cope with a dynamic new dimension of organized learning.

financial options and structural requirements

FRANCIS M. BODDY

Many current discussions of recurrent education from a variety of perspectives suggest modification or radical restructuring of postcompulsory educational institutions.

One suggestion is that action should be taken to permit and simplify the postponement of entry into the next levels of education and training at a number of points within the present educational systems. Some go so far as to suggest that such a break, involving entry into the work force or other activities for some period, be required before the student is permitted to re-enter. Following this logic, it is recommended that institutional structures, techniques, and formats of programs and curricula be greatly modified or that new structures be built to enhance the accessibility and effectiveness of the system for the recurrent student.

Furthermore, reforms in financial arrangements have been urged to bring about more equality of educational opportunity throughout life and that recurrent education can have a significant effect in reducing the inequalities of income distribution.

Another idea is now in fashion that says the system should be more strongly oriented toward specific goals with greater importance assigned to job-entry training, skill development, training for occupational or career advancement, and the improvement of economic productivity than to general study of the humanities.

Finally, it is being argued that the credentialing aspects of the present system be reduced or restricted, or that nontraditional and experiential ways to satisfy credentialism be vastly expanded, validated, and accepted.

Critics charge that the present system prevents intermittent or part-time attendance. Yet there is evidence that the current institutions of postsecondary education are at least somewhat adaptable to this pattern.

Present Intermittent Pattern

Although it is far from ideally responsive to those desiring intermittent attendance patterns, the present system is not completely inflexible.

The Report on Higher Education notes that while in large state universities only 35 to 45 percent of the entering students graduated within four years at that institution, within 10 years 60 to 70 percent graduated from some institution; for state colleges the corresponding figures were 15 to 25 percent within four years at the initial institution, and 35 to 50 percent within 10 years at some institution.[1]

At the University of Minnesota, a very large multiversity in a large urban area, 10 percent of the students enrolled in undergraduate colleges were between 26 and 35 years of age and 2 percent were 36 years of age or older. In the graduate and professional colleges, 30.6 percent of those enrolled were between 26 and 35 years of age, and 5.6 percent were 36 or older.

A Minnesota survey of statewide adult and continuing education by the higher education institutions of the state in the academic year 1968-1969 reports 81,000 individual enrollments in 3,100 credit courses in that year.[2] In fall quarter of the same year, some 140,000 students were enrolled in the regular programs of these institutions.[3]

The difference in median time lapse from the B.A. to the Ph.D. between the total elapsed time and the registered time shows wide variations across different fields. For Ph.D. recipients in 1971 in the U.S., this difference (a possible proxy for "time-out") varied from a low of 7/10 of a year in physics, astronomy, and chemistry to highs of 4.5 years in professional fields and to 6.6 years in education.[4]

---

1. Frank Newman, Report on Higher Education (Washington, D.C.: Government Printing Office, March 1971), p. 2.

2. Continuing Education in Minnesota (St. Paul: Minnesota Higher Education Coordinating Commission, 1970).

3. Public College Enrollment in Minnesota's Changing Population Pattern (St. Paul: University of Minnesota, Center for Urban and Regional Affairs, January 1973).

4. National Research Council, Summary Report 1971 Doctoral Recipients from United States Universities (Washington, D.C.: National Research Council, April 1972): 8-9.

It seems evident that efficiency considerations would strongly indicate that at some appropriate point, attained education and skills should be put to active use in the world of work or in other spheres. As obsolescence occurs and the acquiring of new knowledge and skills becomes necessary, re-entry into the educational process will be indicated along with a new consideration of trade-offs. Foregone earnings and other costs to the student continuing in the system necessarily come to be compared with the possible increased earnings and other benefits to be captured at a later stage in his life. The trade-offs are between possible diminishing returns in educational or skill outcomes in the future and the immediate further investment of time and effort for retraining.

Structuring For Re-Entry

Turning now to the patterns of possible re-entry into the system--as it now stands, or as it may be substantially modified or reconstructed--it is clear there is a wide variety of perceived needs for recurrent education. Among these perceived needs or desired programs are:

--special skill training to improve job prospects;

--upgrading of skills and knowledge for improved performance and for advancement;

--retraining to meet changing market demands;

--special training or retraining to adapt to new processes and techniques;

--continuing education in the underlying disciplines of the occupation or profession;

--re-entry to complete an unfinished program;

--re-entry to complete an additional stage in the educational system; and

--continuing education to improve the quality of the individual's life, to develop avocational interests, to improve understanding of social and political forces, to enhance more effective contributions to the social and political structures, and to expand the opportunities for personal development and fulfillment.

No one system could respond effectively to all those valid demands for recurrent education. Many are met by our present systems in their more formal programs, or by extension divisions, nontraditional and experimental programs and structures, off-campus and outside the classroom delivery systems, and relatively new additions to the institutional

532-819 O - 74 - 18

structures such as the community college, technical schools, and other even more flexible options.

Not only is there a wide variety of possible demands by the re-entering students but also there are wide differences among the circumstances and future prospects of the potential clientele. Data from a study of the 1960 census[5] show that there are substantial differences in both the expected pattern of lifetime earnings and the relationship to levels of schooling completed among men in broad occupational groups in the U.S. These data imply differences in the types of recurrent education that would be occupationally effective, in the possible economic trade-offs of such re-entry and in the appropriate times of re-entry.

Seventeen million people have completed less than eight years of elementary education, 21 million have one to three years of high school and 12 million have one to three years of college. While many of these are long out of the educational system and well advanced in years, there are many others, particularly at the "incomplete" high school and college level, still relatively young and for whom the pay-offs for re-entry into formal schooling might indicate substantial advantages for this form of recurrent education.

In short, there are large numbers of adults in the U.S. whose educational needs are not being met by our present educational institutions.

If recurrent educational opportunities are to be opened up to meet better these apparent needs, financial and structural requirements must be examined.

The more feasible and economically viable solutions will lie largely within the present systems of educational institutions, including not only the schools and colleges of the traditional system, but trade schools, extension and correspondence divisions and programs, inhouse programs, and on-the-job training.

New forms of institutions and delivery systems, and the expansion of the use of new means of instruction and methods of communication will offer effective and more efficient ways to meet at least some of the needs for the provision of recurrent education. But these options should not supplant the present system.

Financial Restructuring

One apparent failure of current financing options for students and their families is the lack of an effective system of assisting the

---

5. Herman P. Miller and Richard A. Hornseth, <u>Present Value of Estimated Lifetime Earnings</u>, Technical Paper No. 16 (Washington, D.C.: Government Printing Office, U.S. Bureau of the Census, 1967).

recurrent student. Compared to developments in financing housing and major consumer durables over the past 40 years, progress in financing education has been meager. We have not yet developed a way to provide the security for the loans for educational purposes that is provided by the mortgage on the assets in housing and consumer durables, nor have we developed the appropriate pay-off schedules, such as the monthly payment of interest and principal over a suitable term in these other areas. The current discussions of payback systems, based on a percentage or a sliding scale of percentages of future income, suggests that some much more effective system may be developed. Essential to any such system, however, is a workable solution to the problem of getting the security for the lender and the pay-off of the interest, principal, and administrative costs based on a group of loans and borrowers rather than on an individual basis. Central to this problem is the difficulty of avoiding what in insurance is called adverse selection. For unless the group contains a representative number of prospective high income earners to offset the prospective low income earners, the necessary repayment percentage of income scales will be so high as to discourage those who most need to make use of it because of the lack of other feasible financing options. Moreover, financing the education of women by such a system is biased strongly against them by the patterns of female labor force participation and the income levels of those who do participate.

Such a future income-based loan system would also give overwhelming emphasis to educational programs, especially in recurrent education, that are primarily or even single-mindedly designed for purely economic individual pay-offs, neglecting those programs whose pay-offs would not be directly rewarded by future money incomes. Short of compulsory participation or substantial subsidy (perhaps by way of insurance) by governments, it seems unlikely that solutions will be found which would radically change the current situation.

Increasing tuition levels to a higher proportion of the full cost of instruction is another way to modify the financing of publicly aided institutions. Public savings could be transferred from institutions to students in the form of increased grants and fellowships. Increased individual aid would doubtless affect the current economic calculus of decisions to enter or re-enter the system.

Tuition costs, even if approaching full cost of instruction, are but a part of the cost to the participant. Foregone income remains a powerful factor, and unless grant support takes account of living costs and family needs of the recurrent student, the prospective student from the low income family may not enter. For those higher in the income scale, and hence with smaller or zero grants, the increased tuition costs will be much higher than at present and will weigh more heavily in the total cost of attendance to the student and his family. This in turn will tend to bias decisions against women in family allocations of income or assets to the education of its members.

In countries like the U.S. where educational policy control rests with the state, and to some degree the local or institutional level, the piecemeal adoption of such financing policies in different forms in various states or localities, and lack of complete adoption across the country by all states, would create problems of student migration to low-tuition areas and institutions. In turn, this might result in restrictions on serving out-of-area students and vast complications in defining and enforcing "residence" of the students by those areas that continue to subsidize the institution rather than the student.

Financing of recurrent education by the employer or occupational groups by payments to the student directly or to institutions to bring the program to the student at the place of work has long been practiced in business and industry. But practice is limited. Recurrent education in knowledge and skills not specialized to the employer (or employers or occupational group) may make the employee more valuable to others and increase his mobility. His wage or salary must be raised to match his increased productivity to restrain him from taking other employment. Thus, the investment in the employee cannot be recaptured in added future productivity. This is probably quite a strong restraint to single-firm financing of many forms of recurrent education.

If employer groups can organize and agree on a cost-sharing plan, then the recurrent education programs need not be employer specific, but only industry specific, to provide rational economic justification for employer financing. Many fields require a high level of technical knowledge and skills that are industry specific. Such industry-wide financing is used in those fields and could probably be expanded substantially if the delivery systems and the educational institutions were better adapted to such service.

Since much of the talent and facilities necessary for recurrent education are within the present institutions, it might be better to reform the structural aspects of the present institutions and their educational programs that bar or restrict legitimate access for recurrent education.

Conditions Favorable For Change

One of the reasons for the relative neglect of recurrent education by many of our educational institutions has been a lack of resources. Faced with excess demand, the rationing of entry and programs has been determined largely by the priorities of the internal decision systems. The dominant pattern is to favor the regular degree and curricula programs, and the full-time, continuous student. Moreover, the organizational structures and the processes by which students are admitted to particular programs, and processed through the system, are reinforced by the traditional priorities of the faculty, the administration, and, to some degree, those who finance the institution.

Presently, the educational system is facing a slowdown in demand by traditional students. This phenomenon may present an opportunity to modify the attitudes of the institutions and their structures to recognize and give greater emphasis to the nontraditional or recurrent student.

The recent spread of community colleges and technical schools into areas previously distant from educational institutions is encouraging, for the location and accessibility of an institution close to work or residence is particularly important to the recurrent student. Furthermore, these institutions are less rigid and biased against the nontraditional student.

Moreover, attitudes among faculties and administrations are changing. There is a growing recognition of the unmet needs in the areas of extension, continuing and recurrent education. The relaxation of enrollment pressures by traditional students is making a shift toward those fields more possible.

Recurrent students could be more sought after because they would be additional or replacement students rather than competitors for scarce spaces and resources with the traditional students. Serious consideration along such lines is challenging some of the previously held priorities and opinions on the essential missions of the institutions. Economic factors, once deterrents to recurrent education, could speed its adoption as an alternative to declining demands for traditional study.

The growth of state coordinating commissions for postsecondary education also contributes to the reconsideration of institutional missions and priorities.

In summary, there is significant movement toward serious reassessment of established traditions and policies; conditions are favorable for change.

This process could be strongly reinforced if those involved in institutional re-study had better information about the size, the strength of demand, and the program needs of this new clientele in recurrent education.

Many, if not most, institutions may well discover that this demand is substantial and may conclude that their staff and facilities are most appropriate for the needed service. If such a conclusion is reached, then the financial implications and the internal resource allocations implied by such a shift will have a clearer focus.

For public institutions this may lead to changes in the bases of public support. Under current support policies, the extension or recurrent student is treated and financed as only a by-product of the regular process. If he becomes an accepted member of the academic community, the institution could benefit financially.

If the institution does conclude that the recurrent student is to be a full-fledged entrant into the institution, it will need to redesign its programs, curricula, and perhaps structure to provide the appropriate collegiate home-base for these students.

Reactions to reform ideas on institutional and student financing, educational goals, and resource allocations will be responsive, I believe, to the needs of recurrent education. But I do not believe that such reactions will include massive shifts in priorities or a full-scale restructuring of the basic educational system--nor do I think they should.

french policy on continuing education

JACQUES DELORS

If one is to attempt a definition of "continuing education," two basic points must first be made clear. First, the concept of continuing education did not start to take on definite shape and form in France just with the Law of 1971, or even with those of 1966 and 1968 (though they did play a major role in the developments as we are witnessing today). Even before the Second World War, people were thinking about community development and individual development. Trade unions and social organizations in particular engaged in what they often called "culture populaire" (popular culture), which is what we now call "continuing education."

Second, we in France tend to concern ourselves overmuch with terminology, and believe that we are engaging in something novel when we have invented a new word or acronym. We have to realize that when farmers, for example, get together to form a cooperative--something they have been doing for many years--they are thereby creating a field of action for continuing education. Is not the purpose behind this step, for each of the members, to gain greater intellectual and operational control over their work, over the outlets for their products and over the problems which they have to face?

In order to give a proper definition of continuing education, we are thus forced to widen our terms of reference again and again, since in the final analysis all experience is educational. Life is educational, or can be, and this is undoubtedly especially true of farm life. Any discussion of continuing education should, therefore, be conducted on the basis of a realization that the chief learning situations are provided primarily by life--not only a person's working life, but all the other aspects of his existence as well.

The Purposes Of The Policy

The purposes of the French policy on continuing education will be molded and shaped by society as the policy unfolds. There are four primary purposes:

(1) Mastery of change

Fifteen years ago, the first French congress on sociology had as its theme: "France and Change." At that time, the title may well have surprised some people, but today no one would be surprised by it, since it has become a truism to say that we live in a world of constant change. This change is particularly apparent in our work: who can truthfully say that in his job he is still using the same methods, the same approach, the same ideas as when he started out 20 years ago? Who has not had to cope with on the job change in many different guises? Change in methods of command or of relations with other people, change in methods of production, change in market research, and so forth. A country that has sustained a more than 5 percent per annum growth rate in real terms over a period of 25 years was bound to experience this change, though not exclusively in the economic sphere.

Thus, change in the world of work was inevitable. It is a normal accompaniment to economic growth and the shift from a malthusian, inward-looking society to a dynamic society open to the outside world.

Faced with this change, we are as perplexed as we are by other changes, such as the crisis within the Church, our misgivings about the strength of the family as an institution, and the collapse of part of the educational system.

No one can say a priori, when faced with this change, that he has all the weapons he needs to deal with the resulting challenge. One way of facing change with resolve and determination is through continuing education: the opportunity to step back from the hurly-burly of life for a brief moment, to change one's frame of reference and to think about the world with colleagues and instructors, to look at things from a distance, to regain confidence in oneself, and finally not to get annoyed with inevitable changes but on the contrary to muster one's strength in order to master change. Thus, the number one purpose of continuing education is undoubtedly to equip people to face change.

In the first instance, this purpose takes on utilitarian form: for the miner who has to leave mining, for the skilled craftsman who has to leave his workshop, for the farmer who has to move to the town, change has an unrelenting, ineluctable aspect--that of necessity. There is also the less dramatic but nonetheless constant change which bears down upon our working life, forcing us to deal with daily variations. To cope, it is of course essential to garner new knowledge and to become aware of each new situation--but self-confidence is even more important. When faced with change, there is no point in stamping our feet in angry frustration: we must go out and overcome it.

All of this proves that--over and above the legal and financial guarantees that continuing education provides and that enable all those who need to go on to a new type of training--the content, form and style of an education that enables each person to gain confidence in himself and in his ability to master change are much more important. This is why continuing education can never be equated with mere acquisition of technical knowledge and skills.

Changes, of course, include some that are secondary and can be summarized under the heading "adjustment of working methods." They have to be accepted, but they do not form the "backbone" of continuing education, which is a technical, psychological and mental effort to master change.

At the outset, therefore, we had to show that policy on continuing education is the "tool" that would enable people to gain confidence in themselves, so that they would not remain standing jobless on the sidelines: it marks the starting point of social progress. Before we speak of the quality of life or of the environment, we have to think of the hundreds of thousands of people who, because they have not received the necessary education, because they are not as strong as others, remain on the sidelines, unable to react to events which overtake them. It is for these people that continuing education has in the first place been instituted, since it is designed to provide every person with the means of livelihood. In our day and age, a means of livelihood means having the chance of a job, the chance to make one's way in life. This is one of the major goals of continuing education, and much still remains to be done before it can become a reality.

(2) Struggle against unequal opportunities

Equity is a very tricky problem and is made all the more difficult by the influence of the mass media. There is constant talk of equality as public opinion is swept along, unfortunately for an all too brief period of time, by certain compelling causes. We shall soon reach a situation where we shall be forced to meet the problem of inequality head on. The problem currently centers around policy for initial education. This clearly shows that society is, in a muddle-headed way, seeking equality. But if someone proposes specific steps to achieve equality, many back away because they are afraid of the consequences.

In the face of all these obstacles, our policy on continuing education has become much less ambitious. What it proposes, quite simply, is to give each individual a second or even a third chance; to insure that life does not stop at 20; to insure, once and for all, that when workers leave school between the age of 14 and 20, they are not rigorously separated into two categories--the happy few (those who have been lucky) and the hapless remainder, who will have to make do for the rest of their lives with a less propitious fate. If the latter group's fate were to be reflected solely in lower earnings, it would be rather irritating, but it would not be totally unacceptable. However, it is very often reflected in a dirty, hard, tedious and repetitive job and in a daily grind that is made even less bearable by the degrading nature of the job. Continuing education wishes to offer new opportunities to those who find themselves on the wrong track, so that one day when a person leaves school at 16 or 18 (because his family is unable to continue to support him, or because the cultural environment does not encourage higher education), he can say to himself that all is not lost, that he has a chance to improve his working life in qualitative terms.

(3) The need to rethink the educational system

The suggestion that we need to rethink our present education system is not one which brings joy to the hearts of the teaching profession, but deep down the teachers recognize this need. What the teachers do not want is to be treated as the scapegoats of society, "the people who do not train enough skilled manpower, the people who do a bad job of educating the kids." Here the teachers are perfectly right, because teachers and the education system are merely a reflection of French society as a whole. If children do not respect their teachers, it is because they do not respect their parents either. If the schools do not produce enough skilled manpower, it is because society as a whole does not encourage them to do so. The figures for job supply and demand show that these problems are more complex than one might think.

Continuing education can help us to rethink education policy in several respects: First, there is at present a crisis in relations between teacher and student; in part this crisis is artificial, but much of it is real. As a result, it will not be possible to induce adults to participate in continuing education without a far-going renewal in the dialogue between teachers and students. Should this dialogue represent simply a vertical transmission of knowledge, moving only from top to bottom, from the teacher to the student, or is it an exchange? In the case of adults, it should incontestably be an exchange; this realization opens up new perspectives on teaching methods. Continuing education addressed to people who already have a lifetime behind them, who perceive education as an exchange and not as a passive function, will be the laboratory of this change.

Experiments with continuing education can thus have quite a substantial effect on how the education system as a whole is viewed. It is my belief that in 1980 we shall no longer be talking of initial education on the one hand and of continuing education on the other, but rather of a total system of education. We shall see children going to school up to what may be a lower age than today, but returning periodically to school because society will have given them a "time credit" for continuing education.

(4) Strengthening individual autonomy

As society has developed, each of us has become subject to increasing social pressure which makes us feel that we are less and less free and are less and less able to act on our environment. To counteract this, we must strengthen each individual's capacity for autonomy.

Our purpose is not to abolish the state, but to strike a new balance between the authorities and the regulations they issue on the one hand, and the individual on the other. When the individual becomes a person, a human being able to react autonomously, it will perhaps be easier to speak of democracy. This is certainly the most profound and ambitious of the goals of our policy for continuing education.

The Present Continuing Education System

I shall start by admitting that the system that has been applied to implement continuing education goes counter to all that has been customary procedure in France. The experiment calls for the establishment of an open, pluralistic, decentralized, spontaneous and concerted system, whereas in the past most social progress in France was realized by legislation. Of course, we need laws, but many laws have never been applied because they failed to strike a responsive chord among the population and its leaders.

Again, France has always been characterized by non-dialogue: notably the non-dialogue between employers and trade unions. Whenever a dialogue did exist, it never amounted to much. The dialogue between the State and other groups was not unlike the dialogue between a father and his teenage son. The teenager wishes to discover himself, to develop his own potential. This he can do only in relation to his father, so he gets into an argument with him. His father, cold and confident (since he controls the money, the car and the apartment), lets his son rage and says: "If you don't like it, you needn't stay." The son packs his bag and goes out the front door. His father watches him sarcastically through the window; the boy looks up and continues to rail at his father. After ten minutes, the teenager returns because he has no other choice: he is dependent on his father for his entire existence. This is characteristic of relations in France between the State and the citizenry; until this has been fully understood, it is impossible to fathom why our society is not making progress. We shall therefore have to make adults of our teenagers, and to do this we shall have to create just and proper relationships between the State and our social and professional bodies. In other words, there must be a true dialogue between them, and a sound system of labor relations must be established.

The objects of a system of labor relations are very simple:

(1) to insure that all the problems that arise in connection with work and labor and that all the workers' aspirations are known and discussed. Such discussion would end either in an agreement or in a strike, but if an agreement were reached, all of its provisions would be scrupulously implemented.

(2) to raise problems at the proper level: if 20 workers are laid off at Pezenas, the Prime Minister should not be called upon to deal with this matter.

(3) to promote social progress, by its very existence.

These three points form the basis for the system of vocational training that has been set up. This system is, in the first place, an open system, i.e., no one in any one ministry has exclusive power to plan policy on continuing education. It is necessary to have a society furnished with oxygen and air, rather than a closed society, where those with a monopoly on knowledge decide everything for the French population.

Secondly, the system that we have constructed is pluralistic, i.e., it recognizes that not all Frenchmen hold the same view of society, but that each and every one ought to be able to coexist within France, that their views on society and religion should not be in constant conflict, preventing them from working together.

Furthermore, this system is decentralized. Problems must be raised where they can be solved. The problem of the Chablais area cannot be solved in Paris, but rather in the Chablais itself, in the prefecture of the department of Haute-Savoie of which it forms part, and probably also in the prefecture of the Alpes region. This was why it was decided in 1969, long before there was any talk of decentralization, that the regional prefects could, on their own, commit public funds to subsidize either the equipping or the operation of training centers. They have been doing this ever since 1969 in consultation with the Regional Committee or its specialized agencies.

This system must also be spontaneous. France has more than a million and a half employers, and close supervision would require more than 20,000 inspectors. This would be very expensive for the State and would not accomplish much, for these inspectors would not be as able to judge the situation as heads of enterprises and their associates, the trade unions, and the workers themselves. The entire system is based on the sense of responsibility of the four parties involved:

--the public authorities,

--the heads of enterprises,

--the workers and their representatives, and

--the establishments of public education.

Finally, it is a concerted system: everything depends on cooperation among the parties. Cooperation does not imply integration. The fact that the unions are participating in the policy for continuing education does not mean that they will support the company unreservedly; they are simply defending, from their own position, the spiritual and material interests of the workers. Similarly, the fact that the heads of enterprises cooperate with the unions does not mean that they are in favor of the common program or of worker self-management. The heads of enterprises are simply pursuing a policy of education and training for their staff.

This cooperation is found at all levels of social life:

(1) within the works council: the views of the works council must be mentioned in the statements issued by enterprises employing more than 50 people;

(2) within the departmental committee: the object of this committee is to advise the regional committee of local aspirations, the needs of the department and human needs. Once the regional committee has laid down overall guidelines for the entire region, the departmental committee serves as an active tool for harmonious implementation of this policy. Because the regional committee covers a larger area, it is able to act as arbitrator; it also possesses considerable financial power, which in practice it shares with departmental-level agencies.

(3) on the national level: for the past five years, the top officials dealing with continuing education have met every month with six representatives of the employers' organizations and six representatives of the trade unions to examine jointly all the problems that have arisen.

One could claim that the public authorities are shirking responsibilities that are properly theirs, but this is not true. In a decentralized system, the public authorities have responsibilities of their own, which are of three kinds:

(1) The public authorities must insure that the system does not lose track of the goals listed above. For example: continuing education is designed for all workers and not just for one category. Company efforts to date have, admittedly, focused on graduate engineers and higher level personnel. The public authorities, for their part, devote 4/5 of their allocated funds to programs designed to assist blue-collar and administrative workers, so as to correct this imbalance.

(2) They must help the public educational establishments, the Ministry of National Education, the Foyers de Progres Agricole (rural development centers) and the agricultural centers to play their full role in continuing education. This means that these bodies should be able to offer quality training to all who need it at a cost at least equal to if not less than that of private sector institutions. It would also be desirable for them to undertake programs that no private group would otherwise embark on. For example, if tomorrow the public authorities discover that a type of training that is required in the public interest is not being provided, they will arrange for the public establishments to offer it and will if necessary finance it completely.

(3) They must promote innovation and creativity in continuing education. The authorities are keenly interested in learning of all new educational experiments; they study the results and effects and make them known throughout France.

Results And Future Prospects

It is fair to say that, with regard to the novelty of the system that has been introduced and the difficulty and scope of the subject, it has gotten off to a better start than we dared hope. Figures support this optimistic statement: in 1972, 1.4 million workers participated in training courses, i.e., a little over 7 percent of the working population. In that same year, France spent close to an estimated 6.5 billion francs on continuing education: F 2 billion from the interministerial budget, F 2.5 billion paid by business enterprises, and F 2 billion which the State itself paid to train civil servants. If we look simply at officially approved programs, i.e., the most recent programs financed in whole or in part by the State, we find that the number of trainees has jumped from 60,000 in 1968 to 460,000 in 1972. Over the same period, public expenditure in this field has tripled. The rate of growth has therefore been spectacular.

Another way of preparing a balance sheet is to consider how governments and the other organized groups in society have accepted the system and allowed it to operate. The results are all the more satisfying as the government had decided, in this instance, to break with traditional patterns which had often led to major social reforms being cast in a centralized, state-controlled mold. Contrary to past practice, the Laws of 1966 and 1968, followed by that of 1971, established an open, pluralistic decentralized system with powers delegated to regional authorities; a system, moreover, concerted with business and the trade unions at the national level, passing by way of the department and the region. Here you will also see a very close link with the efforts that have been made since 1969 to provide France with a proper system of labor relations.

The system is, on the whole, working well, and this new approach to social betterment is gaining ground all the time.

Further Problems

The most difficult problems still remain. These may be summarized as follows:

(1) Many workers are not yet inspired with the spirit of continuing education, either because they do not feel the need for it or because they have no desire for advancement. This is particularly true of the valley of the Arve, in Haute-Savoie, where there are a lot of machine works. This work is difficult; it has its own traditions, and the workers themselves often lack motivation. One of today's major tasks is an intellectual, political and educational one--that of deciding what can be done for these workers who are not motivated and to whom one cannot say that if they get some more education they will earn more. What is needed is to make them understand that they simply need moments of repose in their working life, time off to try to complete their general education, to try to gain greater self-confidence. This applies to semi-skilled workers and to skilled workers alike.

(2) It is difficult to know what to do about companies that have few employees. A business that employs only four or five people will be faced with a major problem if it has to do without one or two of its staff even for a few days. Special solutions will have to be sought for enterprises of this type, taking the form either of the training course coming to them (audiovisual aids plus occasional meetings of all concerned for group discussions) or of the organization of courses of proven value outside working hours. The problem is a real one; it is obvious that we cannot be constantly pulling people away from their work.

(3) A number of companies have not yet understood the nature of their obligations with regard to continuing education. Their obligation is not simply to spend 0.80 percent of their wage bill on continuing education. They should look not to the law but to the joint agreement of 1970 signed by the CNPF (Conseil National du Patronat Francais--National Council of French Employers) and the CGPME (Confederation Generale des Petites et Moyennes Entreprises--General Confederation of Small and Medium-Sized Enterprises) on behalf of the French business community. When this agreement has been fully implemented, employers will be spending between three and five percent of their total wage bill on education and training. This is entirely different from the levy of 0.80 percent, which is in fact a "homeopathic" levy introduced to encourage companies which were doing nothing at all to start thinking about training programs. The problem then is not to spend money but rather to draw up a training policy for the enterprise, i.e., to take account of all the economic, social and human needs of the company and to formulate a policy for continuing education which will then be discussed with the works council.

This is certainly no easy task, but this is where the future leads. Workers are becoming less and less willing to work just for money. As living standards rise, people's aspirations are rising too; they want to get ahead in their job, to understand what they are doing--and they are right.

Companies' personnel policies must therefore be policies for human development and not simply for expansion of the business. Seen in this light, the policy for continuing education can have an important role.

As far as small businesses are concerned, cooperative arrangements may provide the solution. Such companies could band together to have training assistants which would enable them to build training programs. All types of cooperative arrangement would be appropriate here, particularly the Fonds d'Assurance-Formation (Training Insurance Fund), which is the most flexible, supportive, and advanced in the field of social harmonization, and in addition offers considerable financial resources for implementation of training programs.

(4) If continuing education has any meaning, it applies to all workers, whether employed or self-employed: the risks of change to which we alluded earlier apply just as strongly to a skilled tradesman, a shopkeeper and a physician as they do to a wage-earner. These

sectors, too, must organize, i.e., make the same effort as the employers and workers did under their agreement of July 1970. The Law of 1971 is a framework law, which must be fleshed out by vital and resolute action on the part of the social groups involved. This is why farmers, craftsmen and traders must organize at the departmental, regional or national level in order to progress in this direction. I am pleased to note, in this connection, that the Haute-Savoie chamber of trade has established a training insurance fund for craftsmen and their journeymen.

One anecdote gives a clear indication of where we now stand with regard to continuing education: When the United Kingdom joined the Common Market, all of the British newspapers devoted several pages to their new partners in the EEC, and some of them had high words of praise for France. One economist stated, in fact, that the most important social reform of the past 20 years was the Law and the employer/union agreement on continuing education.

This must obviously have pleased those who are building up our present system, but their satisfaction must be tempered by awareness of the path that still lies ahead before the goals we have listed are achieved, and the realization that the most difficult part of the job still remains to be done.

U.S. public policy and the evolutionary adaptability of postsecondary education

STEPHEN P. DRESCH

Following a well-established tradition of fadism in matters educational, "continuing," "recurrent," or "non-traditional" education has recently come into vogue as a subject of discussion and debate among those concerned with educational policy. As is often the case, a perception of very real strains and imperfections within higher education underlies this developing concern. However, true to historical form, the dominant response has been to ignore the underlying sources of dissatisfaction, focusing instead on the easier task of prescribing new modes of educational delivery without regard to the underlying causes of observed institutional failure. Unfortunately, the academic-policy community finds it easier to invent a palliative measure, such as Recurrent Education, agonize over its content and meaning, and attempt to create a demand for it by manipulation of policy instruments (financing, accreditation, etc.).

The Issue Of Public Policy

The thesis of this note is that the central issue in the development of a policy toward recurrent education is not, primarily, to determine what new educational opportunities ought to be developed. It is not, primarily, to determine how these should be financed. It is, rather, to identify, first, the means by which existing public (and private) policies have served to preclude the adaptive evolution of the postsecondary educational system, and secondly, the changes in these policies which are necessary if such an adaptive evolution is to be possible. In short, the fundamental issue is that of removing those barriers to educational diversity which are incarnate in the traditional educational processes which dominate postsecondary education.

A specific discussion of this dimension serves a vital purpose, for the real threat is that the effort to develop a "well-behaved" system of recurrent education, in any guise, may be thwarted by an inflexible traditional system, if existing policy is not altered. More seriously, such an effort may itself serve to preserve a larger

532-819 O - 74 - 19

dysfunctional system, as have virtually all prior policy initiatives in this general area.

Whatever else it may achieve, recurrent education fractures the lockstep of the traditional educational structure. Why have alternative options not been made effectively available by "the market?" Certainly there are many dimensions of market failure operative in this case, among them imperfect knowledge and uncertainty, labor market rigidities, and capital market imperfections, to list only a few which would necessarily enter into a comprehensive analysis. However, one of the most important factors is public higher education policy itself.

The fundamental fact is that a recurrent education "policy" is necessitated primarily by the existence of a highly structured, static educational environment which owes much of its form and stability to a perversely supportive policy nexus. That is, recurrent education, both its supply and demand, cannot be viewed apart from the broader postsecondary educational context.

It is remarkable that educational attainments during the past 25 years in the U.S. could have been so radically increased and broadly diffused with very little change in the educational process itself. Increasing proportions of the high school population have continued their educations, and yet the menu of offerings has remained virtually static. The only accommodation to the increasing diversity of the student population has been in "quality."

We have attempted to provide everyone with the opportunity for at least the illusion of a quality education. But even in this rather fraudulent enterprise we have failed, as the first-year attrition rates from two-year colleges shockingly testify. Yet, virtually every significant policy action taken in postsecondary education over the last decade has served predominantly to shore up and protect this status quo of educational homogeneity.

The historical evolution of the modern higher education system, unlike that of prepared foods, is characterized by a progressive narrowing of options over time. The case is closer to that of the automobile, which has progressively driven other forms of local transit into oblivion while itself becoming an ever more standardized commodity. In higher education, "The Teachers College or Mining Institute has become the State College, then the State University...."[1] More recently, the vocationally oriented community college has become the liberally preparatory junior college. The primary goal of new, diverse institutions seems to be to become conventional four-year institutions.

---

1. Newman Report, "Graduate Education," Advanced Draft, U.S. Department of Health, Education, and Welfare, December 15, 1972.

However, the history of the auto is primarily one of product superiority, at least from the point of view of a large proportion of individual consumers, with monopoly entering only in the standardization of the product. In higher education, the case for product superiority, at least from the point of view of the potential student, seems particularly weak. Its monopoly derives not from technology or private market power, but from public policy.[2] The effect of public policy has been to subsidize the dominant mode of educational delivery so greatly as to render alternatives nonviable. Interestingly, every attempt to deal with or resolve the contradictions inherent in the resultant educational arrangements has simply served to perpetuate the underlying sources of dissatisfaction.

Developing a policy for recurrent education means demythologizing the existing educational order. If new forms of postsecondary educational delivery are to evolve, what is required is the effective creation of freedom of choice, an opening up of new possibilities for lifetime paths of education, work and leisure. In short, we need a policy which does not direct or constrain choice. We need one which facilitates but does not bias choice.

Forces For Change

The stability of the existing educational structure is currently threatened by a complex of technological, economic, and social forces. Two factors in particular explain the tendency toward standardization in higher education: the historical role of education as a consumption good and the evolution of a dominant economic-technological commonality. And in both dimensions, major disequilibria are developing.

For most of the present century, increasing enrollments in higher education in the U.S. have been drawn almost entirely from upwardly mobile, socially middle class strata, i.e., groups which subscribed to the values of the upper-middle class even if they lacked the corresponding material means. A cardinal characteristic of this dominant class was that education was viewed not only as a means to a material end, but also as a direct input into well-being, both during the period of education and in later life. Thus, in the perception of this class, education had value not only as an investment in future income, but also as a consumption good in its own right. If the student population was drawn predominantly from groups holding these values, then the extension of educational opportunities would be accompanied by major efforts to emulate the traditional educational

---

2. In the case of auto public policy, as represented directly by highway programs and indirectly by subsidies to middle class suburbanization (e.g., tax subsidies to owner-occupied housing), has also been perversely facilitating, so the two cases may not be truly dissimilar even in this dimension.

order. The agricultural or mining institute might well be sufficient to serve the narrower ends of the student but were insufficient for these larger social, or class, goals.

What is unique in the extension of educational opportunities, occurring in the last decade, is that this view of education was either unshared by or unaffordable to the newly "enfranchized" groups. The conception of "culture," its attainment and its relevance to the individual, has been found to be very different beyond the confines of the middle class. The only value really shared is the desire for improved material welfare.

The other, reinforcing, factor is that education as consumption has value, or is effectively demanded, only at sufficiently high levels of income. Subjected to a much more severe budget constraint, lower income groups place little relative value on this social aspect of education in comparison to the direct and indirect costs of obtaining it.

The most extreme of these costs, and the one public policy has done least to mitigate, is the loss of earnings during periods of full-time educational enrollment. Traditional higher education and its discriminatory tuition policies have done little to facilitate part-time enrollment. The City University of New York, for example, prides itself on free tuition, but tuition is free only for full-time students, with significant charges imposed upon part-time enrollees. Thus, even public subsidy policies have been geared to preserving the dominant middle class ethos of higher education. "Encourage" people to enroll, but only if they subscribe to and sacrifice for the prevailing conception of higher education.

The other dimension of increased educational standardization parallels the experience over the last century of an increasing technological standardization. The educational system which evolved was perfectly suited to the diffusion of broad new technologies and forms of organization. However, this process of evolution is not static, and new directions of evolution have created tensions between economic needs and educational organization. With the latter half of the 20th Century, we find no broad common threat to technological development, but instead an increasing refinement and focusing of technological advance. Furthermore, the very complexity of the new technologies almost necessitates specialization. Finally, the rapidity with which these narrowly defined technologies change has increased the rate at which educationally created skills become obsolete.

The basic fact of the present period is the radical upswing in the rate of narrow technological obsolescence. What was once a slow, incremental process which operated over an individual's lifetime now operates on a year-to-year basis. Traditional educational forms simply cannot meet the implied demands.

Although difficult to observe and measure, it is almost certain that the share of broadly educational activities taking place within the traditional educational sphere is declining markedly. Somehow productive enterprises must be adapting the labor force to these day-to-day changes in technology and practice. When third generation computers give way to the fourth generation, great cadres of workers must be either replaced or re-educated.

An industrial environment of this type must inexorably lead to decline in the role of the formally constituted educational system or change in its structure and content. A continuing, reconstituted set of educational options, paralleling the continuing processes of technological and economic evolution, would seem to be very likely concomitant to a progressive system of on-the-job <u>re</u>training. But in its current form, the educational system is ill-prepared, and apparently unwilling, to meet this need.

A final factor which may be operating is the "rejection" of the assembly line, and related phenomena. If this apparent trend continues, the result will be a demand for a continuing process of skill broadening as well as deepening.

Redesigning Public Policy

Existing programs have excluded alternatives to conventional higher education by focusing subsidies entirely within a narrow range of options.

The solution is neither obvious nor easy, particularly in light of the strong political constituencies dedicated to the preservation of the existing order. However, new directions can be suggested by cataloging options and examining their possible ramifications.

One such option is the "Human Investment Fund," which represents a rather radical departure from existing policy. The proposal is a variant of the National Youth Endowment suggested several years ago by James Tobin and Leonard Ross.[3] The Tobin-Ross endowment would make available to all persons at graduation from high school or at age 18, as a matter of right, a fixed sum of $5,000 which could be drawn upon at any point prior to age 28 for any broadly-defined educational purpose. Any person utilizing his endowment would be committed to pay an income tax surcharge after the age of 28, at a specified rate per $1,000 drawn.

In its reconstituted form, as proposed here, the endowment, increased initially to $10,000, would not be restricted to the 28-year

---

3. James Tobin and Leonard Ross, "A National Youth Endowment," <u>New Republic</u> 160, 2836 (May 3, 1969): 18-21.

limit, but could be utilized at any time.[4] In a major departure from the Tobin-Ross proposal, the full amount would be either taken or declined, i.e., prior to age 25 the individual would have to declare his intention to participate, at which point the full amount would become available (although not necessarily eligible for immediate withdrawal).

Having declared the intention to participate, a tax equal to a fixed percentage of total income, e.g., 6 percent, would be imposed in each year for a period of 30 years, beginning with age 18 (with the tax applied retroactively in case of a later declaration). Thus, surtax payments would cease at age 48. However, if at any prior point, accumulated payments were sufficient to discharge a debt equal to 120 percent of the original total amount advanced, no further payment would be required. The individual would earn interest on the unexpended portion of the advance at the same rate at which interest would accrue on the outstanding debt (presumably equal to the rate then prevailing on federal debt). In any year, if income were zero, no payment would be made, and any positive payment could be made via a transfer from the unexpended endowment. The full proposal is outlined in greater detail in the Appendix.

Drawings from the endowment account prior to age 48 would be limited to broadly defined human capital forming purposes, with limits determined by the level of direct educational costs plus an annual living allowance. The only exceptions would be drawings utilized to make payments required on the basis of income. After age 48, any remaining endowment balance could be drawn upon for any purpose and in any amount. Effectively, after this age the endowment becomes a totally unrestricted asset of the individual.

In the present context, the truly interesting questions concern the implications of this system versus one of direct or indirect subsidy to more-or-less traditional higher education. The essential differences would seem to be the following:

1. Most obviously, the endowment could be drawn upon at any time. The individual would have an incentive, therefore, to consider the trade-offs between a vastly expanded set of optional lifetime paths of education and work.

2. The endowment could be drawn upon for any broadly defined educational purpose, including many which would not be likely to receive direct public support. Particularly in conjunction with a relaxation of the time schedule of education and work, it could be anticipated that a much greater share of relatively formal postsecondary education would be work-related, not necessarily in only a narrowly vocational sense. Rather, an expanded set of work-study arrangements would be expected to evolve which would offer the opportunity of alternating

---

4. Over time the endowment would be increased to reflect nominal income growth in the economy at large.

or concomitant, hopefully reinforcing, periods of education and work. The major barrier to such developments in the past has been the necessity for the employer to bear virtually the total cost of both on-the-job and job-related training, with no assurance that he would continue to benefit from the education and training of the employee, who might leave after being trained at the employer's expense. This risk is even higher in the case of more general, if still job-related, education, with the result that most employer-financed training is highly specific to the individual firm.

3. Even with respect to more traditional, full-time education, this scheme would serve to mitigate the adverse consequences of foregone earnings as a barrier to educational activity by providing funds in excess even of anticipated "full-cost" tuition (which may in fact be lower, at least at some levels of higher education, than is conventionally thought).

What the ultimate implications of such a radical reorientation of public policy might be cannot be easily predicted from today's vantage point. Initially, it is probably safe to anticipate that the responses would be marginal. However, over the long run, as the system (educational institutions, employers, "students") began to respond to the new opportunities, major structural changes in postsecondary education would be likely to evolve. And, while this may be only the economist's bias, the result could be more far-reaching and revolutionary than would follow from a more conscious, explicit policy of educational reorganization.

Appendix

The Human Investment Fund

At the outset, it should be noted that the following presents only a rough sketch of the Human Investment Fund proposal. Specific numbers, e.g., the 6 percent repayment rate, have not been estimated by any formal procedure and are purely illustrative.

Structure

The Human Investment Fund (HIF) would be legally established as a quasi-independent public agency empowered to issue debt guaranteed by the federal government. HIF would contract with other agencies (Internal Revenue Service, Social Security Administration) for administrative services.

Eligible Population

All persons graduating from high school or reaching age 18 would be eligible to participate in the HIF program. The HIF program would be designed to "break even" on any cohort of high school graduates. On account of all participants not high school graduates, the federal government would deposit with HIF an amount equal to the expected loss (present value) on these accounts in isolation.

Interest Rate

The interest rate utilized in all HIF calculations and contracts would be 1 percent plus the three-year moving average rate of growth in expected lifetime incomes of persons with educational attainments of high school graduate or above. Any differential (positive or negative) between this rate and the rate paid on HIF debt would accrue to or be absorbed by the federal government.

Individual Contract

At any point between initial eligibility and age 25 an individual could choose to contract with HIF, a choice which would entail the establishment of (a) an "endowment account," and (b) a "payment account."

Endowment account. At the decision to participate, the endowment account would be credited with a designated sum. Initially established (e.g., in 1973) at $10,000, this designated amount would be increased for each year's 18-year old cohort at the rate of income growth (above). Participation would be assumed to have been initiated at age 18, with the amount available to the individual determined as the designated amount in his 18th year. For every year between age 18 and the age at which he chooses to participate, interest would be compounded at the appropriate (floating) interest rate. Once established, the endowment account could be drawn upon at any time. Any positive balance in the account would earn interest at the appropriate interest rate.

Payment account. The payment account would be established simultaneously with the endowment account. The amount of the payment account would represent the individual's debt to the HIF. On establishment (as if at age 18), the payment account would be debited at 1.2 times the amount by which the endowment account was credited (e.g., $12,000), the additional 0.2 representing a "premium" for income insurance. The balance in the payment account would accrue interest at the then-effective interest rate. The payment due to the payment account in any year (each payment reducing the amount outstanding in the payment account) would be six percent of adjusted gross income in that year. For those deciding to participate after age 18, the payment due in any prior year (on the basis of income in that year) would be treated as having been made by a transfer from the endowment account to the payment account in that year. If, at age 48, a positive balance remained in the payment account, this amount of debt would be forgiven and no further payment liability would exist.

For a married couple, if both were liable, the payment due in any year would be six percent of joint adjusted gross income; if only one were liable, payment due would be the larger of (a) six percent of own adjusted gross income, or (b) three percent of joint adjusted gross income.

income contingent loans for recurring education

KENNETH R. BIEDERMAN and BRADLEY B. BILLINGS

The essence of recurrent education is the distribution of education over the lifetime of the individual, as opposed to the concentration of education in the early years, prior to any period of work experience. The present educational system in the United States is highly structured toward the syndrome of education first, followed by a continuous period of work, and ultimately retirement.

Arguments for the encouragement and development of an educational system which formally recognizes the existence and need of recurrent education are varied.[1] Some form of continuing education seems essential in any technologically advanced economy where changes require frequent and often significant occupational adjustment on the part of individual members of the labor force. Economic efficiency and growth mandates the avoidance of technological obsolescence among productive factors, yet the current system of institutional education is not adapted to the problems of depreciation and technological obsolescence of human capital. Recent research indicates that the divorce of formal education from job experience, which typifies most educational systems, is not the most efficient approach to the technological development and maintenance of human capital.[2] The question arises then as to why the educational system has evolved as it has, why a formal system of recurring education has not developed.

---

1. See J. Alan Thomas, "Financing Adult and Continuing Education," Johns-Alexander-Jorden, ed., in Planning To Finance Education (National Educational Finance Project, III, 1971): 147-60.

2. For example, see Lester C. Thurow, Poverty and Discrimination (Washington, D.C.: The Brookings Institution, 1969).

To a great extent, the product has evolved to meet the demand, and that demand depends upon the financial arrangements and income maintenance provisions available. If existing financial markets were made more available to the educational needs of adults, the preference of adults translated into market demand for continuing education would clearly be different, reflecting both a shift in the demand for adult education services as well as movement along a given demand curve as a result of lower expenditures immediately required for these services. Many adults pursue educational goals through continuing education in an inefficient, and thereby costly, manner because of financial limitations.

This study looks at the financial limitations to continuing education which are likely to exist for adults of various age and income levels, and suggests ways in which current loan markets might be altered or restructured in order to accommodate the educational needs of adults in a more efficient manner. Specifically, consideration is given to the adaptation of the income-contingent loan scheme--which has received considerable attention as a method for financing higher education[3]--to the educational needs of adults.

Student Loans For Adults

Presently structured lending institutions are not amenable to recurrent education. Personal loans in general must be secured by nonhuman capital and generally require short-term payback (three to five years) accompanied by relatively high rates of interest. Thus, loans of several thousands of dollars for purposes of obtaining additional education for many adults would impose excessive payback burdens, assuming the loans were made available in the first place. Current lending markets do little toward removing existing financial inequities that exist between high income-low income, younger-older, and less educated-more educated adults desirous of continuing their education.

Beyond personal financing, adults desirous of education simply do not find the present educational system financially receptive. Federal support for adult education is limited in both scope and

---

3. See Robert W. Hartman, Credit for College: Public Policy for Student Loans (New York: McGraw-Hill, 1971); and Shell et al., "The Educational Opportunity Bank: An Economic Analysis of a Contingent Repayment Loan Program for Higher Education," National Tax Journal 21 (March 1969): 2-45.

expenditure, with nearly two-thirds of the $4 billion being spent in 1971 for veterans' education and programs directed toward the disadvantaged.[4]

The only common ground that exists among the various states with regard to adult education is that all states participate in the Adult Basic Education (ABE) Program.[5] Besides the ABE Program, financial support for adult education varies from no support in the case of Kansas to very limited support in some southern states as well as Massachusetts, Missouri, and Oregon to relatively extensive financial and program support in Florida and California. Local government support is equally diverse, from extensive state-local sharing in adult education programs to no local government support whatsoever.

Among all students, adults have the greatest financial obligations and the highest opportunity costs. Yet, tightly structured labor markets, limited governmental support, and restrictive or nonexistent financial markets prevent the pursuit of continuing education through an optimal mode or time pattern.

On the surface, self-financing government supported loan programs appear as a viable solution to many of the financial limitations and inequities that exist with regard to recurrent education. There is presently little inclination on the part of legislators to expand educational cost financing through state and local taxes, particularly to levels suggested by a widely expanded, government financed adult education system. Self-financing personal loan programs circumvent

---

4. U. S. Office of Education, Perspectives of Adult Education in the United States and a Projection for the Future, report for the Third International Conference on Adult Education, Tokyo, Japan, July 25-August 7, 1972 (Washington, D.C.: Government Printing Office, October 1972), p. 22.

5. The Adult Basic Education Program (P.L. 89-750, Amended) was established under the Adult Education Act of 1966 and is administered by the U. S. Office of Education. The program is open to persons of 16 years and older for purposes of attaining reading, writing, and computational skills up to an 8th grade equivalency. Funding is shared with the states (and/or local governments), providing 10 percent of the program costs and retaining responsibility for planning, supervision, evaluation, staffing, and other related essential services. For a detailed, statistical analysis of the program, see National Center for Educational Statistics, Adult Basic Education Program Statistics--Students and Staff Data, July 1, 1969-June 30, 1970 (Washington, D.C.: Government Printing Office, 1971).

this problem, while at the same time allow for testing the market demand for recurrent education. The problem thus becomes one of developing a viable loan program amenable to the educational needs of adults who differ considerably with regard to financial limitations to continuing their education.

The procedure followed here was to determine the payback burden that would be imposed upon adults borrowing funds under various loan programs.[6] Two forms of income contingent loan programs were considered: A fixed term payback, and a variable term payback dependent upon the age of the borrower.

An adult's ability to borrow funds under any given program would be contingent upon current and future financial obligations during the payback period, as well as income anticipations. These in turn are dependent upon the age, education, and present labor market situation of the borrower, as reflected in current income.

The first loan program is an adaptation of the Educational Opportunity Bank proposed by the Zacharias Panel on Educational Innovation.[7] For exemplary purposes, a cohort of 1,000 borrowers was assumed, having income levels representative of relatively high, relatively low, and average income for any given age and education of the borrower.[8] Borrowers were distributed by three different age categories: 25-34, 35-44, and 45-54. Current population distributions and mortality tables were used to form this representative sample of individuals participating in recurring education and to trace their numbers over time.

In order to provide some basis for comparison of the different educational pursuits of adults and the corresponding impacts on their future incomes, it was assumed that adults would enroll in courses leading to either high school graduate or college graduate

---

6. This format was suggested in Hartman, Credit for College.

7. Educational Opportunity Bank: A Report of the Panel on Educational Innovation to U. S. Commissioner of Education Harold Howell, Director of the National Science Foundation Leland J. Haworth, and Special Assistant to the President for Science and Technology Donald F. Hornig (Washington, D.C.: U. S. Government Printing Office, August 1967).

8. Low income--income levels 25 percent below average in population of adults identical by age and education; high income--income 25 percent above the same mean.

equivalencies.[9] It was also assumed that the initial payback year for each age category would be at the beginning year of that category and that payments would not be required during the period an adult was out of the labor force for purposes of continuing his education.[10]

The basic concept involved in the Educational Opportunity Bank for Adults (EOBA) loan program is a fixed term repayment schedule with the amount contingent upon future incomes. Adults borrowing under this plan would agree to make repayments of t percent of their income per year for x years for each $1,000 initially borrowed. In order to avoid unexpected losses to the lending institution resulting from participation of only those anticipating low incomes, an "opt-out" rate would be built into the program such that no individual borrower would have to pay back more than the loan principal compounded at some designated rate R. Thus, relatively low income borrowers would be subsidized by relatively high income borrowers, but the disincentive to borrow implicit in such a system for borrowers with high incomes or high income expectations would be lessened by the opt-out provision.

In calculating the tax rate t (payback rate), the Bank is assumed to operate on a zero profit condition, any deviation from zero profit implying either a subsidy or higher tax. To achieve the zero profit, the Bank is required to earn an internal rate of return consistent with the rate at which the government can borrow. Differences in Bank borrowing rates and rates charged borrowers are to cover administrative and associated costs of operation.

The method of solution for the tax rate is similar to that used by Shell et al. and Dresch and Goldberg.[11] Basically, it involves

---

9. Equivalency levels are measured in terms of potential earnings at these levels of education; it does not necessarily imply the actual holding of degrees.

10. This is an administrative problem that cannot be resolved with the ease that it has been in loan programs for full-time undergraduates. For purposes here, we skirted the issue by assuming initial loan repayment being made during the beginning period of re-employment after education has been completed; or, during education if it is being pursued while the adult maintains his regular employment schedule.

11. Shell et al., "The Educational Opportunity Bank"; and Stephen P. Dresch and Robert D. Goldberg, "Variable Term Loans for Higher Education--Analytics and Empirics," Annals of Economic and Social Measurement 1, 1 (January 1972): 59-92.

solving for the opt-out year for each category of participants and calculating the payments for each year and group of borrowers who vary by age, income, and assumed educational pursuit. The total amount borrowed is compared with the payment stream, and through repeated iterations, the solution value of the tax rate is found which equates borrowing and payments. To put both borrowings and payments into comparable terms, borrowings are compounded forward to the first year of payment and payments are discounted back to the initial year. The discounting factor is the specified internal rate of return.

The opt-out year for each category is calculated by finding the inter value N small enough so that:

$$(1) \quad 1000/M[(1+r)^{m} + (1+r)^{m-1} + \ldots + (1+r)] \leq v \sum_{t=1}^{N} (1+r)^{-t} Y_{it}$$

where M is the number of years of borrowing, r is the specified opt-out rate, v is the tax rate per $1,000 borrowed, Y_{it} is the income for class i in year t, and m is the year index.[12]

The schedule of payments is calculated by:

$$(2) \quad P_{it} = \begin{cases} vY_{it} \; ; \quad t < N(i) \leq T \\ (1+r)^{N(i)} [1000/M \{(1+r)^{m} + \ldots + (1+r)\} \\ - \sum_{t=1}^{N(i)-1} P_{it}(1+r)^{-t}] ; \quad t = N(i) \leq T \\ 0 \; ; \quad t > N(i), \text{ or } t > T \end{cases}$$

where N(i) is the opt-out year for the ith class, P_{it} the payment of each person in the ith cell in period t, T is the ending year and other terms as defined above. The middle term calculates the residual payment left in the final year under the opt-out provision.

The zero profit condition can be stated as:

---

12. See Shell et al., "The Educational Opportunity Bank," for further discussion of this and the following equation.

$$(3) \qquad S = \sum_{t=1}^{T} (1+i)^{-t} \left[\left[\sum_{i=1}^{NL} N_{it} P_{it} \right] \right]$$

where S is the sum of borrowings by all groups (assuming $1,000 per person) compounded forward, i is the internal rate of return, N_{it} is the number of persons in each group, NL is the number of classes, and P_{it} is the payment by the ith group in the tth year. The payments are calculated according to equation (2)--the tax rate times income for each group for all time periods less than the ending year, or less than the particular group's opt-out year. Once the opt-out year is reached, the payment is simply the remainder of the loan outstanding compounded by the opt-out rate. After either the opt-out year or the ending year for a group is reached, payments are zero.

Growth rates in income were determined as a sum of two parts:

a. an expected increase in income within an educational category due to increases in real wages which result from job experience, productivity increases associated with such experience, and other job related factors besides changes in education over time; and

b. increases in real income resulting from additional formal education--an educational premium.

Differences in income resulting from additional education were determined from income data on yearly earnings by age and formal education levels. (For this purpose, it was assumed that 12 years of education were completed at age 18, and 16 years [college degree] were completed at age 22.) It was observed that income differentials by levels of education widened with increasing age categories, with greatest income differences between 8th grade and 12th grade education, and 12th grade and 4 years of college occurring 25-35 years after completion of formal education in each case. For our purposes here, we assumed a 30-year lag between the completion of the formal education and the peak income differentials observed between differing levels of such education. Since it is unreasonable to assume income would increase by the full amount of this differential upon completion of education, average annual rates of increase in income were calculated resulting from increased formal education, determining the aforementioned educational premium. Combined, the rates of income increase captured expected increases in real income as a result of normal job experience as well as increases in formal education, or its equivalent.

532-819 O - 74 - 20

Table 1 shows the estimated tax rates t which adults opting to use this income contingent plan would have to pay per $1,000 borrowed under various assumptions regarding length of repayment and opt-out rates. Thus, a cohort of borrowers with the income, age, and education characteristics described previously would pay a tax rate of .66 percent of adjusted gross income per $1,000 borrowed under a 20-year payback contract with an assumed real internal rate of 2.5 percent and real opt-out rate of 4.5 percent. The insurance rate figure reflects the amount tax rates are increased due to the burden of loan repayments of those borrowers in the cohort who die before full repayment; that burden being distributed among the remaining borrowers. Consequently, if the EOBA were designed such that full loan repayments were made either by the borrower or some designate (such as immediate family), the rates shown in columns (3) and (5) of table 1 would be lower by the corresponding rates in columns (4) and (6), respectively.

Increasing the repayment period has the predictable effect of lowering the applicable tax rates and raising the insurance rate. The sensitivity of the tax burden for variations in Bank borrowing costs is evidenced in comparison of column (1) with columns (3) and (5).

The income contingent plan as envisioned in the Educational Opportunity Bank Program involved a subsidization of relatively low income borrowers by their more successful undergraduate colleagues, with degrees of subsidy dependent upon the opt-out rate and the program tax rate.[13] Although this same subsidy element exists in the income-contingent loan plan for adults, there is an additional subsidy in this program which merits consideration. It was assumed in determining the rates shown in table 1 that no repayments would be made after age 65. The reasoning behind this assumption was that high mortality risks would prevent the lending institution from extending terms on human capital loans much beyond age 65. In addition, rapidly falling income levels which occur due to retirement would make repayment particularly burdensome. Since inclusion of the after age 65 repayment consideration into the loan program would have the mutually adverse effects of decreasing the supply of loans in the former instance and decreasing demand for loans--and thereby adult participation in continuing education--in the latter, the assumption seems reasonable.

However, an immediate consequence of this assumption is the subsidization of the education of relatively high income, older adults by the relatively low income, younger adults as would be reflected in higher tax rates. Since increased tax rates imply

---

13. For an analysis and evaluation of this subsidy element in income contingent loan programs for higher education, see Dresch and Goldberg, "Variable Term Loans."

Table 1. Educational Opportunity Bank For Adults.

(1) Internal Rate of Return [a] (%)	(2) Opt-Out Rate [b] (%)	(3) Tax Rate (t): [c] 20-year Payback (%)	(4) Insurance Rate: [d] 20-year Payback (%)	(5) Tax Rate (t): [c] 30-year Payback (%)	(6) Insurance Rate: [e] 30-year Payback (%)
2.0%	4.0%	.62%	.04%	.47%	.08%
2.5	4.5	.66	.03	.50	.08
3.0	6.0	.69	.03	.54	.08
4.0	6.0	.79	.03	.63	.08

a. Real rate.

b. Real rate.

c. Rate per $1,000 of loan principal.

d. Amount by which tax rate in column (3) would be lowered if no accounting were made of mortality and early retirements in calculation of t.

e. Amount by which tax rate in column (5) would be lowered if no accounting were made of mortality and early retirements in calculation of t.

earlier opting out by high income borrowers, an additional regressive element is introduced through a corresponding reduction in the subsidization of low income borrowers by high income borrowers in any given age category.

To compensate for this--and thereby introduce a progressive tax rate structure into a variable term, income-contingent adult education loan program--a variation of the above loan program was considered. This variant, although basically an income-contingent plan, consists of variable term repayments dependent upon the borrower's age. The program would operate similarly to a cash-value, life insurance policy in which payments per $1,000 of policy (loan) vary inversely with age and are paid up at age 65. Each cohort of adult borrowers would be treated by the lending institution independently of borrowers of different ages. Terms of the loan would consist of a payback period determined by the difference in the borrower's age and age 65--the point where the "loan policy" is fully retired. Consequently, for any given opt-out rate and internal rate of return to the lending bank, a rate structure would be introduced in the repayment pattern which would:

a. increase with the age of the borrower, thereby eliminating the subsidy of relatively high income older adults by low income younger adults; and

b. maintain the desirable property of future high income borrowers subsidizing the less successful borrowers within any age category.

Table 2[14] shows the tax rate structure which would result from this variable term, income contingent loan program for a similar cohort of adult borrowers as was considered in the EOBA loan program.

By extending the payback period for the younger borrowers, as well as eliminating the inherent subsidy of older borrowers by the young, the Paid-Up, Age 65 Plan provides significantly lower tax rates for younger adults than does the Educational Opportunity Bank for Adults (EOBA) Plan. For example, under assumed real opt-out and internal rates of 4.5 percent and 2.5 percent, respectively, the EOBA Plan would assess a tax rate to all borrowers of .50 percent per $1,000 under a 30-year payback period, and .66 percent under the 20-year payback scheme. Given similar assumptions, the tax rate per $1,000 loan would be only .36 percent for borrowers in the age category

---

14. The techniques for solution of this loan program as shown in table 2 are essentially the same as those described previously for the EOBA.

Table 2. Paid-Up, Age 65 Plan.

Opt-Out Rate[a] = 4.5%		Opt-Out Rate[a] = 6.0%	
Internal Rate[a] = 2.5%		Internal Rate[a] = 4.0%	
Age	Tax Rate[b] %	Age	Tax Rate[b] %
25-34	.36%	25-34	.49%
35-44	.44	35-44	.55
45-54	.64	45-54	.77

a. Real rates.

b. Rate per $1,000 of loan principal.

25-34 under the Paid-Up Plan.[15]

As to the feasibility of either loan program, at least from the standpoint of the borrower, it is not only necessary to determine the level of payback required for any given loan, but to arrive at some benchmark as to what constitutes an excessive repayment burden upon the borrower. A basis of comparison then would exist in this matter not only between loan programs, but within a given program as to reasonable repayment levels for borrowers.

We adopted the criterion that rates or levels of repayment of a loan which exceeded personal savings would be considered an excessive repayment requirement. Although to a certain extent such a criterion appears arbitrary, this condition would call for a repayment schedule for adults of differing income, demographic, and expenditure characteristics which would not impinge upon their current consumption patterns or abilities to meet existing financial obligations.

Table 3 shows relative burdens of the EOBA and Paid-Up, Age 65 Plan for borrowers of alternative sized loans by age and income level. Repayment ratios are calculated for each lending plan, indicating what the level of loan repayments required under a particular program would be compared to payments which would be equivalent to levels of savings.[16] Thus, the burden of repayment of a $5,000 loan, for example, under the EOBA Plan, borrowed by an adult age 25 earning below average income, and repaid over a 20-year period would be more than 3 times his average savings propensity during this same period. In comparison, the repayment burden of the same loan under the same program but with repayment extended over a 30-year period would be but 1.7 times the individual's savings.

---

15. These absolute figures are contingent on our simplifying assumptions that payback commences on the first year of a given age category and that payments cease beyond age 65. Excepting mortality considerations, an individual in the age category 25-34 is assumed to have a 40-year payback horizon. Altering this assumption in order to more evenly distribute loans by age would increase the tax rates under both plans, but should not significantly alter the relative figures in and between tables 1 and 2.

16. Savings defined as net changes per period in assets less liabilities. Savings rates by income and age categories estimated from U. S. Bureau of Labor Statistics, <u>Survey of Consumer Expenditures, 1960-61. Consumer Expenditures and Income Cross-Classification of Family Characteristics Urban United States</u>, Supp. 2--Part A to BLS Report 237-38 (Washington, D.C.: Government Printing Office, July 1964).

Table 3. Ratios of Payback Burden Of Loan Programs To Personal Savings For Various Sized Loans: Borrower Categories By Age and Income.

Plan and Borrower Characteristics	Size of Loan: $5,000 Loan[a]	$10,000 Loan[a]	$15,000 Loan[a]
I. EOBA Plan[b]			
Age 25-34			
Low income	3.07	6.14	9.21
High income	.74	1.48	2.22
Age 35-44			
Low income	2.95	5.90	8.85
High income	.61	1.23	1.85
Age 45-54			
Low income	2.33	4.66	6.99
High income	.48	.97	1.45
II. EOBA Plan[c]			
Age 25-34			
Low income	1.70	3.41	5.11
High income	.46	.93	1.40
Age 35-44			
Low income	1.58	3.16	4.74
High income	.40	.81	1.21
Age 45-54			
Low income	1.27	2.54	3.81
High income	.34	.68	1.01
III. Paid-Up Age 65 Plan			
Age 25-34			
Low income	.97	1.94	2.91
High income	.30	.60	.90
Age 35-44			
Low income	1.39	2.78	4.17
High income	.35	.71	1.07
Age 45-54			
Low income	2.26	4.52	6.78
High income	.47	.94	1.41

a. Burden ratios were computed by using the savings rate across time and income classes to form the denominator, and the percentage of income which would have to be paid under each plan for a $5,000, $10,000, and $15,000 loan as the numerator. Real opt-out and internal rates of 4.5 percent and 2.5 percent, respectively, assumed in all calculations.

b. 20-year payback period assumed.

c. 30-year payback period assumed.

Implications, Conclusions, And Recommendations

Ideally, a loan program constructed for the purpose of serving the educational needs of adults should be structured with repayment conditions that would not impose undue financial hardships upon the borrower. As to what in fact constitutes financial hardships is in itself arbitrary; we have adopted a repayment schedule equivalent to average savings over time as indeed an arbitrary, but reasonable, basis for comparison of relative financial hardships imposed in the repayment of loans under alternative lending structures.

In general, the financial profile of young adults is one of relatively low income, small holdings of liquid assets, and considerable indebtedness relative to older adults. This pattern is indicative of a high average propensity to consume among young adults[17] (age 18-35), and a relatively high average propensity to save among older adults (45-65). The distribution of holdings of liquid assets by families whose head is under age 35 is heavily skewed at the lower end, with 70 percent of families holding less than $1,000 in liquid assets.[18] For older adults (age 45 and above), a somewhat different financial resource picture evolves, with nearly 25 percent holding liquid assets in excess of $5,000.

As evidenced then in table 3, a long-term, income-contingent loan program for continuing education is suited to the needs of young adults. This is true for both high and low income categories, and as might be expected, is particularly adaptable to those having relatively high incomes.[19] Of the two programs considered, the Paid-Up, Age 65 Plan is preferable due to the longer repayment period and the removal of the subsidy of older adults inherent in the EOBA, income-contingent plan. Loans much in excess of $5,000 are likely to prove burdensome for low income, young adults, whereas those enjoying relatively high income levels could easily borrow up to $15,000 under the Paid-Up Plan without incurring serious repayment burdens. Of the two programs, neither would likely prove excessive to the relatively high income young adults borrowing up to $5,000.

Older adult participants (age 45-54), on the other hand, would find that of the loan plans considered, the EOBA Plan with a 30-year

---

17. A ratio which Thurow has shown would in fact be higher but for institutional constraints; L. Thurow, "The Optimum Lifetime Distribution of Consumption Expenditures," American Economic Review 59, 3 (June 1969): 324-330.

18. Katona, G. et al., 1969 Survey of Consumer Finances (Ann Arbor: Survey Research Center, University of Michigan, 1970), p. 103.

19. The reader is reminded that high income refers to income levels 25 percent above the mean income for a given population.

payback would prove more ideal for them. Since adults in that category would cease payment after 20 years at the most, this program would provide them with the greatest amount of subsidy. Also, the EOBA Plan dispenses the tax burdens of mortality among borrowers of all ages, unlike the Paid-Up, Age 65 Plan. Because of the relatively high incidence of mortality in the oldest age group, the EOBA Plan provides added subsidy in the form of partially paid group insurance.

High income borrowers among the older adults would not be heavily burdened by repayments of loans up to $15,000 in either plan. Since the figures in table 3 do not take into account the relatively favorable position of older adults with regard to liquid asset holdings and small indebtedness, the burden ratios are undoubtedly overstated for this age group. Even among low income, older adults, the borrowing situation is likely to be brighter than is indicated under any given loan plan. Regardless, the EOBA, 30-year Plan would still prove preferable to these individuals as a group.

Middle-aged adults (35-44) are confronted with many of the financial barriers to recurring education that their younger colleagues face; namely, small liquid asset reserves and high levels of indebtedness.[20] The advantage of a longer repayment period exists for adults in this age category for the EOBA, 30-year Plan and the Paid-Up, Age 65 Plan. There is a noticeable burden difference between the two, particularly for low income borrowers. This reflects the advantage of not having to subsidize older borrowers under the Paid-Up Plan. Both plans appear to impose rather severe payback rates on low income, middle-aged borrowers even for loans as low as $5,000. For high income, middle-aged participants, either plan requires reasonable repayments for $5,000 and $10,000 loans and only the EOBA 20-year payback plan involves excessive repayments for loans of $15,000.

In table 3 the burden ratios are calculated for loans of $5,000, $10,000, and $15,000 to give some idea of the sensitivity of the borrowing restrictions as loan size increases. Of course, these loan amounts may or may not be sufficient to cover the financial burden of undertaking more education in desired time patterns. More needs to be known of the relative benefits associated with adults pursuing an educational goal full-time versus part-time, and for what time intervals, before these questions concerning individual levels of indebtedness can be answered. From what we have determined and in accordance with our notion of the burden of any loan scheme, a loan plan which involves repayments not in excess of savings propensity is preferred, because it is formulated on the idea that a person should pay back his education loan in a manner congruent with his preferences for

20. This is particularly true in the early years, 35-40. Katona et al., 1969 Survey of Consumer Finances, pp. 21-35 and 103.

present versus future consumption.[21] However, there are serious technical administrative problems associated with such a plan. A major drawback of a loan program of this nature is that as the loans increase, the period of repayment lengthens. For example, we found that a $15,000 loan would require a repayment period in excess of 40 years for all cases considered but one. Even a $10,000 loan requires a 35-year repayment horizon in most instances, which puts the 35-44 and 45-54 groups past retirement, hence employing a heavy subsidy from young to old.

The Paid-Up, Age 65 Plan appears to be the best alternative to this since its burden ratios are generally lower than the EOBA 20-year and 30-year schemes. The administration of this plan would not be significantly more difficult than for the EOBA plans, since both are based on the same concept--income contingent loans collected through the Internal Revenue Service.[22] The EOBA appears less desirable than the Paid-Up, Age 65 Plan since it incorporates the intergenerational loans; this is a drawback from which only our version of the Educational Opportunity Bank suffers. The version proposed by the Zacharias Panel does not incorporate any such subsidy since its borrowers are assumed to be of uniform age.

Our results are sensitive to our data and calculations, which are quite aggregated. Thus, these results can be refined if a more detailed study were undertaken. For example, we are in need of far better data showing participation in recurring education by age and income categories, and the true income bonuses resultant upon such education. More knowledge is needed as to what constitutes educational obsolescence and how it in fact is measured. Until more is known about this concept, thereby permitting insight into ideal consumption patterns of education over time, an optimal lending scheme for purposes of recurring education cannot be determined. But we feel that our results do point out many of the problems and limitations imposed upon a program of this nature, and do provide guidelines as to what directions reasonable financing schemes must take in order to eliminate current finance market imperfections and thereby facilitate expression of demand for recurring education.

---

21. To an extent, current savings indicate this. One reason that early age savings are so low is relative high purchases of consumer durables which in fact are consumed over many years. However, the effect of the budget constraint is unchanged regardless of the actual time pattern of consumption of such durables.

22. See Shell et al., "The Educational Opportunity Bank," for a more complete discussion of the administration of income contingent loan plans.

summary

an agenda for research: a summary analysis

SELMA J. MUSHKIN

The past decade produced new and unprecedented efforts to restructure educational systems for more efficiency and equity. Among those new approaches is "recurrent education" which is a system for acquiring modular segments of knowledge and skills beginning at the end of compulsory education and continuing throughout a lifetime at the option of the individual.

Presently, many educational offerings meet such conditions. Adult and continuing education are part of the familiar educational scene. There are governmental manpower training programs for the poor and unemployed, and industrial training programs for workers, executives, and customers.

There is nothing new in the components of recurrent education; what is new is that the concept is being grasped by policymakers of advanced nations as a possible solution to several major problems--or awakened demands--that have developed.

Perhaps the major problems that have arisen and given impetus to the concept of recurrent education are the finances of the colleges and universities. The whole question of financing education has come to the forefront with the declining growth of the market for preparatory education for the young in universities and colleges, and the resistance to tax support for secondary schools and postsecondary education.

At the same time, the old notions that "the more education, the better," and "get a good job, get a good education," are being challenged by an unfavorable job market.

There is also concern about the lengthening of education, without links to work careers or emphasis on market demands for workers. Furthermore, there is awakened concern for equality in education and special opportunities for the poor and those disadvantaged by educational practices.

As a consequence of these issues, re-examination of familiar institutional patterns is now in process. It comes as government is developing a self-consciousness about its own services and is asking about the quantity, quality, successes, and failures of its various services in achieving the public purposes sought.

Member nations of the Organisation for Economic Co-operation and Development (OECD), and nations in other parts of the world as well, are examining recurrent education as a part of their evaluations of education in general. The OECD has put its emphasis on a strategy for change toward a recurrent or more flexible pattern of learning, earning, and playing. Such an emphasis accords with the nature and scope of the changes involved for most of the member nations. Is it the right course for the United States? Is incremental modification toward a recurrent system over the long term "right" for the U.S.? And toward what scope and with what special purposes are the incremental modifications to be made?

A. Policy Considerations

Apart from the controversial questions involved in the implementation of recurrent educational programs, there are a number of important policy motives for recurrent education.

In fact, recurrent education is being promoted for achievement of so many and such varied purposes that a classification of objectives appears to be needed. Such a classification is set forth as an illustrative one.

Higher Education Institutional Objectives

1. Improving the quality of higher education, by:

   ...greater maturity of student bodies.
   ...better information about ongoing scientific and engineering problems in industry and government.
   ...better formulation of new research tasks.

2. Safeguarding the finances of institutions of higher education, by:

   ...additional student revenues.
   ...lower costs per student of existing faculty offerings.
   ...lower costs by better use of existing facilities.
   ...additional persons qualifying for GI benefits as learners.

3. Providing experience and also job access for young students, by:

...participation of those in the work force in courses of study.
...broadening the circle of student acquaintanceship for young students to include those who recruit.

4. Motivating young students, by:

...lessening the ivory-tower atmosphere of the classroom.
...reducing the ever present tension to complete and not drop out by the option of recurrent education.
...reducing immediate financial pressures involved in completing school.
...offering less traditional options.

Economic Stability And Growth Objectives

5. Increasing productivity in the economy, by:

...increasing numbers qualified to fill available vacancies.
...facilitating worker participation in work place decisions.
...motivating workers to stay on the job with resulting lower turnover costs.
...facilitating job restructuring, job enrichment, and co-determination of work place rules.

6. Reducing economic wastes of unemployment and underemployment, by:

...retraining for new jobs.
...upgrading of skills.
...re-educating for new advances in knowledge.
...re-educating for new careers.

7. Easing transitions between military and civilian pursuits, by:

...training for civilian jobs and conversion of military skills.
...training for civilian life.

8. Improving decision-making, by:

...encouraging middle management training.
...facilitating training for job enrichment.
...facilitating worker education.

Greater Equity Objectives

9. <u>Providing a second educational chance for women, older persons, minority groups, and blue collar workers, by</u>:

...facilitating learning experience for such groups.
...maintaining income during study and guaranteeing jobs for blue collar and other workers.
...implementing study support programs, for example, child-care services, home health aids, etc.
...facilitating study required for job credentials.

10. <u>Encouraging literacy and work habit education, by</u>:

...providing general incentives for study.
...removing stigma of special treatment under work incentives programs.

11. <u>Encouraging upward bound education, by</u>:

...making educational timing, methods, and certifications more flexible.
...crediting and building on work experience.
...maintaining income and implementing study support programs.

Secondary School Objectives

12. <u>Improving the quality of secondary education, by</u>:

...facilitating termination of schooling by some at compulsory school-leaving age.
...reducing the tensions created by emphasis on not dropping out.
...enforcing re-examination of high school curriculum content, and learning cycle in light of current information about maturity and growth of high school students.
...encouraging review of high school to higher education transfer practices.

13. <u>Reducing the costs of secondary schooling, by</u>:

...limiting high schooling to compulsory years.
...reducing costs and losses due to school absenteeism.
...reducing vandalism in schools.

14. <u>Motivating student performance, by</u>:

...removing the stigma of "drop out."
...reducing the possibility of employers screening on basis of high school graduation.

...providing a later second chance.
...opening the way to choice about working and learning.

Personal Development And Self Fulfillment

15. <u>Improving chances of physical self-improvement, by</u>:

...providing a breather during which harmful habits (smoking, excessive drinking or eating) can be corrected.
...new information can be acquired on nutrition and other daily living modes and consumption patterns that affect health.
...facilitating maintenance of income during career adjustment, thus reducing chance of stress as a cause of illness.

16. <u>Providing opportunities for new learning, by</u>:

...developing appropriate modes of study.
...maintaining income.
...assuring job rights.

17. <u>Enriching jobs and leisure, by</u>:

...facilitating job enrichment.
...improving access to learning in "off" hours.
...improving consumption methods and choices.

18. <u>Improving relations between generations, by</u>:

...parent and child sharing of learning experiences.
...broadening the age groups on campus.
...gaining a common understanding of the requirements of study.

19. <u>Improving parental education, by</u>:

...providing new learning opportunities.
...emphasizing educational purposes.

The conference examined several of these motives. One is that recurrent education is a means for personal development or self fulfillment in careers as well as in areas quite apart from vocational interests such as public service, governmental affairs, literature, art, hobbies or even homemaking and homecrafts. Research questions could be addressed to the roles recurrent education could play in self-fulfillment and developing stronger participation. However, the policy considerations which the conference dwelt on were recurrent education as a means for improving economic, educational, and social equality and improving

532-819 O - 74 - 21

economic productivity through upgrading skills and fostering worker participation in decision-making.

Recurrent education was considered in depth as a policy option for upgrading knowledge and skill, retreading or redirecting skill when technology, or worker tastes about work environment change, and "second-chancing" for the economically or socially "by-passed."

In the context of the education system, recurrent education may be viewed as a part of educational reform, a method for broadening choices and making more flexible the structure within which decisions to work and study are defined. In a larger context the purposes may be stated as improving the stability and output of the economy, as reducing poverty and otherwise improving the equity of the system, or as a means of improving the quality of life.

In the pages that follow an agenda for research is outlined in terms of policy and implementation questions. In each instance the research problems draw upon the papers prepared for the Georgetown Conference on Recurrent Education and the research needs identified or suggested by those papers.

The long list of purposes and the consequences for policy decision of the lengthy enumeration were not considered in their totality. High on our agenda, however, is an examination of the effectiveness of recurrent education not only for each of the purposes but for the many. If recurrent education is a second best solution for some purposes but could contribute at small incremental cost to others, should proposals for recurrency be given a new priority consideration? Is it possible that quantification of the multiple purposes would assist in the determination of cost in relation to the full range of output? Would such costing provide documentation for the required concensus on action?

1. Equality

Educational opportunities have been viewed from a policy standpoint as a second chance for those by-passed by society. Such policy considerations have been applied as well to recurrent education. The 1969 address of the then Swedish Minister of Education before the European Ministers of Education is sometimes credited with launching the notion of a recurrent education system. "Recurrent education," he said, "should help us on the way toward equality in society."

Halsey, in his paper for the Georgetown Conference, traces the history of this concept of equality through education. He views the 19th Century origins of compulsory education from the perspective of the desire of workers for liberation and industry for a literate working force. The 20th Century doctrine of equality tries to bridge the gap between classes, but for many nations it is an equality within an elite society. Expansion of access in that elite structure without other changes will not result in greater economic equality, as the study of Jencks makes plain. Halsey looks to a program of positive discrimination through stipends and a curriculum adjusted to the needs of the immediate community. Such methods have been instituted in some countries for certain disadvantaged groups.

Recurrent education, in its broadest definition, is considered a policy option to foster greater equality by reaching those groups bypassed by conventional education. Such groups include: older or retired persons, women released from years of childrearing, the unemployed or underemployed, young drop-outs, the poor, and all of the various minorities of race, religion or culture.

There are numerous groups of possible students to which a recurrent education program could address itself. Major groups for which "second-chance" education has been institutionalized in the U.S. are veterans, the unemployed, and minority youth. Other examples are possible. For instance, Bengtsson's paper notes the great importance--political and social as well as economic--attached to intergenerational equality of educational opportunity. Poorly educated older adults are likely to turn away from conventional education. He summarizes a demonstration of approaches to educational offerings to older workers in an overall program addressed to "overbridging" the educational gap between youth and the older worker.

Women also represent a special constituency for recurrent education. Among the special problems faced by women that lead them to attempt re-entry into an educational stream are these:

(a) widowhood or divorce with young children,

(b) disablement of primary wage earner,

(c) extraordinary family expenses and need for supplementary earnings, such as college-going of children, or high medical costs,

(d) widowhood or divorce in middle age,

(e) early marriage and child bearing of women who drop out but seek re-entry when children go to school, and

(f) child-rearing activities come to an end and children leave home for school or marriage.

In summary, greater equality through recurrent education needs to be carefully assessed, "equality" defined, and its conditions specified. The following research questions are posed by discussions in the conference:

1. How is the objective of greater equality to be defined? Does it mean uniformity in resource inputs per person,

learning outputs, income chances, or greater economic and social mobility?

2. What impacts do financing, location, curriculum, scheduling, and credentialing have on "equality?" How are such factors measured?

3. Can greater equality be achieved through recurrent education programs? Under what conditions? Or would those already endowed by wealth, income, and earlier educational attainment become the primary beneficiaries of such programs?

4. How is equality of output--in terms of economic or social achievement--to be measured?

5. Are there differences in such achievement depending upon whether educational status is attained early, later, or on a recurring basis?

6. Which target groups are to be selected for "equalization aid" through recurrent education? Would attempts at equalization work?

2. Productivity

The familiar paths of formal education, as now structured, provide most inadequate arrangements to upgrade work skills and keep professional skills up to current knowledge. This gap creates, in turn, a productivity problem.

The President, recognizing the importance of improving productivity as an economic stabilization device, established in June 1970 a National Commission on Productivity composed of representatives from industry, labor, agriculture, the public, and federal, state, and local governments. Among the specific aspects of productivity to which the Commission gave its primary attention was education. More specifically, the Commission stated its views that added experimentation and innovation were necessary in education and especially incentives for group participation, job enrichment, and similar practices to improve productivity.

Skill development through recurrent education has come to be viewed as an essential tool of anti-inflation policy. The research of Charles Holt and his colleagues deals with Holt's concept of unemployment and inflation. Manpower programs, it is argued, have anti-inflation impact when they are concentrated on alleviating skill shortages and removing bottlenecks to production. Under these circumstances output is increased at any given level of employment and inflationary pressures are decreased.

But little quantification has been carried out that would suggest the magnitude of the effect of a recurrent education program upon production and inflation. Nor is the question an easy one to tackle. A complexity of factors are involved in productivity of which skill creation is only one.

For example, vacancy ratios may be high in some labor markets and not in others pointing to movement of workers as an option to additional training. High vacancy ratios create bottlenecks impairing the achievement of optimum production levels and thus reduce supplies of goods below the potential levels. But high vacancy levels can be due to many factors including worker dissatisfaction and company policies.

Furthermore, economic growth can be slowed by the numbers of persons unemployed due to special circumstances of youth and discrimination. Many young persons available for work are out of a job due to inexperience, and the adverse incentives for employer recruitment of youth. Racial, religious, and sex discrimination take their toll by increasing the period in which jobs remain vacant while those who might be qualified remain unemployed.

Worker attitudes and company policies also have definite effects. Why cannot recurrent education approach these factors of working attitudes? Indeed, that has been advocated and tried out.

In the U.S. high absenteeism, turnover, and conflicts on the job have pointed to new arguments for less, rather than more, division of labor, and to broadening of worker participation in decision-making. Training to achieve such purposes has gained new importance. Research on worker participation and training for such participation has been carried out by Thorsrud at Norway's Institute for Industrial Environment Research. Thorsrud has experimented to determine the prerequisites for creating a higher degree of personal involvement in the job and in decision-making in plants. While those studies were directed to a better understanding of the workings of industrial democracy, the product is reported to include "higher worker productivity." Personnel management concepts applied in the U.S. also suggest that there may be improved output and less absence from work when job content is broadened and when employees are equipped to participate in management-type decisions. The U.S. appears to have done far less by way of experimentation and demonstration than other industrial nations on training for job enrichment and job-structure reorganization despite the marked concern about the competitive position of its industries.

In trying to appraise education and training as economic production tools, we need to understand better the potential of worker participation and the educational requirements for such participation. The findings from Norway and Yugoslavia endorse education for adults as a part of the production process. However, such endorsements may not be based on hard scientific evidence. If valid for Norway or Yugoslavia, these studies may have little bearing on worker behavior in the U.S. Such education may not yield sufficient economic output in the U.S. to take seriously any formal structuring of education for such purposes.

Still another policy motive for recurrent education--and perhaps the most important--is the need to combat the kind of unemployment caused by obsolescence of skills. This is a social as well as an economic consideration. Indeed, much of the impetus for recurrent education comes from the school of "Future Shock" which emphasizes the need for continual re-education for the economic and social worlds of tomorrow.

Technological change and scientific advance have been from the outset important factors in advocacy of a system of recurrent education. The argument essentially boils down to the fact that new technology, new methods of organizing markets, and new knowledge as a consequence of scientific advance make obsolete preparatory education and even skills learned earlier on the job. A system of recurrent education by which those threatened with educational obsolescence could retread and upgrade their knowledge and skills is one answer to such advances in technology and science.

However, analysis of the option "recurrent education" to overcome skilled labor shortages also demands that alternatives to new technology be reviewed together with their relative costs. For example, one alternative might be the downgrading of skills, rather than upgrading, to achieve a higher production volume and at lower cost. This downgrading goal could become an ingredient in the design of new production methods.

In summary, we know altogether very little about the extent of educational obsolescence--obsolescence of knowledge and skills used on the job. Not only is there little quantification but the conceptual framework for assessing and quantifying has not been fully worked out. We need to know more about how such obsolescence, in addition to other factors relating to learning, influence productivity.

The following research questions are posed by the issue of productivity improvement through recurrent education:

1. What is the rate at which knowledge and skill become obsolete and require "replacement?"

2. If all those when faced with the risk of obsolescence were to enter an educational stream, what proportion of the work force would be going to school?

3. How large are the jumps in technology and in knowledge?

4. How long would it take to retool a worker? What are the differences in timing for retooling at each occupational and professional level?

5. What effect does recurrent education have on productivity and enlarging the volume of output to reduce inflation? Would a system of recurrent education achieve these economic stabilization aims?

6. If a recurrent education system offers a means for increasing productivity and output, by how much? Quantification of the overall impact on productivity and the volume of production of a system of recurrent education remains to be undertaken.

7. Is educational obsolescence a predictable risk, that is, is the risk sufficiently identifiable and unchanging that insurance principles can be applied to its quantification and to financing the risk?

8. Would industry-by-industry cases of educational obsolescence yield important data on the nature of the risk, the educational background of those affected, and the extent of the risk for management?

9. What are the factors that contribute to the rate of educational obsolescence? And what are the determinants of each of those factors?

10. What groups in the population are especially subject to educational obsolescence? What are optional methods of reducing risks for those vulnerable groups? And what effect would those methods have?

11. Is career changing becoming a part of economic life? Do career changes in selected markets require much training? Of what kinds in terms of a "market?"

12. Are there factors other than skills that lend themselves to manipulation through recurrent education aimed at improving productivity? Can workers' attitudes and management policies be changed to improve productivity through a recurrent education program?

B. Implementation

1. Strategy Of Implementation

Recurrent education can be implemented as a substitute for educational services following the years of compulsory schooling. For most nations, and certainly for the U.S., this approach is only a contingent possibility. As a substitute it would involve a radical revision in the educational system encompassing formal learning from the end of compulsory schooling through the remaining years of life and including not only the upper grades of secondary level education, technical education, university education and professional education, but also the more familiar forms of adult and continuing education.

The alternative to a structured system that starts at the end of the period of compulsory schooling and continues at the option of the individual throughout life is one designed as a supplement to other forms of education thus requiring few if any changes in existing educational patterns and thus facilitating the incremental move toward a new approach to continuing or adult education.

Whether a recurrent education scheme is going to be a substitute or supplement is a question of degree of implementation that elicits the following questions:

1. Would recurrent education serve as a break on the mounting creditialism that calls for ever enlarging the period of education?

2. Would such a system facilitate a vitalization of the high school permitting youth greater opportunities for beginning work careers earlier or moving more easily between learning to do a job and doing a job?

3. Could the period of formal high schooling be shortened? What would be the cost savings?

4. What would be the impact on the quality of postsecondary education of younger persons in freshman classes--those graduating at an earlier age from high schools, and those who choose to go immediately on with their studies?

5. Would those who come from professional families and higher income groups elect in larger numbers to continue preparatory education and not pick up the option of a period of active employment away from studies?

6. How could the potential inequities resulting from any selective choosing between income groups be overcome?

7. How could incentives be built in for recurrency, rather than continued study?

In general, if we view recurrent education as a system of change --both in secondary and in higher education--we need to assess cost impacts, and the extent to which present patterns of education can achieve policy purposes better (or worse) than a coordinated system which would be modular in design, informal in physical plant, less strict on admissions and purposively structured for the recurrent adult student.

2. Components

The actual components of a recurrent education program are identical to those in any educational system: students, teachers, curriculum, scheduling, physical plant, and financing. Credentialing can be an optional ingredient.

These supply characteristics involve questions

<u>on physical plant</u>:

a. Where will the students and teachers assemble? In traditional educational institutions, libraries, places of work, churches, recreation centers, homes, etc.?

b. Can a comprehensive system be designed to encompass all physical plant possibilities? Or will recurrent education necessarily be a fragmented, individual program due to locational differences in purposes of study, educational choices, age of students, and prior educational experience?

<u>on teachers</u>:

a. Who is to do the teaching? Retired businessmen, regular teachers or professors, labor leaders, plant foremen, artists, writers, etc.? How will they be paid?

b. How is the teaching to be carried out? Should young students be separated from the older students?

<u>on credentialing</u>:

a. What criteria, if any, are to be applied in credentialing?

b. Who is to do the credentialing? Professional societies, employers, labor unions, regular universities or schools, governments?

c. How are the credential criteria to be examined? To be validated?

<u>on curriculum</u>:

a. What is to be taught? To whom? And how? And for what purposes?

b. In what sequence are curriculum items to be taught?

c. How does a proposed sequence fit into knowns about adult learning?

Illustrative questions about several other components are dealt with in detail by this paper: scheduling, student selection, demand, and financing.

3. Scheduling

We need to understand far better than we do the timing of resource inputs into learning and the output gained at each timing period. We are far from understanding the most effective timing required to achieve gains in knowledge and skill for adults.

The initial results of the National Assessment of Educational Progress indicate in some areas, particularly science, significant loss of knowledge between the high school and young adulthood. (Alternatively one could of course conjecture that schools as institutions for imparting knowledge have markedly improved over the last decade or so.) If the results of National Assessment can be interpreted to mean a loss of information in a decade both the question of curriculum content and the timing at which that information is imparted has to be reassessed.

Questions are raised about when individuals learn best what kinds of things and the sequences of learning. Has mankind structured learning as a preparatory imparting of knowledge and skill in the right time-frame? Is this same timing appropriate for the different knowledges and skills?

Further knowledge and skills are now taught in small doses divided frequently in 45 or 50 minute intervals and for younger children in briefer periods still. Is this kind of learning schedule suited to adult requirements? Generally the answer appears to be "no." The study that has been given to imparting skills for some work indicates concentrated, immersed study, over relatively short periods. What indeed is lost and what gained by way of outputs for any given amount of teaching and student time if concentrated study in adult years is substituted for study early on. Questions of learning facility and agility and perception come into play as well as other aspects of learning. Much research is needed at this fundamental level.

4. Students

Obviously, a recurrent education scheme must consider as part of its design stage the potential students. The underlying issue is how to design a set of programs suitable to widely differing groups in the population and their special characteristics and, at the same time, keep avenues open for transfer over a time period between programs.

Whether the potential students are veterans, the unemployed, or a racial minority, the kinds of questions that should be posed are similar in approach to those presented in the following discussion of recurrent education for women. In each case, the basic issues concern: (a) what are the special educational requirements of the group? (b) how can educational services for the group best be encouraged, and supported? (c) what would be the results for education? and (d) what would be the results for the group?

A number of questions are posed by the special needs of women. Women need services that give them time for study. What supporting services are required to give women access to educational services after a period away from preparatory schooling? For those with children in their care, preschool programs are needed that match in quality, proximity and cost the requirements of the trainee and later the woman worker. In addition, extended school programs are required that not only look after Johnny while mother goes to school, but to aid Johnny in completing his home work satisfactorily. Home nursing services or health aids to provide housekeeping services are required to give temporary assistance when children become ill and Mother cannot take leave of her studies. Similar services are required when a disabled spouse or aged parent is at home and needs care. What would be the cost of various optional services? How well would each assure access of women to education and later to the employment and earnings that often motivate re-entry?

What is the impact of educational activities of the mother on the educational achievement of the children? This is a second band of studies about which little information exists. It was quite a while before pay-off from education of women was taken seriously, and then only after quantification of the dollar value of educational services provided by the mother for her child (boy child presumably). But there is reason to think that mothers who attend school at the same time or nearly the same time as their children have a very different effect on the child's motivation to learn, the child's perception of learning, and the requirements of learning. Do children learn more (or less) when their mothers also go to school? All we have to judge this on is anecdotal.

5. Demand

Demand for a specific recurrent education program can be assessed, but with some few exceptions has not been. A starting point for research on demand in the U.S. is now provided by the demand survey of the Educational Testing Service. Estimates made for the sample survey of persons 18 years of age through 60 (excluding full-time students) indicate that some 32 million persons are actually engaged in education. Almost 80 million persons indicate an interest by responding "yes" to the questions: Is there anything in particular that you would like to know more about or would like to learn how to do better? Vocational subjects are reported to have attracted the greatest interest.

Miller in his conference paper outlines three types of demand--backlog, derived, and awakened. To awaken a demand, program design should take full account of cost, accessibility, relevance, and attractiveness. He suggests that underutilization of recurrent educational opportunities is not a fundamental problem. It presents primarily a problem of design with demand being a function of design.

He then proposes that demand estimates be made for local areas rather than nationwide and that the estimates be based on:

(a) demographic characteristics of potential students,

(b) extrapolation from current programs,

(c) income and price elasticity of demand,

(d) models of work histories and rates of job obsolescence, and

(e) attitudinal changes toward education.

Eligibility and the conditions under which the educational offerings are made available clearly have much to do with demand. As has been suggested, rights to re-employment, income maintenance while studying, supporting services for those with family responsibilities, the appropriateness of the educational offering, all are determinants of demand.

Job guarantees and income are important particularly to the male worker who is in the middle of his working life. In this regard, it should be noted that union benefits in the U.S. provide funds only toward tuition and similar fees, and do not meet the requirements of income maintenance. Industrial middle management training in Europe under the British or French public programs, or in the U.S. under managements' own programs, maintain incomes, in whole or part; guarantee jobs; and, in some instances, provide for job advancement on completion of training. But the record has not been quantified and analyzed.

The requirements that have evolved to meet adult demand have been briefly examined by Biederman and Billings. They write:

> if existing financial markets were made more available to the educational needs of adults, the preference of adults translated into market demand for continuing education would clearly be different, reflecting both a shift in the demand for adult education services as well as a movement along a given demand curve....

Essentially we remain ignorant of the conditions under which demand for recurrent education is generated for the different groups in the population and the size of that demand along with its price elasticity characteristics. Research to establish the size and characteristics of demand for recurrent education is an important step. The following basic questions on demand require research:

1. What is the size of the demand? Under what conditions? What is its price and income elasticity?

2. Who demands recurrent education?

3. What motives are behind such demand? What do the users study, and why?

4. How is demand dependent upon the design of a program, including its subjects, location, timing, teachers, credentialing, and financing?

5. How is demand dependent upon such supportive services as child care for mothers and work release time, job guarantees?

6. What amounts of income maintenance are essential, particularly for those already working?

Harder information about demand for recurrent education can perhaps be obtained by experimentation, that is, the design of small-scale demonstrations each with the appropriate control groups to provide answers to such questions.

Ingredients of recurrent education already exist in such examples as adult and continuing education programs, correspondence schools, management and labor training programs, and certain federal programs. Therefore, another approach to research might be better analysis of such diverse programs to understand how demand is generated and in what volume, for what kinds of study, and under what price conditions.

6. Financing

Questions about financing center on the familiar (a) who should pay, (b) what costs, (c) with what priority, and (d) under what type of financial arrangements? And in the case of recurrent education the issue about appropriateness of the financial methods in a strategy of implementation is especially important because the long run purpose toward which the strategy is designed can be achieved only within a suitable financial framework.

Who should pay?--Most studies of recurrent education financing assume that the students will pay all or part of their own direct costs on a pay as you go basis, by a prepayment, or by a postpayment of loans. For direct cost financing, certainly tuition fees are the main source proposed for the U.S. But even the Edding paper from Europe calls for a large margin of student financing.

Boddy in his paper for the conferences notes the long standing practice of employer payments to the student or to institutions. He suggests that if employer groups could organize and agree on a cost-sharing plan, the educational programs need not be employer specific, only industry specific, to justify the industry funding. Industry could finance the whole or part of cost, or a share by industry could be introduced in other ways--by provision of faculty, participation in training, sharing facilities such as research laboratories or computers, and so forth. Total industrial outlays for education and training are not easily compiled. In most of the European nations it is reported that industry finances its own training programs and uses little of the facilities and services of the university. This is not so universally. Preparation of persons for the public service, for example, in some nations such as France is provided by branches of the university.

There are additional questions on who pays--and when--that relate to less direct outlays. How are the purposes to maintain income, maintain rights to jobs, and to provide such service supports as day care, home health aids, and so forth to be financed? At present employers finance the costs of educational leave under the limited firm or industry programs. But most of the education is financed by those who go through training. Full-time study is thus very difficult for those in their mid-life work years.

The optimum distribution of costs between industry, learner, and government--federal, state, or local--remains a question for further study. More information is needed as part of this study about the benefits from education and the portion of the costs now borne by each group.

In summary, the following questions require additional study:

1. What share of student teaching (and related overhead costs) should be borne by the recurrent education student? Tuition at full cost in a recurrent education system not only helps to finance the system but also assures that the courses of study are worth buying and suitable for the users. It introduces a responsiveness in the educational system and enlarges the area of competition between the more formally structured education and the less formal. If the knowledge and skills adults seek can be obtained at lower costs and equally well, the students will use the cheaper program of study.

2. If all direct costs are borne by the adult student or his employer, what will be the effects on the finances of private colleges and of public colleges, two-year institutions, and four-year institutions? What would be the effect under alternate demand conditions? If at any one time one out of each ten students in colleges and universities were full-time, full cost tuition, recurrent education students, clearly the finances of the schools would be changed. The state tax subsidy for student higher education could be reduced with adult fees, assuming one out of ten students pay them, representing the equivalent of an eight percent rise in revenue. The amount of state taxes now used for subsidies for an

equivalent number of students could be used for added scholarship aid, or for other purposes. For the private college, the competitive position would be improved by accommodating adults who pay their own way.

3. What would be the tax revenue loss, net cost to the student, and other tax consequences of an educational cost deduction under the federal income tax? Tax treatment of human investments made by adults on their own behalf might be brought more closely in line with tax treatment of physical capital investments or existing deductions eliminated. When families finance the tuition charges, the investment purposes of education are obscured, and at best indirect, but when the student pays and does so with the clear concern that vocational purposes be furthered, it becomes more appropriate to view charges and related costs as a capital investment. A review might well be undertaken of the tax treatment of education expenditures under current law and costs of the educational deductions that are business expenses. What would be the revenue impact, and what would other tax consequences, including distributive effects, under a recurrent education program in which the individual student covers educational costs regarded as vocational, capital investments.

4. What is the current continuing education experience on tuition charges as a share of cost? And what does the experience suggest about price elasticity of adult demand for study? Indepth assessment might suggest the limits on the adult market for education if there are no changes in incentives to study.

5. What share of direct educational costs are borne by employers? Are these direct costs for in-plant, on-the-job training, or for external study? Collective bargaining provides educational payments for external study. Levine estimates these payments at $17 million per year.

What are the costs?--Costs for recurrent education include (a) direct teaching costs, (b) income maintenance and income foregone costs, (c) costs of maintaining rights to job, and (d) costs of service supports for education and training.

Despite the decade or so of discussion of recurrent education, there does not seem to be a full scale cost calculation of recurrent education anywhere that matches the broad scope envisioned in discussions. Perhaps the failure to carefully cost the optional systems grows out of a conviction that recurrent education as an all inclusive system beyond the compulsory years of schooling is not a practical option other than perhaps in the vision of a strategy for change.

But to come to grips with recurrent education, cost approximation is needed. In the course of estimating costs, the range of problems involved would come into sharper focus.

To illustrate, cost estimating would require information to the extent to which recurrent education is stimulatory, and additive of resources now used, or is simply a substitution for existing educational services and their costs. (For the U.S. such cost estimating would put in bold relief the inadequacies including time lags of data on costs for teaching of students even in the colleges and universities, and the paucity of information about other forms of education such as costs incurred by industrial firms for education and employee and customer training.) And the cost estimates would have to include estimates of immediate cost, both gross and net, and the longer term growth in costs that takes account of the numbers of potential users, the strategy of the developmental educational program, trends over time in costs per program unit and costs per student participating where these costs are not fixed but vary either with program, or with numbers of users.

Without attempting to assess real demand, we offer this cost analysis by way of illustration. If one to three percent of the labor force were to elect to participate in a recurrent education program, the costs at 50 percent, 75 percent, and 100 percent of earnings loss would be $3.5 to 10.6 billion; $5.3 to 15.8 billion; and $7 to 21.1 billion respectively for 1972 and would rise as total earnings rose. Other costs such as administrative costs of maintaining job rights and service supports would be additional.

The question of net added costs of a full scale program of recurrent education needs to be carefully analyzed. From one perspective, gross costs would be the cost of income maintenance out of which tuition costs would be paid. Current costs of ongoing programs would be deducted. Deductions would include part of the tax subsidy of the universities and colleges, employer on-the-job training, union apprenticeships, community and other adult education measures (public and private), and other ongoing educational programs for adults. Net costs would be smaller still if there were substantial reductions in length of the secondary schooling period as a consequence of the availability of later educational opportunities. And one might assume fewer students in preparatory education in the colleges and universities.

It could turn out that the recurrent education system is essentially a means to give those who are continuing their education beyond the period of compulsory schooling a different kind of choice, a choice about the time in which formal education takes place without added cost. Or the intent may be, as it appears to be in some countries, to reduce the pressures of social demand for expansion of college and university opportunities and to substitute the somewhat less costly, more sporadic, less formal education. Recurrent education could be designed mainly as a means to reduce the financial load of education by offering options that are cheaper but are now made unattractive by the lack of official recognition, and by the views held of such programs by educators and employers.

Recurrent education, of course, could be defined differently and costed differently. In concept, recurrent education could be defined in such a way that there is no direct tie to ongoing programs other than the continuing education programs of the colleges and universities. Recurrent education would thus be an add-on with separate costs and separate financing, including special methods of financing. Any strategy for financing would have to start at least in the U.S. at such a point, and perhaps the incremental approach is called for in Europe as well.

With what priority?--There are many reasons why large added expenditures for recurrent education do not have high priority in the educational community. Deficiencies in early education, it is urged, have first claim on added funding. More costly patching in adulthood may achieve far less by way of equality of opportunity and access to further self-development. The educational establishment does not directly see gains to teaching staff or faculty out of maintaining income of persons in the work force so that they can decide if, when, and how much additional educational offerings they would claim.

Furthermore, the administrative decision tool of cost-benefit analysis gives little support to a priority for recurrent education financing. Cost-benefit analysis or relative investment returns of preparatory and recurrent educational paths cannot but favor preparatory rather than recurrent education. The analysis is typically structured to count as costs earnings foregone and as benefits added earnings over a lifetime (discounted at specified interest rates). Potential earnings, if any, of young persons are low, and the period of work upon completion of education is the full duration of the working lifetime. In contrast, the costs of earnings foregone of adults are high and the duration of a work lifetime after completion of an education program for adults is less.

But such assessments are at present crude and most approximate. Many aspects of educational returns are set aside--or neglected--and costs of the present preparatory work arrangement in productivity loss, lack of motivation, wastages in working time and in materials by those caught in a "job trap" not to their liking are omitted from the calculus. Other costs are omitted too. These costs include:

--alienation of youth and its social costs--by the long period of isolation of youth from real life during preparatory education;

--disruption of family life and its social costs when women find it difficult to return to the work force on separation, death, or disability of their spouse;

--incomplete use of remaining adult competence when unemployment, or downgrading, occurs due to lack of access to retreading and refreshment of professional and technical knowledge; and

532-819 O - 74 - 22

--errors and wastes due to lack of experience of those with technically current skills.

Far more study needs to be given to identifying the cost components and to quantifying them so that indirect costs of maintaining the existing structure are better understood. At the same time investment returns from altered educational pathways have to be carefully researched and quantified taking account of the several possible discount periods and rates. The studies so far are incomplete and have not been subject to an assessment of their validity or changes in findings with alternative assumptions.

Types of financial arrangements--Many prescriptions have been written with varying dosages for recurrent education. Even a partial listing of the major ones gives perspective to the size of the analytical effort required.

Improving the capital market for recurrent education by:

(a) loans made by a newly created education development bank with authority to lend up to a specified sum, to be repaid with interest as an ordinary bank loan, or out of income as a fixed predetermined percent of income, or in other specified ways;

(b) guarantees of bank loans to individuals undertaking recurrent education with interest at market rates or subsidized rates; and

(c) investment of unemployment insurance or OASDI trust fund reserves in educational loans to those covered under the insurance systems with or without a ceiling on the amount of the reserves to be so applied, and with, or without, federal standards governing educational program specifications.*

Providing a tax reduction that would in effect encourage educational undertakings by those with tax liability. The tax reduction could take one of several forms:

(a) tax computed after averaging income over a three-year period with educational expenses incurred in the year of schooling taken as a deduction from average annual income for the period;

(b) a tax credit up to some amount, e.g., $50 a month for each month enrolled in full-time study in an accredited educational institution;

---

* In some ways this proposal is more advanced in terms of legislation largely due to the efforts of Herbert Striner.

(c) a tax deduction for educational outlays taken as business expense up to some specified sum, or without a ceiling; or

(d) a depreciation allowance for educational capital costs based on the size of such costs (direct and perhaps also indirect).

Expanding social insurance protections to include insurance against the risk of educational obsolescence * by:

(a) adopting a new federal social insurance program financed by employers and employees by an additional payroll levy of one percent on each (or optionally one-half of one percent on each) with appropriate measures for determining benefits and limiting benefits paid out in any year to the amount raised by the new tax;

(b) adopting a new federal social insurance program financed by an income tax of one percent on adjusted gross income with personal exemption allowances as currently provided. Benefit levels would have to be set as well as methods of restricting outgo to the amount of funds available;

(c) broadening the unemployment insurance program to authorize payment of educational leave out of the funds in the unemployment insurance system representing in effect an add on benefit under the system. Additional taxes would be an option; or

(d) establishing a national or nationwide cooperative system calling for a standard educational allowance plan; benefits to be purchased privately, or by industry for its employees and at the option of industry to be purchased from a governmental insurance plan or a private insurance plan.

Lifetime educational credit plan might be set up to broaden educational choices by:

(a) calling for federal credits of, for example, $200-$400 per person per year for 16 years to be paid into a fund out of the proceeds of a special tax and to be paid out at the option of each family for child care or other educational services to children from age six on, or to be retained in a reserve and accumulated at interest, with an annual decision made by the family about the use

---

* This idea has been cast in a larger framework by Edward Clarke in his plan for educational allowances, and by Lee Rainwater in his plan for a comprehensive social security system.

of the credit and the accumulated reserves;

(b) calling for federal credits, for example, of $200-$400 per person per year from age 16 to 22 to be paid into a fund out of general revenue for those families whose income is under $10,000 per year. The annual amount to be adjusted progressively downward for families with incomes of $10,000 or more so that no payments are made on behalf of children whose families have incomes of $18,000 per year. The amounts paid into the fund would be paid out each year at the option of the family to buy child care or other educational services from age 16 on, or to be retained in the reserve and accumulated at interest with an annual decision made about the annual allowance to the fund and accumulated reserves;

(c) calling for credits financed by special earmarked income taxes only for periods beyond the years of compulsory schooling, e.g., age 16, and perhaps be available in large sums for the period of college and university education for those from families with low or modest incomes;

(d) calling for credits financed alternatively out of general revenues of the federal government, or a special federal income tax to be paid by those with children (by those with children over a specified age, etc.), or a special state add-on to its income tax; and

(e) conditioning payments of credits by requirements that states adopt more equitable systems of elementary and secondary school finance, or more competitive tuition fees in public colleges and universities; or both conditions could be set.

---Structural and other changes could be made to encourage recurrent patterns of education but without direct government provision for maintaining income by:

(a) more flexible work schedules with inplant educational offering, or cooperatively arranged industry-union-educational institution offerings;

(b) time release for study;

(c) alternate work-study provision with blocks of time devoted to work and then to study; and

(d) adoption of a 30 hour work week together with eight hour study time each week.

The need for more research on financing is evident in the extensive review of the literature. And the gaps must be considered alongside the many proposals for implementation of a recurrent education program.

Despite a decade or more of emphasis on educational obsolescence and educational aspirations of target groups, the research base for policy option is very narrow. For example, until more work is done on the demand for recurrent education and financial risk of educational obsolescence in relation to technological change, assessment of a plan for financing based on tax deductions or social insurance financing will have many uncertainties.

Furthermore, the exchange of information between nations has not yet provided the analytical tools we need to answer important questions about demand. How many workers qualify for educational allowances paid out in France and in the Federal Republic of Germany? What groups in the work force benefit most? Mid-management? Skilled workers? Unskilled? Men? Women? Why is there not a larger demand? Or is there an unmet demand that leads to rationing of benefits? How is that rationing carried out? And the experience in the United Kingdom with sandwich courses and work-release time needs to be better understood.

What, then, are the prospects of recurrent education, asked Halsey in summarizing the conference for the London Times. "One fear is that it may be trivialized into gestures towards a more generous provision of adult education, sabbaticals, day release, Open university and sandwich courses." This possibility emerged in the discussion as the frequent turning of prospect into retrospect: "The new idea is domesticated by giving it a history....But if recurrent education is to be taken seriously as a citizenship right, like social security or pensions, then the transformation of the established system is at issue, requiring ambitious institutional inventiveness, much more flexible relations between work and education, more optimistic definitions by teachers of educability and curriculum, a vast development of ccommunity schooling and ever more bounteous educational budgets."

Selected Bibliography

General

American Academy of Arts and Sciences. A First Report: The Assembly on University Goals and Governance. Cambridge, Mass.: American Academy of Arts and Sciences, 1971.

American Council on Education. Higher Education and the Adult Student, an ACE Special Report. Washington, D.C.: ACE, 1972.

Ashby, E. Any Person, Any Study. New York: McGraw-Hill, 1971.

Bruner, Jerome. "On the Continuity of Learning." Saturday Review: Education, 1(2):21-24, February 10, 1973.

Carnegie Commission on Higher Education. A Digest and Index of Reports and Recommendations: December 1968 - June 1972. Berkeley: Carnegie Commission on Higher Education, 1972.

Carnegie Commission on Higher Education. Less Time, More Options: Education Beyond the High School. New York: McGraw-Hill, 1971.

Carnegie Commission on Higher Education. The More Effective Use of Resources: An Imperative for Higher Education. New York: McGraw-Hill, 1972.

Carnoy, Martin, ed. Schooling in a Corporate Society. New York: David McKay Company, 1972.

Commission on Non-Traditional Study. Diversity By Design. San Francisco: Jossey-Bass, 1973.

Continuing Education: An Evolving Form of Adult Education. Battle Creek, Michigan: The Kellogg Foundation, 1970.

Coons, John; Clune, W.; and Sugarman, S. Private Wealth and Public Education. Cambridge, Mass.: Belknap Press, 1970.

Csoma, G., et al. Adult Education in Hungary. Leiden, the Netherlands: Leicsche Onderwijsinstellingen, 1968.

David, Marcel. Adult Education in Yugoslavia. Paris: UNESCO, 1962.

Draper, J.A. and Yadao, F. Degree Research in Adult Education in Canada. Toronto: Department of Adult Education, 1969.

Fay, F.A. "Adult Education and Public Policy." Adult Education, 23(4):150-157, Winter 1972.

Fogarty, M.; Rapoport, R.; and Rapoport, R. Sex, Career and Family. London: George Allen and Unwin, 1971.

Forgan, Alan. "A Policy for Culture." Adult Education, 45(6):364-368, March 1973.

Green, Thomas. Educational Planning in Perspective. London: Futures, 1971.

Hardy, Laurent. Adult Education in Quebec. Toronto: Ontario Institute for Studies in Education, 1969.

Houle, C.O. Continuing Your Education. New York: McGraw-Hill, 1964.

International Commission on the Development of Education. Learning to Be. New York: International Commission on the Development of Education, 1972. Unpublished paper.

Janni, H. and Roggemans, M.L. New Trends in Adult Education: Concepts and Recent Empirical Achievements. Series C: Innovations No. 7. Paris: UNESCO, International Commission on the Development of Education, 1972.

Johnstone, J.W.C. and Rivera, R.J. Volunteers for Learning. Chicago: Aldine Publishing Company, 1965.

Kalley, D. "European Views on Recurrent Education." New Generation, 54(4):9-15, February 1972.

Katz, Joseph and Associates. Class, Character and Career. Palo Alto, California: Stanford University Press, 1968.

Knowles, Asa and Associates. Handbook of Cooperative Education. San Francisco: Jossey-Bass, 1971.

Kulich, Jindra. The Role and Training of Adult Educators in Czechoslovakia. Vancouver, B.C.: University of British Columbia, 1967.

Lengrand, Paul. An Introduction to Lifelong Education. New York: UNESCO, 1971.

Leskinen, H. The Provincial Folk School in Finland. Bloomington: Indiana University Monograph Series in Adult Education, No. 3, 1968.

Levin, M.R. and Slavet, J.S. Continuing Education: State Programs for the 1970's. Lexington, Mass.: Heath, 1970.

Love, John. Adult Education in England and Wales: A Critical Survey. London: Michail Joseph, 1970.

National Advisory Council on Extension and Continuing Education. A Measure of Success: Federal Support for Continuing Education, 7th Annual Report and Recommendations. Washington, D.C.: Government Printing Office, 1973.

National Advisory Council on Extension and Continuing Education. A Question of Stewardship: A Study of the Federal Role in Continuing Higher Education. Washington, D.C.: National Advisory Council on Extension and Continuing Education, 1972.

Newman, F. Report on Higher Education. Washington, D.C.: Government Printing Office, 1971.

Paisley, M.B. and Associates. Reaching Adults for Lifelong Learning. I. Final Report and Summary. Palo Alto, California: Stanford University, California Institute for Communication Research, August 1972.

Psacharopoulos, G. The Returns to Education: An International Comparison. Amsterdam: Elsevier, 1972.

Savicevic, D.M. The System of Adult Education in Yugoslavia. Syracuse, N.Y.: Syracuse University Press, 1968.

Sheppard, H.I. and Herrick, N.Q. Where Have All the Robots Gone? New York: The Free Press, 1972.

Smith, A.Z., ed. Education Recaps: Spring 1971, Winter 1971-2. Princeton, N.J.: Educational Testing Service, Spring 1972.

Smith, R.M.; Aker, G.F.; and Kidd, J.R. Handbook of Adult Education. New York: Macmillan, Inc., 1970.

Special Task Force on Work in America. Work in America. Washington, D.C.: Department of Health, Education, and Welfare, December 1972.

Stetson, Damon. Starting in Over. New York: Macmillan, Inc., 1971.

Toward the Educative Society. Syracuse: Syracuse University, Publications in Continuing Education, January 1971.

U.S. Office of Education. Perspectives of Adult Education in the United States and a Projection for the Future. Washington, D.C.: Government Printing Office, 1972.

Vogt, Hartmut. "Adult Education in the U.S.S.R." Continuous Learning, 7:57-66, March/April 1968.

Welden, J.E. "30 Million Adults Go to School." American Education, 5(9):11-13, November 1969.

Yaron, Kalman. Life-Long Education in Israel. Jerusalem: The Public Advisory Council on Adult Education, Ministry of Education and Culture, 1972.

Ziegler, Warren L., ed. Essays on the Future of Continuing Education--World-Wide. Syracuse: Syracuse University, Publications in Continuing Education, July 1970.

OECD and Other European Sources

Burgess, Tyrell and Pratt, John. Technical Education in the United Kingdom. Paris: OECD/CERI, 1971.

Capelle, Jean. The Development of Permanent Education in France. Strasbourg, France: Council of Europe, Council for Cultural Cooperation, May 1968.

Centre for Educational Research and Innovation. Recurrent Education: A Clarifying Report. Paris: OECD/CERI, 1973.

Council of Europe. Educational Leave, a Key Factor of Permanent Education and Social Advancement. Strasbourg: Council of Europe, 1969.

Council of Europe. Permanent Education: Denmark. Strasbourg: Council of Europe, 1968.

Council of Europe. Permanent Education: France. Strasbourg: Council of Europe, 1968.

Council of Europe. Permanent Education: Norway. Strasbourg: Council of Europe, 1969.

Council of Europe. Permanent Education. Strasbourg: Council of Europe, 1970.

Council of Europe. Second Roundtable on Permanent Education. Strasbourg: Council of Europe, 1971.

Eide, Kjell. Permanent Education in Norway: Reflections on Post-Work Education. Strasbourg, France: Council of Europe, Council for Cultural Cooperation, June 1969.

Husen, Torsten. Social Background and Educational Career. Paris: OECD/CERI, 1972.

Manpower and Social Affairs Committee. Adult Training as an Instrument of Active Manpower Policy. Paris: OECD, June 15, 1971.

OECD. Adaptation and Employment of Special Groups of Manpower. Paris: OECD, 1968.

OECD. Alternative Educational Futures in the United States and Europe: Methods, Issues and Policy Relevance. Paris: OECD/CERI, 1972.

OECD. Educational Policy and Planning - France. Paris: OECD, 1973.

OECD. Educational Policies for the 1970's. Paris: OECD, 1971.

OECD. Educational Policy and Planning - Germany. Paris: OECD, 1973.

OECD. Equal Educational Opportunity: 1. A Statement of the Problem, with Special Reference to Recurrent Education. Paris: OECD/CERI, 1971.

OECD. Labour Force Statistics 1959-1970. Paris: OECD, 1972.

OECD. Manpower and Social Policy in the Netherlands. Paris: OECD, 1967.

OECD. Manpower Policy in Belgium. Paris: OECD, 1971.

OECD. Manpower Policy in Norway. Paris: OECD, 1972.

OECD. Mass Higher Education: Trends, Issues and Dilemmas. Paris: OECD, in press.

OECD. Policies for Higher Education. Paris: OECD, in press.

OECD. Recurrent Education: A Strategy for Lifelong Learning. Paris: OECD/CERI, 1973.

OECD. Recurrent Education in Australia. Paris: OECD/CERI, in press.

OECD. Recurrent Education in Belgium. Paris: OECD/CERI, in press.

OECD. Recurrent Education in Canada. Paris: OECD/CERI, in press.

OECD. Recurrent Education in Japan. Paris: OECD/CERI, in press.

OECD. Recurrent Education in Norway. Paris: OECD/CERI, 1972.

OECD. Recurrent Education in the Federal Republic of Germany. Paris: OECD/CERI, 1972.

OECD. Recurrent Education in the State of New York. Paris: OECD/CERI, 1972.

OECD. Recurrent Education in Yugoslavia. Paris: OECD/CERI, 1972.

OECD. Recurrent Education: Policy Implications and Issues. Paris: OECD/Education Committee, 1972.

OECD. Reforms in Yugoslavia. Paris: OECD/CERI, 1970.

OECD. Structure of Studies and Place of Research in Mass Higher Education. Paris: OECD, in press.

OECD. The Swedish View of Recurrent Education. Paris: OECD/CERI, 1972.

OECD. The Utilization of Highly Qualified Personnel: The Venice Conference, 25th-27th October, 1971. Paris: OECD, 1973.

Schwartz, B. A Prospective View of Permanent Education. Report I. Strasbourg: Council of Europe, Council for Cultural Cooperation, August 1969.

Seear, B.N. Re-Entry of Women to the Labor Market After an Interruption of Employment. Paris: OECD, 1971.

Developing Countries

Beeby, C.H. The Quality of Education in Developing Countries. Cambridge, Mass.: Harvard University Press, 1966.

Bhatt, G.P. "Adult Education in Gujarat." Indian Journal of Adult Education, 30:10-12, September 1969.

Coles, E.T. Adult Education in Developing Countries. Elmsford, N.Y.: Pergamon Press, Inc., 1969.

Cunningham, E.L. "A New Approach to Adult Education in Developing Countries." Indian Journal of Adult Education, 33:9-11, August 1969.

DuSantony, P. The Planning and Organisation of Adult Literacy Programmes in Africa. Paris: UNESCO, 1966.

Dutta, S.C. Adult Education in South Asia. New Delhi: Indian Adult Education Association, 1965.

Edstrom, Lars-Olof. Correspondence Instruction in Ethiopia, Kenya, Tanzania, Malawi, Zambia, and Uganda. Stockholm: Dag Hammarkjold Foundation, 1966.

ERIC Clearinghouse on Adult Education. Adult Education in Africa: Current Information Services, No. 12. Syracuse, N.Y.: ERIC Clearinghouse on Adult Education, 1968.

Fraser, Stuart E. Education and Communism in China. London: Pall Mall Press, 1971.

Hely, Arnold S. Adult Education in Nepal. New York: UNESCO, 1966.

Roy, N.R. Adult Education in India and Abroad. New Dehli: S. Chand and Co., Rain Nugar, 1967.

Townsend-Coles, E. Adult Education in Developing Countries. Oxford: Pergamon Press, 1969.

New Structures

Andrews, G.J. A Status Study of Accreditation in Adult and Continuing Education Programs in Higher Education. Atlanta, Georgia: Southern Association of Colleges and Schools, 1973.

Astin, Alexander W. Some New Directions for Higher Education: A Research Perspective. Washington, D.C.: American Council on Education, 1970.

Barker, R.G. "Ecology and Motivation." In: Nebraska Symposium on Motivation. Lincoln: University of Nebraska Press, 1960.

Blakely, R.T. and Lappin, I.M. New Institutional Arrangements and Organizational Patterns for Continuing Education. Syracuse: Syracuse University Press, 1969.

Carnegie Commission on Higher Education. New Students and New Places, Policies for the Future Growth and Development of American Higher Education. New York: McGraw-Hill, 1971.

Carnegie Commission on Higher Education. Reform on the Campus: Changing Students, Changing Academic Programs. New York: McGraw-Hill, 1972.

Carnegie Commission on Higher Education. The Campus and the City. New York: McGraw-Hill, December 1972.

Carnegie Commission on Higher Education. The Fourth Revolution: Instructional Technology in Higher Education. New York: McGraw-Hill, 1972.

Clark, H.S. and Sloane, H.S. Classrooms on Mainstreet. New York: Teacher's College Press, 1966.

Cohen, Audrey C. Human Services Institutes: An Alternative for Professional Higher Education. New York: College for Human Services, 1970.

College Entrance Examination Board. Five Articles on Non-Traditional Education Concepts. New York: College Entrance Examination Board, 1972.

Commission on Academic Affairs, American Council on Education. "Twelve Issues in Non-Traditional Study." Washington, D.C.: American Council on Education, 1972 (multilithed).

532-819 O - 74 - 23

Commission on Non-Traditional Study. "New Dimensions for the Learner - A First Look at the Prospects for Non-Traditional Study." New York: Educational Testing Service, 1971.

Coyne, J. and Herbert, T. This Way Out: A Guide to Alternatives to Traditional College Education in the United States, Europe, and the Third World. New York: Dutton, 1972.

Cross, K.P. Beyond the Open Door: New Students to Higher Education. San Francisco: Jossey-Bass, 1971.

Eurich, N. and Schwenkmeyer, B. Great Britain's Open University: First Chance, Second Chance, or Last Chance? New York: Academy for Educational Development, 1971.

Feinsot, A. Breaking the Institutional Mold: Implications of Alternative Systems for Post-Secondary/Higher Education. White Plains, N.Y.: Knowledge Industry Publications, 1972.

Gayner, S. "The Urban Center: A Step in the Right Direction." Business Education World, 48:20-21, 1969.

Gould, S.B. and Cross, K.P., eds. Explorations in Non-Traditional Study. San Francisco: Jossey-Bass, 1972.

Harlacher, E.L. The Community: Dimensions of the Community College. Englewood Cliffs, N.J.: Prentice-Hall, 1969.

Hefferlin, J.B.L. Cut-Rate Credits and Discount Degrees: Quality Controls of Non-Traditional Study Through State Regulation and Voluntary Accreditation. Princeton, N.J.: Educational Testing Service, 1973.

Houle, C.O. The External Degree. San Francisco: Jossey-Bass, 1973.

Hudson, R.B. Toward a National Center for Higher Continuing Education. Syracuse, N.Y.: Library of Continuing Education, Center for the Study of Liberal Education for Adults, 1968.

Maclure, S. "England's Open University." Change, 3:62-66, 1971.

Madsen, D. The National University: Enduring Dream of the U.S.A. Detroit: Wayne State University Press, 1966.

Marien, M. Beyond the Carnegie Commission: Space-Free/Time-Free and Credit-Free Higher Education. Syracuse, N.Y.: Educational Policy Research Center, 1972.

McKeachie, Wilbert J. Offering Course Options: Personality, Preference and Course Outcomes. Washington, D.C.: American Educational Research Association, 1970.

Medsker, Leland L. and Tillery, Dale. Breaking the Access Barrier: A Profile of the Two-Year Colleges. New York: McGraw-Hill, 1971.

Meloni, A. Transfer of College Credits and Off-Campus Learning. Philadelphia: U.S. Association of Evening College Students, St. Joseph's College, 1972.

National Center for Educational Research and Development. New Thrust in Vocational Education. Washington, D.C.: Government Printing Office, 1971.

Perkin, H.J. New Universities in the United Kingdom. Paris: OECD/ CERI, 1969.

Perkins, J.A., ed. Higher Education: From Autonomy to Systems. New York: International Council for Educational Development, 1972.

Price, Charlton R. New Directions in the World of Work: A Conference Report. Washington, D.C.: W. E. Upjohn Institute for Employment Research, 1972.

Ruyle, J.; Geiselman, L.A.; and Hefferlin, J.B.L. Non-Traditional Education Opportunities and Programs in Traditional Colleges and Universities, 1972. Princeton: Educational Testing Service, 1973.

Ruyle, J.; Geiselman, L.A.; Hefferlin, J.B.L.; and Kirton, A. Non-Traditional Programs and Opportunities in American Colleges and Universities, 1972. Princeton: Educational Testing Service, 1973.

Sexton, W.E. and Spencer, A. Less Than Baccalaureate Level Technical Education Programs in Higher Education. Washington, D.C.: American Association of State Colleges and Universities, 1971.

Sharon, A.T. College Credit for Off-Campus Study, Report No. 8. Washington, D.C.: ERIC Clearinghouse on Higher Education, 1971.

Smith, G.K., ed. New Teaching, New Learning, AAHE Current Issues in Higher Education 1971. San Francisco: Jossey-Bass, 1971.

Spurr, S.H. Academic Degree Structures: Innovative Approaches, Principles of Reform in Degree Structures in the United States. New York: McGraw-Hill, 1970.

Stein, Bruno and Miller, S.M. "Recurrent Education: An Alternative System?" New Generation, 54:1-8, 1972.

Troutt, R. Special Degree Programs for Adults: Exploring Non-Traditional Degree Programs in Higher Education. Iowa City: American College Testing Program, 1971.

University of California, Office of the President. Degree Programs for the Part-Time Student. Berkeley: University of California Press, 1971.

Valley, J.R. Increasing the Options: Recent Developments in College and University Degree Programs. Princeton: Educational Testing Service, 1972.

Vermilye, D.W., ed. The Expanded Campus: Current Issues in Higher Education 1972. San Francisco: Jossey-Bass, 1972.

Walkup, B.S. "External Study for Post-Secondary Students: Original and Supplement." New York: College Entrance Examination Board, 1972 (multilithed).

Walton, W.W. New Paths for Adult Learning: Systems for Delivery of Instruction in Non-Traditional Programs of Study. Princeton: Educational Testing Service, 1973.

Warren, J.R. Credit and Measurement in Non-Traditional Study. Princeton: Educational Testing Service, 1973.

Wirth, Arthur G. Education in the Technological Society: The Vocational-Liberal Studies Controversy in the Early Twentieth Century. Scranton, Pa.: Intext Educational Publishers, 1972.

Zetterberg, H.L. Museums and Adult Education. New York: Augustus M. Kelley, 1969.

Identifying Target Groups

American Council on Education. Higher Education and the Adult Student: An ACE Special Report. Washington, D.C.: American Council on Education, 1972.

American Vocational Association. Research Visibility, 1968-69: Reports on Selected Research Studies in Vocational, Technical, and Practical Arts Education. Washington, D.C.: American Vocational Association, 1969.

Astin, Helen S. The Woman Doctorate in America: Origins, Career, and Family. New York: Russell Sage Foundation, 1969.

Atwood, H.M. and Ellis, J. "The Concept of Need: An Analysis for Adult Education." Adult Leadership, 19:210-212, passim, 1971.

Belitsky, Harvey A. Private Vocational Schools and Their Students. Cambridge, Mass.: Schenkman Publishing Company, Inc., 1969.

Bell, Daniel. "Meritocracy and Equality." The Public Interest, 29: 29-68, Autumn 1972.

Bernard, Jessie. Women and the Public Interest. New York: Aldine Publishing Co., 1971.

Brinkman, F.J. Analysis of the Characteristics of Selected Vocational Students with Implications for Guidance and Counseling. Ann Arbor: University of Michigan Microfilms, 1970.

Carlson, C.R. "Serving the Needs of Retired Persons." Community and Junior College Journal, 43(6):22-23, May 1973.

Carnegie Commission on Higher Education. A Chance to Learn: An Action Agenda for Equal Opportunity in Higher Education. New York: McGraw-Hill, 1970.

Carnegie Commission on Higher Education. Education - Quality and Equality. New York: McGraw-Hill, 1971.

Carnegie Commission on Higher Education. Quality and Equality Revised Recommendations. New York: McGraw-Hill, February 1972.

Carp, A.; Peterson, R.E.; and Roelfs, P. Learning Interests and Experiences of Adult Americans. Princeton, N.J.: Educational Testing Service, 1973.

Civil Service Commission, Bureau of Training. Off-Campus Study Centers for Government Employees. Washington, D.C.: Government Printing Office, 1971.

Coleman, J.S. Equality of Educational Opportunity. Washington, D.C.: Government Printing Office, 1966.

Coombs, Philip H. New Paths to Learning for Rural Children and Youth. West Haven, Conn.: International Council for Educational Development, 1973.

Dowling, W. "How to Identify Needs of Groups for Continuing Education." American Journal of Pharmaceutical Education, 33:721-728, Spring 1969.

Draper, James. "Towards a Participating Society." Indian Journal of Adult Education, 23(11):11-14, November 1972.

ERIC Clearinghouse on Adult Education. Continuing Education in the Professions: Current Information Source, No. 24. Syracuse, N.Y.: ERIC Clearinghouse on Adult Education, 1969.

ERIC Clearinghouse on Adult Education. Residential Adult Education: Current Information Sources, No. 25. Syracuse, N.Y.: ERIC Clearinghouse on Adult Education, 1969.

Farmer, M.L., ed. Counseling Services for Adults in Higher Education. Metuchen, N.J.: The Scarecrow Press, 1971.

Fisher, J.A. Educational Counseling for Adults. Des Moines, Iowa: Drake University, 1969.

Green, Robert. Minority Groups at Predominantly White Universities: Needs and Perspectives. East Lansing, Michigan: Michigan State University, Center for Urban Affairs, 1970.

Hansen, W. Lee. "Income Redistribution Effects of Higher Education." Paper presented at the annual meeting of the American Economic Association, New York, December 1969.

Hiestand, Dale L. Changing Careers after Thirty-Five. New York: Columbia University Press, 1971.

Husen, Torsten. Talent, Opportunity and Career. Stockholm: Almquist and Wiksell, 1969.

International Labour Office. Notes on the ILO and the Employment of Women for Use by Technical Co-operation Experts. Geneva: ILO, 1969.

International Labour Office. Summary of ILO Standards Relating to Women's Employment. Geneva: ILO, 1972.

International Labour Office. The Vocational Preparation of Girls and Women. Geneva: ILO, 1970.

Jencks, Christopher. Inequality; A Reassessment of the Effect of Family and Schooling in America. New York: Basic Books, 1972.

Kay, E.R. Vocational Education: Characteristics of Teachers and Students, 1969. Washington, D.C.: U.S. Office of Education/ National Center for Educational Statistics, 1971.

Keyserling, M.D. Continuing Education for Women: A Growing Challenge. Chicago: National Conference on Higher Education, 1967.

Kreps, Juanita. Sex in the Market Place: American Women at Work. Baltimore: Johns Hopkins Press, 1971.

Kuder, J.M. Past Trends in Student Personnel Services for Adults in Higher Education. Ft. Collins: Colorado State University, 1971.

Luton, M.C. and Rohfeld, R. "Social Change Through Adult Education." Adult Leadership, 21(10):325-327, April 1973.

Marcson, S., ed. Automation, Alienation and Anomie. New York: Harper and Row, 1970.

Matthews, E.E. "The Counselor and the Adult Woman." Journal of the National Association of Woman Deans and Counselors, 32:115-122, 1969.

Medsker, Leland L. and Tillery, Dale. Breaking The Access Barrier: A Profile of the Two-Year Colleges. New York: McGraw-Hill, 1971.

Merideth, E. and Merideth, R. "Adult Women's Education: A Radical Critique." Journal of the National Association of Women Deans and Counselors, 34:111-120, 1971.

Minority Student Access to Higher Education. New York: Ford Foundation, 1970.

Motives for Recurrent Education. Stockholm: Swedish Ministry of Education, 1968.

Mulligan, Kathryn L. A Question of Opportunity: Women and Continuing Education. Washington, D.C.: Government Printing Office, 1973.

National Center for Educational Statistics. Adult Basic Education Program Statistics--Students and Staff Data, July 1, 1969 - June 30, 1970. Washington, D.C.: Government Printing Office, 1971.

National Institutes of Health, Office of Program Planning and Evaluation. Special Report on Women and Graduate Study. Washington, D.C.: Government Printing Office, 1968.

Nattress, LeRoy, Jr., ed. Continuing Education for the Professions. Chicago: Natresources, 1970.

Nye, F.I. and Hoffman, L.W. The Employed Mother in America. Chicago: Rand McNally, 1963.

Olivo, C.T., ed. Research Visibility: Vocational Education Is People With Educational Needs Beyond High School. Washington, D.C.: American Vocational Association, 1967.

Pateman, Carole. Participation and Democratic Theory. Cambridge, Mass.: Cambridge University Press, 1970.

Paul, W.J. and Robertson, K.B. Job Enrichment and Employee Motivation. London: Gower Press, 1970.

Pucinski, R.C. and Hirsch, S.P., eds. The Courage to Change: New Directives for Career Education. Englewood Cliffs, N.J.: Prentice-Hall, 1971.

Ribich, T. "The Problem of Equal Opportunity: A Review Article." The Journal of Human Resources, 7(4):518-526, Fall 1972.

Spaeth, J.H. and Greenley, A.M. Recent Alumni and Higher Education. New York: McGraw-Hill, 1970.

U.S. Department of Labor, Women's Bureau. Continuing Education, Programs and Services for Women. Washington, D.C.: Government Printing Office, 1971.

Willingham, Warren W. Free-Access Higher Education. New York: College Entrance Examination Board, 1970.

Young, Michael. Rise of the Meritocracy. New York: Random House, 1969.

Manpower and Job Training

Berg, I. Education and Jobs: The Great Training Robbery. New York: Praeger, 1970.

Cross, K.P. Occupationally Oriented Students. Washington, D.C.: American Association of Junior Colleges, 1970.

Davis, Rennard. "Retraining the Unemployed: Skill Improvement Training for Electricians and Plumbers." Monthly Labor Review, 84: 628-629, June 1964.

Decarlo, C.R. and Robinson, O.W. Education in Business and Industry. New York: Center for Applied Research in Education, Inc., 1966.

Goldstein, Jon. The Effectiveness of Manpower Training Programs: A Review of Research on the Impact on the Poor. Washington, D.C.: Government Printing Office, 1972.

Hackman, Ray C. The Motivated Working Adult. New York: American Management Association, Inc., 1969.

Holt, C.C.; MacRae, C.D.; Schweitzer, S.O.; and Smith, R.E. The Unemployment-Inflation Dilemma: A Manpower Solution. Washington, D.C.: The Urban Institute, 1971.

International Labour Office. Labor and Social Implications of Automation and Other Technological Developments, Report VI. Geneva: International Labour Office, 1972.

Janni, H. and Roggemans, M.L. Educational Systems and the New Demands of Industrialized Societies. Paris: UNESCO, International Commission on the Development of Education, 1971.

Johnson, D.F. "Education of Adult Workers: Projections to 1985." Monthly Labor Review, 93(8):43-56, August 1970.

Levine, H.A. "Education: An Emerging Fringe Benefit." Federationist (AFL-CIO), 77:11-16, March 1970.

Levine, H.A. "Educational Opportunity: A New Fringe Benefir for Collective Bargaining." Changing Education (AFT AFL-CIO), 2:5-12, Fall 1967.

Levitan, Sar; Mangum, Garth; and Marshall, Ray. Human Resources and the Labor Market: Labor and Manpower in the American Economy. New York: Harper and Row, 1972.

MacRae, C.D.; Schweitzer, S.O.; and Holt, C.C. "Job Search, Labor Turnover, and the Phillips Curve: An International Comparison." In: American Statistical Association. 1970 Proceedings, Business and Economic Statistics Section. Washington, D.C.: American Statistical Association, 1971.

Mushkin, S.J. "Resource Requirements and Educational Obsolescence." In: Robinson, E.A. and Vaizey, J.E., eds. The Economics of Education. New York: St. Martin's Press, 1966.

Olean, S.J. Changing Patterns and Continuing Education for Business. Syracuse: Syracuse University Press, 1967.

O'Meara, J.R. Combatting Knowledge Obsolescence. II, Employee Tuition-Aid Plans. New York: National Industrial Conference Board, 1970.

O'Meara, J.R. "Going to School Becomes Part of the Job." The Conference Board Record, 7(9):51-56, September 1970.

Price, R.G. and Hopkins, C.R. Review and Synthesis of Research in Business and Office Education. Columbus: Ohio State University/Center for Vocational and Technical Education, 1970.

Rehn, Gosta. "Trends and Perspectives in Manpower Policy." In: Gordon, M.S., ed. Poverty in America. San Francisco: Chandler, 1965.

Reubens, B.G. "Manpower Policy in Western Europe." Manpower, 4(11): 16-22, November 1972.

Weisbrod, B.A. "Benefits of Manpower Programs: Theoretical and Methodological Issues." In: Somers, G.C. and Wood, W.D., eds. Cost-Benefit Analysis of Manpower Policies: Proceedings of a Non-American Conference. Kingston, Ontario: Queen's University Press, 1969.

Finances

Aspirations, Enrollments and Resources, The Challenge to Higher Education in the Seventies. Washington, D.C.: Department of Health, Education, and Welfare, 1970.

Becker, Gary. Human Capital. New York: Columbia University Press, 1964.

Bowen, H.R. and Douglass, G.K. Efficiency in Liberal Education: A Study of Comparative Instructional Costs for Different Ways of Organizing Teaching-Learning in a Liberal Arts College. New York: McGraw-Hill, 1971.

Charters, Alexander N. Real Estate Tax Exemption for Continuing Education Programs. Syracuse: Syracuse University Press, 1972.

Dresch, S.P. and Goldberg, R.D. "Variable Term Loans for Higher Education--Analytics and Empirics." Annals of Economic and Social Measurement, 1(1):59-92, January 1972.

Educational Opportunity Bank: A Report of the Panel on Educational Innovation to U.S. Commissioner of Education Harold Howell, Director of the National Science Foundation Leland J. Haworth, and Special Assistant to the President for Science and Technology Donald F. Hornig. Washington, D.C.: Government Printing Office, August 1967.

Hansen, W. Lee and Weisbrod, Burton. Benefits, Costs, and Finance of Higher Education. Chicago: Markham, 1969.

Hartman, R.W. Credit for College: Public Policy for Student Loans. New York: McGraw-Hill, 1971.

"Income Inequality." The Annals of the American Academy of Political and Social Science, 409, September 1973.

"Investment in Education: The Equity-Efficiency Quandry." Journal of Political Economy, 80(3, Part 2), May-June 1972.

"Investment in Human Beings." Journal of Political Economy, 70(5, Part 2), October 1962.

International Labour Office. Paid Educational Leave, Report VI(1). Geneva: ILO, 1973.

International Labour Office. Paid Educational Leave, Report VI(2). Geneva: ILO, 1973.

Machlup, Fritz. Education and Economic Growth. Lincoln: University of Nebraska Press, 1970.

Miller, H.P. and Hornseth. Present Value of Estimated Lifetime Earnings. Washington, D.C.: Government Printing Office, 1967.

Robinson, E.A.G. and Vaizey, J.E., eds. The Economics of Education. New York: St. Martin's Press, 1966.

Shell, K.; Fisher, F.M.; Foley, D.K.; Friedlander, A.F.; and Associates. "The Educational Opportunity Bank: An Economic Analysis of a Contingent Repayment Loan Program for Higher Education." National Tax Journal, 21(1):2-45, March 1968.

Striner, Herbert E. Continuing Education as a National Capital Investment. Washington, D.C.: W.E. Upjohn Institute for Employment Research, 1971.

Thurow, L.C. "The Optimum Lifetime Distribution of Consumption Expenditures." American Economic Review, 59(3):324-330, June 1969.

Torpey, W.G. "Company Investment in Continuing Education for Scientists and Engineers." Educational Record, 45(4):408-413, Fall 1964.

Voronov, O. "Paid Educational Leave in the USSR." International Labour Review, 107(6):529-538, June 1973.

Library

Allison, A.M. "The Role of the Community College Library in Continuing Education." Continuing Education, 4:53-54, 1971.

American Library Association. A Strategy for Public Library Change: Proposed Public Library Goals Feasibility Study. Chicago: ALA, 1972.

Gould, S.B. "New Era for the Public Library." American Library Association Bulletin, 60:585-590, 1966.

Lee, Robert E. Continuing Education for Adults Through the American Public Library, 1833-1964. Chicago: American Library Association, 1966.

Monroe, Margaret E. Library Adult Education. New York: The Scarecrow Press, 1963.

Reich, D.L. "A Public Library Becomes a CLEP Learning Center," College Board Review, 81:29-31, 1971.

Bibliographies

Adult Education Association of U.S.A. Continuing Education of Women. Washington, D.C.: Adult Education Association of USA, 1970.

Astin, H.S.; Suniewick, N.; and Dweck, S. Women: A Bibliography of their Education and Careers. Washington, D.C.: Human Service Press, 1971.

Blaug, Mark, ed. Economics of Education. Oxford, New York: Pergamon Press, 1966.

Elkin, A. Resources for the Employment of Mature Women and/or Their Continuing Education: A Selected Bibliography and Aids. New York: Federal Employment and Guidance Service, 1966.

ERIC Clearinghouse on Higher Education. Bibliography on Aspects of Non-Traditional Study in Higher Education. Washington, D.C.: George Washington University, 1972.

Flaugher, R.L.; Mahoney, M.H.; and Messing, R.B. Credits by Examination for College Level Studies: An Annotated Bibliography. Princeton: College Entrance Examination Board, 1967.

Fletcher, M.A. The Open University, The External Degrees, and Non-Traditional Study: A Selected Annotated Bibliography. Bryn Mawr, Pa.: American College of Life Underwriters, 1972.

Goldslaub, J. , ed. Manpower and Educational Planning: An Annotated Bibliography of Currently Available Materials. Pittsburgh: University of Pittsburgh, School of Education, 1968.

Grabowski, S.M. Research and Investigation in Adult Education: 1971 Annual Register. Syracuse: Eric Clearinghouse on Adult Education, 1972.

Mahler, W.A. Non-Traditional Study: A Critical Review of the Literature. Princeton: Educational Testing Service, 1973, in preparation.

Mills, G.H. Bibliography on Barriers to Effective Vocational-Occupational Education. Denver: Education Commission of the States, 1972.

Spiegel, J. Continuing Education for Women: A Selected Annotated Bibliography. Washington, D.C.: Business and Professional Women's Foundation, 1967.

Whipple, James B. Community Service and Continuing Education: A Literature Review. Syracuse: Syracuse University Publications in Continuing Education, 1970.

INDEX

D

H

I

J

K

L

M

U.S. GOVERNMENT PRINTING OFFICE : 1974 O - 532-819